Clever Batch

Clever Batch

Brilliant wholefood batch-cooking recipes to save you time, money and patience

Susan Jane White

Gill Books

Gill Books
Hume Avenue
Park West
Dublin 12
www.gillbooks.ie

Gill Books is an imprint of M.H. Gill and Co.

978 07171 8494 1

Designed by www.grahamthew.com
Photography © Joanne Murphy (www.joanne-murphy.com)
Food styling by Orla Neligan (www.cornershopproductions.com),
assisted by Clare Wilkinson and James Gavin
Copy-edited by Kristin Jensen
Proofread by Susan McKeever
Indexed by Eileen O'Neill
Printed by Printer Trento, Italy

PROPS
Meadows & Byrne: T: (01) 2804554/(021) 4344100;
E: info@meadowsandbyrne.ie; W: www.meadowsandbyrne.com
Avoca: T: (01) 2746939; E: info@avoca.ie; www.avoca.ie
Article Dublin: T: (01) 6799268; E: items@articledublin.com;
W: www.articledublin.com
Industry Design: T: (01) 6139111; W: industrydesign.ie
The Props Library: E: studio@thepropslibrary.com;
W: www.thepropslibrary.com
Marks & Spencer: T: (01) 299 1300; W: www.marksandspencer.ie
Dunnes Stores: T: 1890 253185; W: www.dunnesstores.com
Karen Convery: @karenconvery2016

This book is typeset in Freight Micro Pro Light.
The paper used in this book comes from the wood pulp of
managed forests. For every tree felled, at least one tree is
planted, thereby renewing natural resources.
5 4 3 2 1

About the Author

Susan Jane White is an award-winning food writer and columnist with *The Sunday Independent*. When Susan was 25, she developed a serious immune disorder which marked the beginning of her nutritional pilgrimage. Her first book, *The Extra Virgin Kitchen*, debuted at No. 1 while her second book, *The Virtuous Tart*, bagged an Irish Book Award. Susan Jane is also published in America and Italy. As a financially squeezed, time-pressured mum, cooking from scratch every day was good for her health, but also a serious challenge to her sanity — until she discovered batch cooking. She now lives blissfully in Dublin with her husband, two bandits and a never-ending supply of almond butter brownies.

Acknowledgements

This is the incredibly inadequate space where I get to high-five my team for their incorrigible fizz and commitment. Thank you, thank you, thank you …

My gratitude to commissioning editor Nicki Howard and your continued faith in my crazy-assed rhythm. Thank you for your unflinching support in everything I do – and for wanting to sit beside me at dinners.

A heartfelt thanks to Catherine Gough and your seismic forbearance with my potty mouth. Forgiving me must have been a constant process. Teresa Daly, your creativity matters so much to the success of this cookbook and your dedication makes my heart implode. Thank you.

Design-genius Graham Thew, for his inimitable style and magical ways. You're a total wizard.

To my serenity sister Kristin Jensen – this book would be bonkers without you. A thunderous thanks.

My rock-star colleagues Jo Murphy and Orla Neligan, who whipped these images into shape and gave each dish wings. I feel extremely lucky and forever grateful for our time together. Knitting these images into a cookbook felt closer to a playdate than a job.

My gracious literary agent, Sharon Bowers, for always making me laugh, raising my spirits through life's sticky parts, and for being table-thumping gorgeous.

To all the small-scale stockists and independent bookstores across the country, I thank you for your cheer, your advice and your dependability. Keep rocking our world! I'm looking at you too Paul Neilan!

Christine, Fergal and Dash, whose friendship and generosity are truly more nourishing than anything I could conjure on my stove. Thank you for abandoning all sensibilities and letting me turn your beautiful kitchen into a mini Hogwart's adventure.

All the Instagrammers who have tagged their creations from my first two cookbooks – I see you! Thank you for bringing me into your kitchens and into your lives. Your support is invaluable to me – catch my telepathic love bombs and heart-pumping hugs.

To my darling little boys, for being a constant feed of joy and amusement. The way you think inspires me every day. There is nothing more delicious in my kitchen than your snuggles.

Mum, and your reckless enthusiasm for everything I do.

And finally, to my husband Trevor – you still drive me crazy.

To you, my reader —
I am your biggest ever
fan. You fill me with
magic and pinball me
around my kitchen.
This book is for you.

Contents

Introduction

AS AN UNDER-CAFFEINATED, financially cramped, time-pinched mum, my kitchen management needed re-evaluation. Sometimes I got it right, but most evenings I felt like a wine gum in a combine harvester. **Being short on time, money and patience, I had a problem.**

I wanted to cook badass nourishing meals, but I didn't want to cook every single night. I wanted to reduce the honking stress at 6 p.m. in our home. I wanted to spend less time in the grocery store looking for arcane ingredients and more time at home, high-fiving my genius. I didn't need another freaking meditation app. What I needed was to get through the month without maxing out my Visa or adrenal glands.

So these days, my freezer plays an Oscar-worthy role. Developing a relationship with my freezer was a breeze. Suddenly I was saving on shopping, cooking and washing up. My personality finally felt like an update was being installed. Life just flowed much easier. It's a new-age nirvana. Fancy joining me there? **This cookbook is a fun blueprint for readers who struggle with everyday meals.** It doesn't matter if you're living on your own or in a family of six, you control the inventory! From cauli korma to lentil Bolognese, I'm batch cooking for sanity.

Let me take you through each section with reasonable haste and giddiness. The first section is dedicated to breakfasts that will sit in the fridge all week long or hang out on your kitchen shelves. You'll find a handy guide on page 8 to help your kitchen find its own rhythm and sass. There are some helpful symbols along the way too, designed to help your wallet and your watch (see page 2).

Part two celebrates your freezer (and your newfound free time). There are tips on how to start, what you'll find useful, easy labelling and the ideal-sized freezer (spoiler alert: small is best).

In the third part of the book, I introduce you to some of the greatest game changers for mediocre midweek meals. Think of them as a sort of culinary Band-Aid. There are flavour grenades to freshen up plain eggs, rice or fish; freezer dressings to excite any vegetable, because let's be honest, getting kids and truculent adults to eat their greens is about as easy as pirouetting on a pin; and there's a suite of nutritious yogurts and cultured foods to bring mealtimes up an octave. Think of these recipes as your microbiome's very own Electric Picnic.

In the final section, you and I will meet over a sweet treat. Instead of white flour, I use wholegrain flours like brown rice, chickpea and oat flours. Instead of white sugar, let's dance with maple, Medjools and muscovado. And in place of butter or margarine, we party with tahini or nutritious oils like extra virgin olive, coconut and sesame. I'm all about turning those pesky sugar cravings into a nutritional slam-dunk. The swag of treats that follow

Clever Clues

are dastardly good. Any words that come to mind to describe the effect they have on my happiness are frankly far too intimate to be printed in a cookbook. **This might be as close to enlightenment as I'll ever get.**

What I love most about playing in my kitchen is the connection I make with myself and with nature. I live in a busy city. It's hard to escape the circus of pollution, car alarms, traffic and suffocating concrete. So slicing into a juicy orange and spraying citrus mist into the air, scooping out the licky-sticky yumminess of an over-ripe mango, hunting for seeds in a crisp, fragrant watermelon – each experience fuels my connection with nature. It feels grounding amid the fug of modern city living.

Cooking for yourself reaches beyond physical nourishment. Cooking provides emotional nourishment too. It's a form of self-respect. Ask any cook. Ask any parent. It's how, for generations, we've shown love and adoration to the people around us.

When words fail to console a friend, freshly baked brownies do the trick. When my presence is exhausting at a relative's hospital bed, chicken broth speaks instead. And when my heart and paws need pampering, I show them love by choosing deeply nourishing and earthing food.

Eating well is not just about upgrading your food choices. It's about upgrading your life.

I've designed some visuals throughout the book to give you nifty tips on time (an hour glass) and spending power (one, two or three coins).

Hope it helps!

⊕

On a budget

⊕

Reasonable

⊕

Feeling flush

⧗

Particulars to that recipe regarding time

Meathos

MY ETHOS ON MEAT

We're a nation of animal lovers. I know I certainly am. It's hard to pass my neighbour's cat without lovebombing him.

So perhaps I should reconsider the packages of dismembered animal limbs for sale in supermarkets then. Gross, right? Think about it. There's a palpable difference between passing the colourful kaleidoscope of fruit and veg that tickle your nostrils as well as your eyes and passing the meat counter, which makes my children want to cry. At least they have a sense of justice more acute than my own. And I'm ashamed of that. But I can change. And I want to.

I'd like my meat to come from dedicated butchers who pride themselves on buying from local Irish farms with integrity. I'd like my meat to be wrapped by a professional, not a factory. And I'd like to celebrate the animal through mindfulness ... mindful of not eating one every day. Mindful of not supporting an industry that savages animals to feed our dull, accidental complicity. Mindful that we signed the animal's death warrant with the simple act of purchasing. This is my resolution. Will you join me?

I'm not suggesting we give up meat. I'm just suggesting we look at this industry for what it is: an amoral misadventure, possibly the worst of our generation. It's time I stopped supporting it with my wallet. That's why most of these recipes are heavy on veg.

So what am I doing including recipes for bone broth or beef cheeks? Eh, good question. Hear me out. I've found myself suddenly using up every bit of our weekly meat feast. I often threw away oxtail bones or chicken carcasses, but now that we don't buy as much meat, I'm making stock from the remains and maximising every gram.

Meat is not bad. No need to swear off it altogether. Scientists warn that the quantity we eat is unhealthy and unsustainable. Therein lies the problem. For climate reasons, for financial reasons and for health reasons, meat shouldn't be a daily feature in our lives. Bone broth and chicken stock will get you through the days you give meat a well-deserved break.

What My Week Looks Like

AN IDEA OF a week's evening menu? Basically, this week involves three meals from the freezer, one evening of pure dossing and three evenings where I make a meal and freeze the rest so it can save my sanity another night. And every single dish rocks our taste buds as well as our bods. I try to have an artillery of freezer dressings at the ready to improve any salad, soup or boring rice dish.

MONDAY

Aubergine rendang from the freezer and brown basmati rice. Easy.

TUESDAY

Do a big batch of Romesco sauce and freeze half of it in ice cube trays (this will snazz up roasted vegetables and fried halloumi some other night or will be great on toast with feta for a quick lunch).

Serve the remaining half with roasted butternut and pumpkin, fried eggs, loads of coriander and some popped capers for the adults (page 214). Piddle easy.

WEDNESDAY

One-tray roasted red pepper soup from the freezer. Pile on organic corn tortillas with grated cheese, avocado and chilli. Hunks of sourdough. Baked sweet potatoes. Minimum effort.

THURSDAY

Defrost one portion of beet Bourguignon from the freezer (my husband, Trevor, will be away) alongside natural yogurt. Cheddar and kale mash with chicken wings for the boys (make stock from bones and scraps).

FRIDAY

Neighbour making a ragù to share. I'll drop her half of my pot next Friday. We do this in turns. Score.

SATURDAY

Make a roasted cauli korma and freeze the leftovers in individual portions. Natural yogurt to serve. Pot of black sticky rice. If the boys don't eat the korma, I have a packet of smoked mackerel on stand-by in the fridge and peas in the freezer. Catch up on podcasts while cooking.

SUNDAY

Whip up a big batch of sourdough lamb meatballs and freeze most of the batch for busy days. Serve on Sunday with smooth hummus, cucumber ribbons, fresh olives if we have some or the black olive crumb on page 000 if not. Defrost a freezer dressing such as chimichurri if I have any left. Make some if not. Get the boys to roll the meatballs.

If there's one thing I have learned since assembling and expelling two human beings from my body, it's the power of planning.

I'm referring specifically to a weekly meal planner. Without plotting ahead, family mealtimes can sometimes feel like an AGM for dehydrated vampires. My meal planning happens every Sunday evening. I choose the recipes I'd like my boys to tango with during the week, then figure out where I can squeeze in a shop. Snoresome? Not when you're maxing Hozier on full volume and caressing a bottle of Tempranillo like a lost kitten at a stranger's leg. This is one of my favourite domesticated chores. I own it.

Examples include breakfasts to store in the fridge all week, such as waffle batter, cheat's shakshuka, cold brew coffee, green tea brack, pimped-up harissa for scrambled eggs on toast – anything that won't impose on my brain cells early in the morning. There will always be a platoon of moreish snacks for when fangs start to sharpen or when bribes need fulfilling. In reality, I usually fall back on two or three home-cooked freezer meals so I can take those nights off.

Then I make the tedious shopping list. That Tempranillo and I are a good team. We make Mary Poppins look lame.

The result? I don't freak out at mealtimes, my little family ends up both physically and emotionally nourished and my adrenal glands are back on speaking terms with me.

RECIPES TO REFRIGERATE ALL WEEK INCLUDE:

Saffron and mandarin apricots

Waffle batter and pancake batter

Chia jams and a healthier marmalade

Green tea brack

Custard pud with amaranth, white chocolate and cherry

Lapsang souchong fruit cake

Hallelujah banana bread

Cold brew coffee

Freezer flaxseed focaccia, 5 ways

100% rye sourdough

Roasted butternut for poached eggs

Black polenta fingers (great with fried eggs)

Shakshuka base (great with eggs)

Hummus (with eggs or toast)

Healthier Jam, 3 Ways

Blackberry Liquorice Jam

MAKES 10–12 SINGLE SERVINGS . . . . .

2 small punnets of blackberries . . . . .

3 Medjool dates, stones removed (or use pre-soaked regular dates) . . . .

2 tablespoons chia seeds, whole or milled . . . .

Pinch of ground liquorice root (optional) . . . .

Squeeze of lime . . . .

Raspberry Ginger Jam

MAKES 10–12 SINGLE SERVINGS . . . . .

300g frozen raspberries, left to defrost . . . .

3 Medjool dates, stones removed (or use pre-soaked regular dates) . . . .

2–3 tablespoons chia seeds, whole or milled . . . .

1 teaspoon minced fresh ginger . . . . .

Squeeze of lime . . . .

Strawberry Cardamom Jam

MAKES 10–12 SINGLE SERVINGS . . . . .

300g frozen strawberries, left to defrost . . . .

3 Medjool dates, stones removed (or use pre-soaked regular dates) . . . .

2–3 tablespoons chia seeds, whole or milled . . . .

Pinch of ground cardamom or seeds from 1 pod . . . .

Squeeze of lime . . . .

⊕ Buy frozen fruit, to bring costs down

. . . .

⧗ Takes 20 minutes to set

Research confirms that scoffing more than 35g of dietary fibre a day can result in a 40% chance of living longer. Jeesh.

Here's what happens in our very own waste plant. Insoluble fibre from our food acts like a traffic warden, clearing jams and keeping junctions clear. His job is to keep things moving. If nothing moves, waste can build up and re-enter the bloodstream. One way of ridding toxins is to sweat them out on a treadmill. Or visit the village sauna. But I think I'd rather fight with my fork.

These jams are criminally good and much more refreshing than the commercial store-bought stuff. One taste will ignite your dimples, like kissing Bradley Cooper or giving Michael Flatley a wedgie live on stage.

Pelt the fruit (blackberry, raspberry, strawberry) in a food processor or use a hand-held blender. Add your licky-sticky dates, the chia seeds, additional spice or flavour and the lime juice. Purée until smooth.

Scoop into a pristine-clean jam jar. Allow the chia seeds to thicken the jam for 20 minutes before using. I like to stir it every 5 minutes to prevent clumps from developing.

Store in the fridge all week and slather over brown bread and butter. Your frontal lobe is gonna love this one.

Raspberry Ginger Jam

Strawberry Cardamom Jam

Blackberry Liquorice Jam

A Healthier Marmalade

MAKES 8–10 SERVINGS . . . .

3 unwaxed organic oranges . . . .

3 tablespoons psyllium seed husks . . .

2–3 tablespoons (raw) honey . . . .

Pinch of flaky sea salt . . . .

⊕ Cheaper and better than the commercial, sugar-laden stuff

. . . .

⧖ Whizz and set

If you're not eliminating waste from your bowels, you'll end up wearing it on your face. The skin is our body's largest excretory organ. Crazy but true. You want luminous skin? Make sure your pipes are on speaking terms with you.

Cranking up the fibre in your diet will have you shaking your booty like Lady Marmalade on the dance floor. By fibre, I don't mean a bowl of wholemeal pasta – that stuff poses as a big shot when really it does very little. When you want fibre, you need to call in the services of black belts like flaxseed, bran, oats, prunes, beans, hummus and psyllium.

Psyllium seeds can be purchased in savvy pharmacies or health food stores nationwide. They help to set the marmalade. Prunes, shmunes – psyllium is the King Kong of the colon.

Start by grating the zest from two of your oranges into the bowl of a food processor, then slice the bum off all three of your oranges and sit them on a chopping board. Carefully carve off and discard the white pith from your first two oranges using a paring knife. Chop the orange flesh into chunks, checking for pips. Drop into the food processor.

With your final orange, carve away the skin and pith (but don't go too crazy – much of the health benefits lie in the skin and white pith). Discard the skin and pith, then chop the orange flesh into chunks, again checking for pips. Add to the food processor bowl along with your psyllium husks, really good honey and sea salt. Pulse until jammy but not entirely smooth. You still want beautiful blobs of orange in there.

Scrape into a scrupulously clean jam jar and leave to set for 30 minutes before spreading over hot, buttery toast. Refrigerate for up to one week – it will set even more when chilled.

Green Tea Brack

MAKES 1 LARGE LOAF . . . .

320g sultanas and/or raisins . . . .

350ml cold, strong green tea . . . .

220g sprouted spelt flour or 200g
regular whole spelt flour . . . .

120g light muscovado sugar . . . .

1½ teaspoons baking powder . . . .

1½ teaspoons ground allspice or
mixed spice . . . .

1 teaspoon ground cinnamon . . . .

1 large egg . . . .

Zest of 1 orange . . . .

⊕ Sprouted flour will bump up
the cost

⧖ Pre-soaking required. Freezes
beautifully in slices.

On any occasion that my husband is not overburdened with sweetness and light, I offer him green tea brack. It works faster than paracetamol. Within moments his face becomes improbably buoyant and I'm sure I hear him squeaking like a hamster in heat.

Soak your little army of dried fruit in the cold, strong tea overnight (or for 8 hours). Hot tea may sound preferable, but you'll end up with no soaking liquid, resulting in a drier dough – snoresome but important fact.

The next morning, fire up your oven to 180°C. In a large bowl (or a saucepan if you haven't got a big enough bowl), tumble in the flour, sugar, baking powder and your selection of spices. Rake through carefully.

Quickly beat the egg and orange zest in a cup, then add to your puddle of soaked fruit. Scrape the wet mixture into the dry mixture. Work it through until lusciously glossy.

Transfer into a loaf tin lined with non-stick baking paper, ideally a 1½lb tin. Specifics drive me crazy, so you're on the right track if it looks like a loaf. Only half filling a long loaf tin? It's probably a 2lb loaf tin, so bake your brack for 45 minutes, until a skewer comes out dry when gently pierced into the centre. Be aware that 1lb loaf tins will need extra time in the oven to make sure the centre is cooked all the way through. When I use my 1lb loaf tin, I bake the brack for 70–75 minutes.

And if you hit the 1½lb loaf tin on the bull's-eye, bake for 60 minutes.

Remove from the oven once cooked and leave to cool in the tin for 20 minutes before unveiling onto a wire rack.

Serve it as is or toasted with a scrape of butter and a hot cuppa. If you want it to look really shiny on top, professional bakers brush it with a simple sugar syrup, which you can too.

Rye Sourdough (p.59)

Green Tea Brack (p.24)

Hallelujah Banana Bread (p.69)

Custard Pud with Amaranth, White Chocolate and Cherry

MAKES 8 SERVINGS . . . .

180g amaranth grain . . . .

375ml water . . . .

1 teaspoon vanilla paste or good-
quality extract. . . . .

¼ teaspoon flaky sea salt . . . .

3 tablespoons maple syrup, honey or
date syrup. . . . .

3 tablespoons tahini . . . .

2 eggs, beaten . . . .

50g good white chocolate (e.g. Green
& Blacks), roughly chopped into
chunks . . . .

50g dried Morello cherries . . . .

2 very ripe bananas, chopped, or 2
teaspoons psyllium husks . . . .

500ml your preferred type of milk . .

Not cheap, but goddamn delish

. . . .

Lasts all week in the fridge

This amaranth pudding is packed with unexpected pleasure: crunchy, sweet flecks of white chocolate chased by the sour smack of juicy cherries and gorgeous creamy custard. It's the sort of thing I find very necessary to keep in my fridge for surviving this ridiculously demanding world we live in.

For a relatively shy grain, amaranth has more muscle than wheat, with four times the calcium and twice as much iron. And with this grain's cargo of lysine, you can kiss sayonara to cold sores. Pretty good deal for half a cent per gram.

Preheat the oven to 165°C.

In a small saucepan with a tight-fitting lid, bring the amaranth, water, vanilla and salt to a soft boil. This means a gentle putter rather than a violent bubble that will blow the lid off and scare the bejaysus out of your dog. Cook for 15 minutes, until the water has been fully absorbed. Amaranth is not a dry, fluffy grain when cooked, so expect something that looks like a sneezy couscous.

While the amaranth is doing its thing, prep the rest of the gear. In a large bowl, beat your preferred syrup into the tahini and eggs until smooth. Sprinkle the chocolate chunks into the egg mixture along with your cherries and chopped banana or psyllium. Slowly whisk in the milk.

Remove the amaranth from the heat, stir briskly with a fork and add to the eggy party.

Pour and scrape your custardy mix into a medium-sized pie dish. You're aiming for a pudding no deeper than 2.5–5cm. Cook in the oven for 40–50 minutes. It should wobble slightly in the centre when done, like a baked custard. I make this on a Sunday evening and look forward to breakfast all week.

Nut Pulp Granola with Chai and Pistachios

MAKES 12–16 SERVINGS . . . .

125ml extra virgin coconut oil . . . . . .

125ml good honey, maple syrup or
barley malt syrup . . . .

Flurry of flaky sea salt . . . .

300g nut pulp left over from making
nut milk (or use ground almonds) . . . .

250g jumbo oats . . . .

120g salted pistachios . . . .

5 caffeine-free chai spice blend
teabags, torn open . . . .

(+) Repurposes nut pulp from
making nut milk (see page 100,
for example)

. . . .

⧗ Little effort, big return

For security purposes, I like to keep a jar of homemade granola in my cupboard at all times. I'm a better human being when my belly is busy.

The older I get, the more I need my food to fill an emotional crypt too. I get a better burn from lovingly crafted granola than the store-bought stuff. I get a theatrical high knowing my corner café hand-roasts their coffee beans to Shostakovich. Or that my daily loaf is blessed with a wave from the baker himself. It's the love and adoration bestowed upon ingredients that really grips me, like a tummy rub for a homeless puppy. Food is more than fuel. There's no love in highly processed food – it's just conveyor belt crap and cannot service you physically or emotionally. Not the way this granola can.

Plus, I finally found a worthy way of repurposing nut pulp left over from making nut milk. Namaste.

Fire up your oven to 160°C. Line your largest baking tray, or two smaller ones, with non-stick baking paper.

In a big saucepan, gently melt the coconut oil, your chosen syrup and a smattering of salt. You want them to smooch each other, not violently grumble. Parachute the remaining ingredients into the pan, turn off the heat and stir to thoroughly coat.

Spoon onto your prepared tray and bake in the oven for 30 minutes. Toss the granola twice while baking to prevent the edges browning. This recipe requires a longer cooking time than regular granola because the wet nut pulp needs to dry out in the oven. If it's not dry, it won't store well.

Remove from the oven once cooked. Clouds of warm spices and honey will waft through your house, reminding you (and the apartment block) of your culinary wizardry. Cool before shelling your pistachios and tumbling into the granola.

This granola can be stored for up to three weeks in a tightly sealed jar, to be sprinkled over despondent salads or eaten on languorous mornings.

Lapsang Souchong Fruit Cake

MAKES 1 LARGE CAKE . . . .

Olive oil, for greasing . . . .

200g roasted hazelnuts . . . .

210g regular pitted dates . . . .

75g dried dark unsulphured
apricots . . . .

375ml hot, strong lapsang souchong
tea, divided . . . .

375g raisins . . . .

1 tablespoon vanilla extract . . . .

1 teaspoon ground cinnamon . . . .

¼ teaspoon freshly grated nutmeg . .

¼ teaspoon ground allspice . . . .

Zest of 1 unwaxed orange . . . .

180g walnuts or salted pistachios (or
a mix of both) . . . .

⊕ Reasonable
. . . .

⧖ Freeze in slices

Amy Chaplin was the midwife of this genius. New York City (and my elevenses) is a better place because of it. Feel free to use Earl Grey or chai tea instead of the smoky lapsang souchong.

This fruit cake will keep for three or four weeks in the fridge. You can find almost all the ingredients in your local four-letter German supermarket. Serve in thin slices with a shot of coffee – or brandy butter and a Christmas photo album.

Fire up your oven to 150°C. Line a 30cm springform cake tin with some oiled non-stick baking paper.

Grind the hazelnuts in a food processor. Tip into a large mixing bowl and set aside. No need to clean the food processor – you'll be using it later.

Now soak the dates and apricots in 250ml of the hot tea for 10 minutes. Drain well and set aside.

Boil your raisins in the remaining 125ml of hot tea. As soon as they reach the boiling point, stir, cover the pot, reduce the heat to low and simmer for 10 minutes. Remove the lid and continue to cook for a few more minutes, until all the tea has cooked off and the raisins are bursting with plumpness. Juicy juicy.

Spin the cooked raisins in your food processor with the vanilla extract, all the spices and the zippy zest. Blend until smooth. Tumble this paste into the bowl of ground hazelnuts along with the drained dates and apricots. Fold really well. Now stir through your walnuts and/or pistachios.

Press the cake mix into your prepped tin and smooth the top. If you have extra nuts, you can decorate the edges. Bake for 1 hour, until set. Eject from the oven and allow to cool completely before removing from the tin.

Popped Amaranth

MAKES 6 SERVINGS . . . .

8 tablespoons whole amaranth . . . . . .

Patience (not optional) . . . .

⊕ On a budget

. . . .

⧖ 60 seconds

Amaranth is dirt cheap, delightfully odd and indecently healthy. What more could you ask of a superfood? This popped cereal is regularly dropped onto kitchen tables and into conversations to impress even the most stubborn of hipsters.

Which got me thinking – the word *superfood* is misleading. Every food is super. No, honestly. Listen. Studies consistently show that over 80% of us eat convenience foods on a daily basis. In other words, highly processed 'pseudo' foods, or foods pretending to be foods. Investigative journalist and author Felicity Lawrence reveals that we each neck about 4.5kg of sneaky food additives every year. Gross.

So the term *superfood* is actually missing the point. All fresh food is super in comparison to the lab-created junk packaged under the pretence of being 'convenient'. Convenient for whom, exactly? Instead of asking why fresh food is expensive, we should be asking why 'convenience' food is so cheap. Therein lies your answer.

You'll need a reasonably high-sided, heavy-based saucepan for popping, as amaranth tends to jump out of small pans.

I find gas flames perfect for popping because we need to heat the heavy-based saucepan rather high – 60 seconds does the trick. If you have an electric hob, just leave the dry pot (no oil) on the ring a little longer to achieve a scorching hot temperature – 3–4 minutes normally achieves this. The heavier the base of the pan, the better the result.

Add a few grains of amaranth and watch it pop over 5 seconds. If it takes any longer, chuck the batch, leave the pan until it's hotter and start again. Don't worry – your first time popping amaranth is messy. The second time, like anything else, is a cinch as you'll know what you're aiming for.

Once popped, circa 5 seconds, pour onto a plate to cool and continue with the remaining grains.

Sprinkle onto granola in the morning, eat plain with cold milk, parachute onto salads or keep stored in a jar for up to four weeks.

Chocolate Buckwheat Granola

MAKES ENOUGH FOR 1 MASSIVE
KILNER JAR . . . .

125ml extra virgin coconut oil or
ghee (page 194) . . . .

125ml rice malt syrup or barley
malt syrup . . . .

1 teaspoon ground cinnamon . . . .

1 teaspoon vanilla bean paste or
good-quality extract . . . .

150g oat flakes . . . .

150g barley flakes (or more oat
flakes) . . . .

150g whole buckwheat groats (not
flakes) . . . .

100–130g hazelnuts or pecans

4 tablespoons raw cacao nibs
(optional) . . . .

Pinch of flaky sea salt . . . .

200g regular pitted dates, chopped . .

100g dark chocolate, such as Green
& Blacks cooking chocolate, chopped
into chunks . . . .

Pricey, but still cheaper than
store-bought stuff

. . . .

Lasts for weeks on your kitchen
shelf

The number of expensive granolas to choose from in our supermarkets is unprecedented in the history of *Homo sapiens*. Trust me, you can make a much better one for a fraction of the price at home. This one has three different grains, making it a complete protein by virtue of its amino acid permutation. That's bench presser speak for 'high-five'. Sporty teens will go mental for it.

Find rice malt and barley malt syrup in savvy delis and health food stores nationwide.

Fire up your oven to 160°C. Line your largest tray (or use two smaller trays) with non-stick baking paper.

In your biggest pot, melt your preferred fat, your syrup, cinnamon and vanilla over a timid heat. Turn off the heat.

Now tumble in all the remaining ingredients except the dates and dark chocolate. Scrape the contents of the pan out over your lined tray(s).

Bake in the oven for 25 minutes and not a minute longer. Allow the granola to cool completely before stirring through the chopped dates (Medjools are even more magnificent, but can bump up the price) and glorious chunks of chocolate. Store in a tall glass jar on the kitchen counter. Stunning stuff with ice-cold milk.

Golden Amaranth Porridge (p.26)

Saffron and Mandarin Apricots (p.57)

Three-Grain Porridge (p.26)

Carrot Cake Porridge (p.27)

New Age Porridge, 6 Ways

Autumn is porridge party season. That steaming bowl of goodness before an icy walk to work; that comforting smell of the kitchen as your oats happily burp on the stove; that sweet syrupy mess you so love to launch on your porridge like a giddy orchestra conductor. We're a nation that loves our oats.

This grain's platoon of soluble and insoluble fibre has the nifty ability to service our pipes in more ways than one. There ain't nothing sexy about constipation, especially given that our skin often takes over as an excretory organ. Yes, oats will make you regular, but they'll also sat nav our pipes for cholesterol and escort it out of our bodies like a bad-tempered bodyguard. Bonus!

Here are some sonic ways to tart up your porridge so that your pipes continue to party ...

Cacao Butter Porridge

SERVES 1 . . . .

130ml your preferred type of milk. . .

1 tablespoon raw cacao butter, roughly shaved. . . . .

4 tablespoons rolled oats . . . .

Pinch of flaky sea salt . . . .

Whipped honey or a dusting of coconut sugar, to top . . . .

⊕ On a budget
. . . .
⧗ Cooks so quickly

Cacao butter will take your porridge to a whole new level. Soon you will wonder how on earth you ever had oats without it. We serve our cacao butter porridge with coconut sugar scattered on top. This new exotic sugar is tastier than white sugar and sufficiently pretentious to earn bragging rights with that annoying athletic dude in your office. Nowadays, you'll even find coconut sugar in your local four-letter German supermarket.

I bet you have a particular way of cooking porridge, attentive to your own neuroses. Me too! This recipe will work whichever way you choose to cook it. For everyone else, I recommend bringing your preferred milk (mine is oat milk) and the cacao butter to a gentle heat, below simmering point. Add the oats and flaky sea salt and cook for 5 minutes, until the oats expand. Add extra milk for a looser porridge (which I prefer). Try not to let the pot boil, burning the taste of the milk.

Serve with great big globs of whipped honey or a dusting of coconut sugar and a cup of Earl Grey.

Three-Grain Porridge

MAKES 1KG FOR YOUR SHELF . . . .

625g regular oat flakes . . . .

125g buckwheat or barley flakes . . . .

125g milled chia seeds . . . .

125g amaranth flakes . . . .

3 teaspoons ground turmeric . . . .

1 teaspoon flaky sea salt . . . .

⊕   Still a budget option per
     portion, but the cost is ramped
     up initially from sourcing four
     different grains

⏳   Stores for months, ready to
     rock your mornings

This three-grain porridge is kickass comforting – whole, unrefined, unadulterated yumminess that takes minutes to prepare, but feeds your body all day long. The best part? It's a complete source of protein too. By socialising oats with other grains and seeds such as amaranth, buckwheat and chia, we achieve a full quota of essential amino acids that otherwise would have fallen short of the bench presser's sweet spot.

Put all the ingredients together in a 1kg jar. Shakey shakey shakey. Store this way for up to six months.

When you fancy a bowl, just treat the mix like regular oats. I like using 1 teacup (250ml) of this three-grain mix to 2½ teacups (625ml) of plant milk, which serves two adults and two nippers.

Simmer gently for 10–15 minutes, until glossy and creamy. Serve with sticky set honey.

Golden Amaranth Porridge

SERVES 1 . . . .

150ml your preferred type of milk
(rice, oat, almond, cow, soya) . . . .

3 tablespoons oat flakes . . . .

2 tablespoons amaranth flakes . . . . . .

Pinch of ground turmeric or grated
fresh turmeric root . . . .

Pinch of sea salt . . . .

Honey, to serve . . . .

Blueberries, to serve . . . .

⊕   Reasonable

⏳   5 minutes in the morning

I need you to collect yourself. Ready? Gluten is not a poison. Such is the misinformation surrounding gluten, my poor husband thinks we should be taking an insurance policy out against it and our neighbour thinks gluten is something that wild teenagers sniff. If you want to evict something in your diet, ditch the sugar-coated cereals from your cupboard, but leave gluten alone.* I've never seen a herring so scarlet.

*Eh, unless you are indeed coeliac.

Gently heat all the ingredients in your smallest saucepan. Simmer for 3–5 minutes and cook until the flakes swell. Try not to let the pot boil, burning the taste of the milk. It's worth remembering that the milk you choose will dictate the flavour of the porridge. Rice milk is plain but seriously sweet. Oat milk is earthy and sweet. Soya milk gives a more savoury feel.

Serve with extra milk tipped on top and a blob of set honey or blueberries. Pistachios and dried Morello cherries go really well with this combo too, as do strawberries, vanilla and flaked almonds.

Carrot Cake Porridge with Crystallised Ginger

SERVES 1 . . . .

5 tablespoons oat flakes . . . .

300ml (1 mug) plant-based milk, such as oat milk, or regular cow's milk . . .

Pinch of sea salt . . . .

Pinch of ground cinnamon . . . .

Splash of maple syrup (optional sweetness). . . . .

Good pinch of grated carrot (using the finer zesting side of your grater) . . . .

Raisins, to serve . . . .

Pistachios, to serve . . . .

Crystallised ginger, chopped, to serve . . . .

⊕ On a budget

. . . .

⏳ Not demanding

I like oats for their slow-release magic mojo. Have you ever noticed that your body chugs for longer on a bowl of porridge than a plate of toast? That's because oats break down slowly in our system. This makes porridge an excellent breakfast for athletes, chronically hungry teens and anxious cabinet ministers. More importantly, wholefood carbs like oats won't give you the highs and lows associated with sugar-coated breakfast cereals, responsible for many code-red situations in classrooms and Parliament. Yup – oats put the super into superfood.

Gently simmer your oats, milk, salt, cinnamon, maple and carrot for 3–5 minutes over a gentle heat, being careful not to boil the milk and spoil the flavour. It's worth mentioning that oat milk is naturally sweet, so you might prefer to leave out the maple syrup, whereas unsweetened soya milk and almond milk could benefit from a nip of extra sweetness.

Once all the liquid has been absorbed (I prefer mine on the runnier side), pour into your breakfast bowl, top with cold milk and decorate with raisins, pistachios and crystallised ginger. Bloody delicious.

Summer Overnight Oats

SERVES 1 . . . .

6 tablespoons oat flakes . . . .

1–2 tablespoons dark chocolate chunks . . . .

A little grated apple or squeeze of lemon . . . .

Flurry of flaky sea salt . . . .

125ml oat (or other) milk . . . .

A drizzle of runny tahini . . . .

Drizzle of maple or date syrup . . . . . .

⊕ On a budget

. . . .

⏳ Pre-soaking required, but will keep for three days in the fridge

Hot porridge during summer months sounds demented. That's because it is. Here's a new age Bircher muesli recipe, also known as overnight oats. Just assemble the night before a busy day and it will be cool and creamy by morning. Better still, prep it in a jar and grab a spoon as you belt out the door.

Stir the oats, chocolate, fruit, salt and milk together. Cover and allow to 'sleep' in the fridge overnight. In the morning, drizzle with tahini and maple or date syrup.

Hippie Dust

MAKES 1 JAR . . . .

4 tablespoons coconut sugar . . . .

3 tablespoons raw cacao nibs . . . .

2 tablespoons milled (not whole) chia seeds . . . .

2 tablespoons sesame or hemp seeds

Up to 1 tablespoon ground cinnamon .

 Feeling flush

. . . .

 60 seconds. Freezes well.

This stuff should be available on the public health service as PMT potion. It magically dulls the urge to head-butt your way through the Starbucks queue or to reach inside your colleague's gob and take his innards out in your fist. It's really that marvellous.

Hippie dust has sufficient sweetness to feed that sugar monster bubbling beneath itchy skin. You're bound to celebrate the stash of magnesium too, courtesy of the raw cacao nibs. Magnesium isn't an easy mineral to stock up on unless you neck prodigious amounts of Dark Green Leafies. Didn't think so. Magnesium helps with circulation, cramps and other pre-menstrual nuisances like headaches and marriages.

But let's not stop there. Let's get giddy with omega-3 essential fatty acids in the knowledge that these fats flirt with our hormones, not our waistlines. You'll find these in chia and hemp. I feel a poem coming on.

Shake all the ingredients in a clean jam jar and store in a cool dry place for up to six months. That's it! Sprinkle on top of porridge every morning in place of honey or over great clouds of natural yogurt.

I use milled chia instead of whole chia. That's because whole chia seeds need to be soaked for 20 minutes before wolfing – unless, of course, you enjoy getting chia seeds stuck in your molars. Milled and ground chia is a lot softer. You can find packets of milled chia in health food stores, savvy grocers and even your local four-letter German supermarket.

Chocolate Mint Freezer Slice

MAKES 25 SERVINGS . . . .

For the biscuit base

240g walnuts . . . .

8 Medjool dates, stones removed. . . . .

3 tablespoons cocoa or cacao powder

Pinch of sea salt . . . .

For the peppermint cream filling

2 ripe avocados, peeled, stoned and
flesh scooped out . . . .

50–80ml maple syrup (depends on
your sweet tooth) . . . .

80ml coconut oil or ghee (page 194),
melted . . . .

½ teaspoon real peppermint extract .

Raw chocolate frosting (optional)

4 tablespoons coconut oil or ghee . . .

2 tablespoons maple syrup or agave. .

2 tablespoons cacao or cocoa powder

½ teaspoon real peppermint extract .

 Not expensive per portion

. . . .

 Despite having three layers,
it's quick and easy in a food
processor

This chocolate mint freezer slice will help jumpstart your morning. One tiny sliver will deliver a dose of omega-3 fatty acids to your hormones' HQ. Yep. Thank you, walnuts. I make the peppermint cream filling from avocados and maple syrup. No one will know, except of course your cholesterol levels, which should benefit nicely too. Avocados have a jolly fine fat called monounsaturated oleic fat. This is the one your doc wants you to date. Monounsaturated fat has been shown to help lower LDL 'bad' cholesterol, while simultaneously raising your HDL 'good' cholesterol. Fist. Bump.

In a food processor, pulse the base ingredients together until it fraternises into a chocolaty lump. You might need a teaspoon of water to help it along. (A blender really won't work here.) Scrape into a regular loaf tin lined with non-stick baking paper. Press and smooth down.

Using the same food processor bowl, blitz the ingredients for the peppermint cream filling. You're looking for a sumptuous, glossy cream. Pour on top of the base and freeze for at least 30 minutes before slicing little pieces of Narnia from it.

If you want a raw chocolate topping, gently melt the coconut oil or ghee with your maple syrup. Whisk in the cacao or cocoa and the peppermint extract. Pour over the peppermint cream layer. Return to the freezer and hide it behind the fish fingers.

Roasted Butternut, Poached Egg, Furikake and Garlic Yogurt

SERVES 2 . . . .

½ butternut, peeled if not organic . . .

1 tablespoon extra virgin coconut oil
or ghee (page 194) . . . .

Furikake, from your freezer batch
(page 202) . . . .

1 garlic clove, minced . . . .

250g plain yogurt . . . .

A few twists of the salt and black
pepper mill . . . .

2 eggs . . . .

⊕ Reasonable
. . . .
⧗ Weekend treat

Eggs are one of the cheapest and snazziest superfoods on my planet. They're also one of the best sources of protein on Earth. Yolks sport an impressive stash of carotenoids like lutein and zeaxanthin to boost your superhero vision.

Eggs received a bad reputation during the 1980s fat frenzy – one we now know was based on flimsy science and hysterical brain burps. There's no need to fear fat. By all means, raise an eyebrow or two at fats like margarine and hydrogenated crap found in biscuits. But eggs are your friend – and don't forget it.

We often have this for supper on nights I feel compressed. For this reason, it's handy to keep furikake in your freezer or some harissa butter too.

Pump up your oven to 220°C.

Chop your butternut flesh into large bite-sized chunks and tumble onto a baking tray with your preferred fat. Roast for 30 minutes, until slightly caramelised on the edges and delicate on the inside. The cooking time will vary depending on the size of your chunks, so it's really important to keep the chopping uniform so that everything cooks at the same time. You don't want some smaller pieces ready after 15 minutes and larger ones requiring twice the cooking time.

While the butternut is roasting, boil the kettle and prep your remaining bits. Retrieve some furikake from your freezer batch and give it 10 minutes to defrost. Stir your minced garlic through the yogurt, adding some salt and pepper.

When the butternut is cooked through, divide between two plates (or save some butternut pieces for the fridge). Sprinkle with furikake and nestle in some garlic yogurt.

To poach the eggs, make sure your eggs are seriously fresh. You can test this by dropping the egg carefully into a glass of cold water. If it sinks to the bottom, horizontally, straight away, then it's perfect for poaching. If its butt lands on the bottom and its head tilts towards the top of the glass, then it's better to fry the egg or bake with it. If it floats to the top of the glass, it's stale.

Fill a small shallow pan with water and bring it to the boil, then reduce the heat to a steady simmer. Crack your egg into a cup. This makes it easier to slip the egg into the water whirlpool so that the egg white wraps itself around the yolk. Use a spoon to swirl the simmering water, then slip the egg into the centre. Cook for 2–3 minutes. Lift the egg out of the water using a slotted spoon or tea strainer. Briefly drain any residual water on kitchen paper.

Parachute the eggs on top of your butternut plates. Namaste.

Black Polenta Fingers and Gooey Eggs

MAKES APPROXIMATELY 8 SERVINGS . .

200g unroasted buckwheat groats . . .

500ml stock . . . .

Good handful of baby spinach . . . .

Splash of tamari or soya sauce . . . . . .

Extra virgin olive oil, for greasing . .

Eggs, for poaching or frying . . . .

Any spicy salsa from your freezer's
swag or sriracha (page 184), to serve

⊕ On a budget
. . . .
⧗ Good for lunchboxes and will
last all week in the fridge

Buckwheat is a small triangular grain. In Northern Italy, nonnas make polenta from buckwheat, not corn. This 'black' buckwheat polenta will keep in the fridge all week, making it the perfect snack for hungry little hands. Children love this recipe because they can use their fingers to eat it. The more squeamish ones may spot the green flecks of spinach and revolt. That's okay – tell them Adam and Daniel Leavy eat it.

Rinse the buckwheat in a sieve under running water. Transfer the clean buckwheat to your saucepan of boiling stock. Cover and turn down the heat to a gentle putter rather than a raucous boil. Cook for 12–15 minutes, until tender. Remove the saucepan from its heat source and allow the grains to absorb a little more stock under the lid if necessary.

Once cooked, transfer to a food processor (not a hand-held blender) and briefly pulse with the spinach and tamari or soya sauce. Aim for something like a textured porridge, but not a purée. Pour into a small dish or lunchbox greased with extra virgin olive oil. Ideally this polenta will be less than 2.5cm deep. Set aside for 20 minutes at room temperature, until set firm. Cut into fingers and serve alongside poached eggs or keep covered in the fridge until hunger hollers.

To poach the eggs, make sure your eggs are seriously fresh. You can test this by dropping the egg carefully into a glass of cold water. If it sinks to the bottom, horizontally, straight away, then it's perfect for poaching. If its butt lands on the bottom and its head tilts towards the top of the glass, then it's better to fry the egg or bake with it. If it floats to the top of the glass, it's stale.

Fill a small shallow pan with water and bring it to the boil, then reduce the heat to a steady simmer. Crack your egg into a cup. This makes it easier to slip the egg into the water whirlpool so that the egg white wraps itself around the yolk. Use a spoon to swirl the simmering water, then slip the egg into the centre. Cook for 2–3 minutes. Lift the egg out of the water using a slotted spoon or tea strainer. Briefly drain any residual water on kitchen paper before placing the eggs on the polenta fingers and drizzling with salsa or sriracha.

Summer Mango, Date Syrup and Feta Smash

SERVES 4-6 . . . .

2 very ripe mangoes, preferably
Pakistani or Indian Alphonso . . . .

200g feta cheese . . . .

4 tablespoons tahini . . . .

2 tablespoons extra virgin olive oil . .

1 teaspoon lime juice . . . .

½ teaspoon cayenne pepper . . . .

Handful of fresh mint leaves . . . .

Freshly cracked black pepper . . . .

Trickle of date syrup . . . .

 Feeling flush

. . . .

 Mad quick and really easy for
summer months. The ingredients
can sit in your fridge for over
a week before you decide to
make it.

This recipe is guaranteed to deliver alarming amounts of pleasure. Mangos are a good source of vitamin B6 – the vitamin that helps our brain to manufacture serotonin. Cowabunga! And get this – mangos are also hooting with vitamin C to help with the production of collagen and the recovery of damaged skin cells. Your night cream might try to boast the same, but I reckon this recipe is most definitely cheaper and more effective. Isn't it so satisfying to find a food you love that loves you back?

Cut the mango cheeks from each side of the stone. Slice these into strips, like melon, removing the leathery skin with a sharp knife. Try to salvage as much flesh from the stone as possible, but I usually resort to sucking the stone while I read the remainder of the recipe.

Arrange the mango slices on a breadboard and leave to chill in the fridge.

Using a fork, lightly crush the feta cheese into your tahini, olive oil, lime and cayenne pepper. Finely chop the mint leaves and let them loose with the crushed feta. It won't need salt, but a few cracks of the black pepper mill and a sneaky dribble of date syrup will bring it up an octave.

Taste and add more cayenne or mint to suit your mood. Serve in a small bowl beside lashings of fragrant mangos.

Miso Butter Mushrooms

ENOUGH FOR 4-6

3 tablespoons soft butter or melted ghee (page 194) . . . .

1 tablespoon sweet white miso paste . . . .

1 garlic clove, crushed . . . .

4–6 Portobello mushrooms . . . .

⊕ On a budget

. . . .

⧗ Ingredients can laze in the fridge all week until you're ready to commit

Let me tell you why the Japanese have been using miso in their kitchens since forever. (And that's how long they tend to live for too.) Fermented soya beans are rich in isoflavones. These highly intelligent compounds are part of the phytoestrogen clan that proves particularly useful for menopausal felines and for other hormonal quakes, we're told. Could this help to explain why the rate of breast cancer in tofu-eating countries is significantly lower than non-tofu-munching nations? But science is rarely that simple. There is, of course, a suite of measures that the Japanese willingly or unwittingly employ to extend their body's shelf life. This is just one of them. Others probably include green tea, samurai DNA and seaweed.

With a fork, bash the butter, miso paste and garlic against the side of a cup until thoroughly blended. Taste and add more butter if it's too pungent. Ghee also works and is ideal if you're sensitive to milk, as the problematic milk solids, such as casein and even lactose, have been removed. O-M-Ghee.

Fire up the barbecue or hot grill. (A hot oven will also do.) Spread your miso butter around the centre of each mushroom. Wait until the barbecue or grill is sufficiently hot, then cook on the higher shelf of the barbecue for about 8 minutes without turning.

Serve alongside poached eggs, flaked mackerel, hash potatoes or scrambled tofu.

Power Eggs

ENOUGH FOR 1-2 . . . .

2-4 spring onions, chopped . . . .

1 garlic clove, crushed. . . . .

Pinch of chilli flakes . . . .

Pinch of ground turmeric. . . . .

Pinch of cumin seeds . . . .

2 teaspoons coconut oil or ghee
(page 194) . . . .

3 eggs. . . . .

⊕ On a budget

. . . .

⧗ Suitable for any time of day

Spring onions woof. Inside their svelte little figures, you'll find a party of smelly sulphur compounds. That honk is our friend. The lovely allium family contains a pharmacy of goodies like quercetin, sulfides and thiosulfinates for burly bones and fizzing health. Quercetin has been shown to exhibit good leadership in our body's own anti-inflammatory squadron. Yup. This is proving useful for the relief of symptoms like asthma and hay fever. Or hangovers. Honk on!

Gently fry the spring onions, garlic and spices in your preferred fat over a medium heat for 3 minutes.

Break the eggs into a bowl and whisk briefly with a fork. Add to the pan of spices and let the eggs cook halfway through before stirring them. I prefer mine soft and floppy, so I fold the eggs over like a misbehaving omelette and plate up. If you prefer them cooked for longer, stir briskly over a higher heat until the eggs look fluffy.

Plate up with a glorious bunch of juicy baby toms in the summer or a hunk of toasted sourdough and avocado during winter.

Shakshuka, 3 Ways

Shakshuka is a famous pepper dish that originated in North Africa. Did you know that all peppers start off green? As they mature, their colour (yellow, orange, red) and nutritional powers develop. Groovy, huh? Within these colours lurk some radical health-boosting compounds. Peppers are definitely our allies on our journey towards better health and a buzzing body. So is this stonkingly good shakshuka recipe, rich in peppers and toms. Red peppers are the sweetest of all, while their green cousins are the most pungent. Choose whichever variety you fancy.

2-Minute Shakshuka with Black Sesame Salt

FOR 1 . . . .
½ teaspoon mineral-rich salt . . . .
6 tablespoons black sesame seeds. . . .
Enough tomato passata for 1 . . . .
1 egg . . . .

⊕   On a budget
. . . .
⧖   A cheat's version

I am astonished at the volume of love this 2-minute shakshuka can yield at the family table. It's like being mugged by Cupid.

Heat the sea salt in a dry pan over a medium heat. Stir for about 2 minutes, until really dry. Transfer to a pestle and mortar, then repeat with your sesame seeds. They might need a little longer on the pan, until they swell and toast.

Grind both into a fine powder (called gomashio), until the seeds are 70% crushed. Store in a happy clean jar with a tight lid for up to eight weeks.

To assemble the cheat's shakshuka, heat enough tomato passata for each person being served. Poach an egg (see page 32 if you're new to poaching) and drop into your bowl of hot passata followed with a flurry of the black sesame salt.

Smoky Shakshuka Eggs with Coriander Yogurt

SERVES 2 HUNGRY GUESTS OR 4
CASUAL BREAKFASTS..............

2 tablespoons extra virgin olive oil

1 onion, diced....................

2 peppers, deseeded and sliced.....

2 teaspoons ground cumin or cumin
seeds..........................

1 teaspoon smoked paprika.........

1 teaspoon dried oregano..........

Pinch of cayenne pepper...........

6 large extra-ripe tomatoes (not
cherry tomatoes)................

4 (tinned) anchovies..............

4 eggs..........................

Coriander yogurt

1 garlic clove, peeled.............

1 teaspoon whole black peppercorns

½ large tub of natural yogurt......

Handful of fresh coriander, finely
chopped........................

⊕ Reasonable
....

⧖ A weekend treat. Base can be
frozen.

Antioxidants are important little buggers for recovery. They work by disarming those thieving free radicals loitering in our system. Without disarmament, free radicals can wreak havoc on our health, like a game of Space Invaders gone horribly wrong. This is achieved through a process called oxidation. Don't worry, it's not an overnight process.

We simply want to slow down oxidation in our cells and our body, as oxidative stress appears to have a starring role in the theatre of ageing and degenerative diseases. How do we do this? Fresh veggies like pepper and onions are rich in antioxidants and radical nutrients. Think of them as our very own personal ninja army!

Heat a heavy-based frying pan over a low heat. Add the olive oil and sweat the onion until it turns translucent (6–8 minutes). Tip in the peppers and keep sweating on a low heat for another 6–8 minutes, until soft.

Have the spices ready to join the party. Tumble them in, briskly stir and let your nostrils samba. Using a potato masher, add the tomatoes and the anchovies, mashing them into the spicy onion mix. Put a lid on your pan. Gently cook for 15 minutes, until the tomatoes have completely collapsed into a thick sauce. You may need to add a little water to help it along.

As soon as the sauce is thick enough, carve four little wells in the tomato base and break an egg into each. Cover the pan and cook gently over a low-medium heat for 5 minutes, until the egg whites are set.

While the eggs are softly poaching in the sauce, make your yogurt by crushing the garlic and peppercorns together in a pestle and mortar. Stir this garlic paste through your natural yogurt along with the finely chopped fresh coriander. Holler for everyone to take their places at the kitchen table. You need to serve this dish immediately with great big wallops of the garlic and coriander yogurt. Any leftover sauce can be used to excite pasta or despondent lentils the following night.

Borlotti Bean Shakshuka with Harissa Butter

SERVES 2 HUNGRY GUESTS OR
4 CASUAL BREAKFASTS . . . .

Recipe as on page 40, plus ...

250g cooked or tinned borlotti beans

250ml tomato passata . . . .

1 garlic clove, grated. . . . .

1 cube of harissa butter (page 198). . .

⊕   On a budget
. . . .

⧗   Weekend treat, suitable for
breakfast, lunch or dinner

Follow the smoky shakshuka recipe on page 40. Put the drained beans, passata and garlic in a blender and purée until smooth. Add to the smoky shakshuka at the same time as the fresh tomatoes and cook accordingly. The beans will add a more filling element to the meal, making it a great option for midweek suppers too. Drop your frozen cube of harissa butter in at the end of cooking before plating up and serving.

Super Smooth Hummus and Poached Eggs

MAKES 1 LARGE BOWL (15 SERVINGS) .

200–300g dried chickpeas . . . .

½ teaspoon bicarbonate of soda . . . . .

1 x 270g jar of tahini or cashew nut butter. . . . .

3 lemons, juiced. . . . .

4 garlic cloves, crushed. . . . .

1 teaspoon flaky sea salt or soya sauce . . . .

250ml ice-cold water . . . .

1 egg per person, for poaching . . . . . .

Freezer dressings, flavour grenades and ferments to rock your hummus . . . .

Chimichurri (page 183) . . . .

Salsa verde (page 186) . . . .

Romesco sauce (page 187) . . . .

Pistachio and kale pesto (page 192) . .

Nori paste (page 193) . . . .

Black olive crumb (page 210) . . . .

Kimchi (page 229) . . . .

Popped capers (page 214). . . . .

⊕ On a budget

. . . .

⌛ Overnight soaking required. This recipe lasts all week long in the fridge, ready to plunder when the mood yodels. You can freeze it in portions too.

Hummus and poached eggs are ballistically good together. Even fussy toddlers struggle to resist its charms.

Chickpeas are *not* called bloke peas for a good reason. Chickpeas are puffed with feline-friendly compounds. There's magnesium, a mineral many of us crave once a month when we become a crazed version of a slightly-less-bonkers self. Magnesium has the magnificent ability to relieve cramps by helping our blood vessels relax – good news for headaches and varicose veins too.

Then there's isoflavones, a plant-based phytoestrogen that some consider to be ammunition in the fight against breast cancer. It looks like our body converts isoflavones into compounds that mimic some of the effects of oestrogen. Score! Why is this important? Because the female reproductive system is influenced by oestrogen. Phytoestrogens have already been used to improve menopausal symptoms. Some women prefer to take phytoestrogens rather than opt for hormone replacement therapy (HRT). I do like the idea of being prescribed hummus for hot flushes!

If you haven't cooked chickpeas from scratch, you are missing out on one of the creamiest beans on Earth. Tinned chickpeas are fine, but hardly make me breakdance. Try this hummus recipe and make MC Hammer proud.

Start the night before by rinsing the chickpeas and soaking them in cold water.

The next day, drain the chickpeas. Tumble them into a medium saucepan, crank up the heat and add the bicarbonate of soda. Cook for a few minutes, stirring constantly to prevent the bicarb burning. Bicarb helps to make the hummus silky smooth.

Cover with fresh water and bring to a rolling boil. Using a slotted spoon, skim off any funny foam that floats to the top. The chickpeas can take anywhere between 20 and 50 minutes to cook, depending on their size and freshness. Once done they should be very tender, so keep checking.

Drain the chickpeas and transfer to a food processor (you

could also use a hand-held blender). Whizz the chickpeas into a stiff paste with the tahini or cashew butter, lemon juice, garlic and sea salt or soya sauce. With the motor still running, drizzle in the iced water and allow it to mix until you get a very smooth paste.

Cover until ready to serve or chill in the fridge for five to seven days. Also freezes without complaint.

We serve ours with poached eggs (if you're new to poaching, check out page 32). Stamp your signature on it. Swirl some glossy olive oil on top or sprinkle with pomegranate seeds. Perhaps date syrup and fresh coriander? Sweet paprika and chilli flakes? One of my suggested freezer dressings, flavour grenades or ferments? Over to you …

Kimcheese Toastie

PER PERSON . . . .

Non-stick baking paper . . . .

2 thin slices of sourdough bread . . . .

2 tablespoons butter . . . .

2 tablespoons grated Parmesan cheese . . . .

2 slices of Cheddar or Gubbeen, at room temperature . . . .

1 tablespoon kimchi (page 229) . . . . . .

Dressed salad leaves, to serve (optional) . . . .

⊕   Make your own kimchi
     (page 229)

. . . .

⧖   Takes practice to perfect. Can't
     be frozen.

This is my current favourite dish. If you're not pushed on the kimchi, we cannot be friends. Kimchi is a fermented chilli and cabbage salad with a very delicious tang. There's enough heat in this kimcheese toastie to have you prancing like a defected Morris dancer.

The key lies in the pan and parchment paper. You need a lidded, heavy-based sauté pan, but a frying pan and big plate should suffice in a pinch. Also, it's important to use a hard cheese like Parmesan or Cais na Tire for the outside slices and a medium-soft cheese for the centre. We have a thing for smoked Gubbeen or Killeen's gouda-style goat's cheese for the centre. An aged Cheddar is goddamn racy too.

First step is to cut a snug circle of parchment for the bottom of your sauté pan. Weird, but important. A casserole pot or a frying pan will also work.

Heat your pan (and circle of parchment) over a low to medium heat. While your pan is heating up, spread one side of a slice of bread with 1 tablespoon of butter and 1 tablespoon of grated Parmesan, spreading it out over the crusts too. Place on the heated parchment, cheesy side down. Set your stopwatch to 3 minutes.

Now add your slice of Cheddar or Gubbeen on top of the (unbuttered) side of bread while the cheesy side bubbles underneath. Pile the kimchi over the cheese.

Finally, butter the top slice as before, add the remaining Parmesan and place on top of the kimchi. Press firmly on top of your kimcheese and flip so that the top side now becomes the bottom slice.

Place a lid over your pan. Set your stopwatch for another 3 minutes. Try not to let the Parmesan brown and burn – you're looking for a soft caramel colour, so adjust the timing to suit your pan.

Plate up beside a nest of freshly dressed salad leaves (if using). Cut in half and admire your brilliance.

Chestnut Pancakes with Chocolate Chip Ricotta

MAKES 6 LARGE PANCAKES . . . .

1 egg . . . .

1 teaspoon vanilla bean paste or
extract . . . .

250ml your preferred type of milk
(cow's, soya, almond) . . . .

70g buckwheat flour . . . .

50g chestnut flour . . . .

Flurry of sea salt . . . .

Ghee (page 194) or coconut oil, to fry

Chocolate chip ricotta

180–220g Irish ricotta cheese . . . . . .

30g dark chocolate, chopped into
chunks . . . .

2 tablespoons raw runny honey . . . . . .

Feeling flush

Batter lasts for five days
in the fridge

Tuscan chestnut pancakes, called necci, taste sweeter and more wholesome than regular pancakes. That's because those wily Italians use chestnuts as their secret ingredient. Chestnut flour is unquestionably more exciting than white flour.

This version of necci also incorporates Northern Italy's love of buckwheat. Both flours are gluten free and available in savvy delis or health food stores.

Buckwheat is nature's snazziest source of rutin, touted to help with the strengthening of blood vessels in our body. Several studies have shown that flavonoids, specifically from rutin, help to relieve the swelling and pain associated with varicose veins and haemorrhoids. Woohoo! Pancakes for pain!

Rutin is also considered an anti-inflammatory agent within the pharmaceutical sector and is often found in osteoarthritis medication and multivitamins. By golly, those Italians are dangerously smart. No wonder they're still zipping around in their nineties with a speed usually reserved for Boeings. Their entire pantry is like a mini pharmacy – tomatoes, peppers, nuts, olive oil, buckwheat, chestnut, lentils, parsley, basil ... the list goes on.

You'll need two small bowls. In the first, beat your egg and vanilla together, then add the milk.

In the second bowl, sift both flours together. Now slowly whisk the contents of the first bowl into the flours to form a smooth pancake batter. Season generously with sea salt and leave to rest for 15 minutes while you make your sweet ricotta filling.

Beat the ricotta, chocolate chips and honey together. Set aside.

Heat a non-stick frying pan good and hot with a dot of ghee or coconut oil.

Ladle in a little batter, swirling to coat the base of the pan, and cook for 2 minutes. Flip as soon as the underside is stable and cook for a further minute. I find thicker ones work best. As soon as the other side is done, plate up and smother with the chocolate chip ricotta. Fold the pancake in half, then fold again. If you want to drizzle more honey on top, I'm not going to stop you.

Energy Bomb-Bombs
for running out the door

MAKES 15–20 . . . .

2 ginger herbal teabags, torn open (a combo is fine) . . . .

250g gooey Medjool dates . . . .

140g walnuts . . . .

Zest of ½ unwaxed orange (optional flavour) . . . .

3 tablespoons cacao or cacao powder

2 tablespoons extra virgin coconut oil . . . .

1 tablespoon maca powder (optional booster) . . . .

Flurry of flaky sea salt . . . .

Pricey, but still rings in at a fraction of the cost of commercial ones

. . . .

Lasts for three weeks in the fridge. Freezes for four months.

Energy bomb-bombs will happily hibernate in the freezer for up to four months. This will help to upgrade those pesky sugar cravings into a nutritional party. We grab these running out the door and sink our gnashers into them after 4 minutes of defrosting on the car seat beside me.

The swag of ginger and cocoa will supercharge circulation to your brain, so those sleepy eyelids won't stand a chance. Magnesium is a superstar mineral that relaxes blood vessels and increases circulation. Unless you're regularly necking kale and broccoli smoothies, most of us are deficient in this mineral. Magnesium is a pivotal mineral for getting a good night's sleep too – especially if you're prone to waking up in the middle of the night. One of nature's best sources of magnesium is raw chocolate. (Was that a back flip?)

Start by carefully tearing the teabags open and tip them into your food processor.

Remove the stones from each date (compost them if you can). Add the dates to the processor. Blitz with the remaining ingredients until thoroughly socialised.

Roll the dough into little bonbons between your palms. Let them set in the fridge for 2 hours. They'll keep for four months in the freezer, three weeks in the fridge or three minutes in the office.

Turbo Waffles, 4 Ways

Wholefood waffles have become a staple in my kitchen. I'm hooked on the reckless praise they provoke each time I serve them. I think you will be too. My boys go cross-eyed and slack-jawed as soon as they see me taking out my waffle maker.

Cinnamon, Oat, Banana and Nutmeg Waffles with Chocolate Sauce

MAKES 16–24 WAFFLES, DEPENDING ON YOUR MACHINE . . . .

135g oat flour . . . .

1 banana, mashed . . . .

1 egg . . . .

250ml almond milk, buttermilk or regular milk . . . .

Squeeze of lemon . . . .

4 tablespoons coconut oil, butter or ghee (page 194), melted . . . .

1 teaspoon vanilla extract . . . .

½ teaspoon baking powder . . . .

½ teaspoon ground cinnamon . . . .

Scratch of fresh nutmeg . . . .

Pinch of flaky sea salt . . . .

For the chocolate sauce

2 tablespoons melted coconut oil . . . .

2 tablespoons maple syrup . . . .

1 tablespoon raw cacao powder . . . . . .

⊕ On a budget

. . . .

⧖ Batter will laze about in your fridge for up to five days

Oats contain two types of groovy fibre that excites nurses and health scientists alike. This grain's platoon of soluble and insoluble fibre serves our pipes in more ways than one. Firstly, this type of fibre will help keep you regular. Bye-bye haemorrhoids and constipation, hello light-footed daffodil. Secondly, oat's cargo of fibre will help to sat nav your pipes for excess cholesterol like a tenacious traffic warden. Home run!

Blend all the ingredients together and leave for 20 minutes or overnight if possible (soaking flour makes it easier to digest for delicate systems).

Pour ½ cup (around 125ml) of the batter in the centre of your preheated waffle maker. Cook according to your manufacturer's guidelines. This is usually 2–3 minutes, until the machine beeps. Serve hot with thick clouds of Greek yogurt and a smattering of blueberries. Leftovers can be popped into lunchboxes or used as currency around the house.

You can make a fancy pants kapow sauce by whisking together the melted coconut oil, maple syrup and raw cacao powder. It will blow your dimples off.

Cinnamon, Oat, Banana
and Nutmeg Waffles

Teff Waffles with Blackberries
and Sour Cream

Teff Waffles with Blackberries and Sour Cream

MAKES 16–24 WAFFLES,
DEPENDING ON YOUR MACHINE . . . .
280g wholegrain teff flour (brown
or cream) . . . .
500ml your preferred
type of milk . . . .
Squeeze of lemon . . . .
3 tablespoons melted ghee
(page 194), butter or extra virgin
coconut oil . . . .
½ teaspoon baking powder . . . .
½ teaspoon flaky sea salt . . . .
Blackberries, to serve . . . .
Sour cream, to serve . . . .

Feeling flush

. . . .

Store any unused batter in the
fridge and dip into it all week

Teff is the national grain of Ethiopia, where it is fermented and made into savoury pancakes called injera. We've had injera at Ethiopian community centres around Britain that was so large it draped over our setting like a tablecloth. I gracefully milled into it like Homer Simpson in a sea of marshmallows. Teff and I have been best friends ever since.

Your batter should last for up to six days when chilled. Fried eggs are great with teff waffles or crushed avocado and Parmesan. You can make a simple chocolate sauce by melting a bit of butter or coconut oil and mixing through equal parts cocoa powder and maple syrup. Or a beautiful lemon syrup by mixing 1 tablespoon of lemon juice with 1 heaped tablespoon of icing sugar.

You can pelt all the ingredients into a blender or food processor and pulse until creamy. Leave to stand on the kitchen counter overnight, covered, to jumpstart a little fermentation. Or you can use the batter 30 minutes after soaking if necessary. A caveat on teff flour: it doesn't absorb liquid as much as regular flour, so if you try subbing the same quantities for another flour, you'll end up with a stodgy mess.

In the morning, pour the batter into a heated waffle iron as per the manufacturer's instructions. My waffle maker holds four small waffles at a time and takes 60 seconds to cook. There are five settings, but the first setting is plenty hot.

Carefully remove once the waffle iron beeps or the light turns on to signify the waffle is done. No need to flip. Serve immediately with blackberries and sour cream or cooling clouds of crème fraîche and peach slices. The chocolate chip ricotta on page 72 is also ace.

Buckwheat Buttermilk Waffles with Smoked Salmon and Horseradish Yogurt

MAKES 16–24 WAFFLES, DEPENDING
ON YOUR MACHINE . . . .

250g buckwheat flour . . . .

1 egg . . . .

700ml Irish farmhouse buttermilk,
such as Cuinneog . . . .

4 tablespoons melted butter or ghee
(page 000) . . . .

½ teaspoon baking powder . . . .

Generous pinch of flaky sea salt . . . . .

Smoked salmon, to serve . . . .

Horseradish yogurt (page 217), to
serve . . . .

⊕ On a budget

. . . .

⧗ Batter lasts all week in the
fridge to service munchies

The Prince of Wales likes to talk to his cows and give them individual names. Princey says it encourages better milk production. It's not often I like to agree with a monarchy that stuffed our country, but Princey is spot on. Improved 'milking' conditions for cows ensure fewer stress hormones and leads to greater-tasting milk. There's an impressive body of research to back this up. In a country where the chat is almighty, is it any wonder that Irish buttermilk is indecently good? Our beatific herds produce some of the most coveted buttermilk in the restaurant world, appearing on menus across Europe, with buttermilk panna cotta, buttermilk chicken, buttermilk snow and buttermilk ice-cream being some of the favourites. Who knows what makes an age-old Irish by-product into an Instagram sensation, but buttermilk seems to have sealed this transition.

Whisk the first six ingredients together, beating out any lumps. For the bestest of the best results, leave overnight.

Pour half a teacup's worth of the batter (around 125ml) into the centre of your preheated waffle maker. Cook according to your manufacturer's guidelines, but preferably on the low-medium side. This is usually 2–3 minutes, until the machine beeps.

Serve hot with smoked salmon and horseradish yogurt. For snazzy days, we plate up with cold clouds of Greek yogurt, dried lavender buds, honey and blueberries. It's about as weird as I get with my clothes on.

Plain Savoury Waffles

MAKES 16–24 WAFFLES, DEPENDING
ON YOUR MACHINE . . . .

1 egg (or 100ml apple purée
for vegans) . . . .

2 teaspoons vanilla bean paste or
good-quality extract . . . .

2 tablespoons milled chia . . . .

Sprinkle of sea salt . . . .

500ml preferred milk . . . .

3–4 tablespoons ghee (page 194),
butter or coconut oil . . . .

300g gluten-free self-raising white
flour . . . .

Reasonable
. . . .

You can keep the batter all week
long in your fridge

Great with a simple vanilla crème fraîche stirred through any of the healthy jams on page 10. Or with baked beans. Fussy playdates won't refuse these smothered in strawberries and date syrup.

Belt everything in a blender, and leave to ferment overnight. These are the simplest and tastiest of all waffles.

Cook according to your waffle maker machine.

Carefully remove the waffles once the manufacturer's beep or light turns on, to signify the waffle is done. No need to flip. Serve immediately with any freezer dressings such as the harissa butter (page 198), and a sneaky poached egg.

Saffron and Mandarin Apricots with Pistachio Yogurt

ENOUGH FOR 6 . . . .

6 mandarins, peeled . . . .

250g dried dark unsulphured
apricots . . . .

Pinch of saffron threads . . . .

Greek yogurt, to serve . . . .

Handful of shelled salted pistachios,
to serve . . . .

Saffron is dastardly expensive,
so nick your mum's

Sits in the fridge for up to
three weeks

This breakfast will conjure the air around you, making the start to your day pretty magical. It's a spin on an Anna Jones classic. You'll need to track down naturally dried apricots. These are the dark, gooey, unprocessed ones. Health food stores will likely stock them. Bright orange dried apricots have a sheet of preservatives covering them that taste nasty when cooked.

Squeeze the mandarins over your apricots in a pan. Heat to a rolling boil, then add the saffron threads. Turn down the heat and putter away for 10 minutes, until the liquid has reduced and thickened.

Cool and store in the fridge for up to three weeks to make six deliriously happy breakfasts. Serve with thick clouds of Greek yogurt and a smattering of crunchy pistachios.

* See page 24 for photo

Yoga Crumpets

MAKES 12 . . . .

130g brown rice flour . . . .

2 tablespoons coconut flour . . . .

2 tablespoons potato flour . . . .

½ teaspoon baking powder . . . .

Generous pinch of fine or flaky
sea salt . . . .

4 tablespoons leftover cooked quinoa
or lentils (I store these in
my freezer) . . . .

375ml plant milk . . . .

Ghee (page 194) or coconut oil, to fry

⊕ Reasonable
. . . .

⧗ Batter rests all week in the
fridge for snack attacks

My aversion to yoga has finally been crushed. Let's not be hasty – I still keel over doing downward dog and, for the most part, look like a member of a disinherited race on my yoga mat. But I'm over myself.

Being gifted this crumpet recipe by a yogi mum was My Moment. After making the first batch, I quickly wanted to know what else I was missing out on. Repurposing quinoa techniques aside, I wanted to get closer to enlightenment. Because I did not find it in cold brew coffee.

These are scrumptious. We're keeping it vegan so that you can annoy your yoga class with your virtuousness. That's where the real enjoyment lies.

Toss and turn the flours together with your baking powder and a flurry of sea salt. Parachute in your cooked quinoa or lentils. Slowly beat in the milk and leave the batter to swell for 10 minutes.

Heat a frying pan with a scrape of ghee or good coconut oil. I like to use a medium heat – a high heat will disfigure the fat and blacken the crumpets.

Pour in some batter until your preferred size of crumpet is achieved. I like mine small and fluffy, so I generally cook three at a time on the frying pan. When bubbles start appearing on the side nearest you, it's time to flip them over and gently cook the other side. Serve as you go – it's unrealistic to assume your family members will patiently wait.

We top ours with smoked salmon or poached eggs, although set honey and butter can really hit the spot too. These crumpets also work well for kids' lunchboxes.

100% Rye Sourdough

People are so scared of gluten in some parts of California that you could probably rob a bank by waving a baguette in the air. Even in Ireland, it has earned such a bad rep that somebody I'm married to (no names) thinks gluten must be something delinquent teenagers get high on.

I understand how refreshing it feels to ditch bread; how your energy levels hit another stratosphere. I get it. I was there. I thought the culprit had to be gluten, the bad bastard. The reality is far simpler. The fart fests many of us experience with commercial bread has less to do with gluten than with the way industrial bakeries operate. Instead of spending days traditionally fermenting flour, loaves are now spewed out on conveyor belts within minutes and are designed to last for weeks on supermarket shelves. We ditched the bread-making wisdom of thousands of years, but not without consequences.

A popular British brand churns out half a million sliced pans a day – and their market share is less than 10%. Imagine how many cheap loaves bigger competitors are belching out each hour. How can we call this real bread? Is it any wonder that it feels like a civil war is gurgling inside our pipes? Pah!

Try sourdough, which is significantly tastier and easier to digest. Wild yeasts and good bacteria feast on the flour and pre-digest the grain during fermentation. True sourdough is handmade with only three ingredients: flour, water and time. Here's your own kickass starter.

Sourdough Starter

325g wholemeal rye flour . . . .

325g filtered water, at room
temperature. . . . .

⊕   On a budget

. . . .

⧖   Time consuming, but fun and
very rewarding. Freezes well.

This starter can be used to make any sort of sourdough, from
country white boules to spelt loaves.

Day 1:   Start by mixing 25g of your flour with 25g of water. Cover
with a lid and leave to sit at 21–25°C.

Day 2:   Leave alone.

Day 3:   Refresh your starter with another 50g of flour and 50g of
water. Cover with a lid and leave to sit at 21–25°C.

Day 4:   You'll notice a sour smell and air bubbles. Yahtzee! Now
discard or compost 100g of your starter, leaving you with
50g. Sounds counter-intuitive, but it's necessary according
to sourdough Jedis. Refresh your beloved starter with 50g
of flour and 50g of water. Cover with a lid and leave to sit at
21–25°C.

Day 5:   Repeat Day 4.

Day 6:   Ready to scale up and bake? Add 150g of rye flour and 150g
of water, mixing thoroughly. See the method overleaf to start
your bake. Or you can put your starter in the fridge to slow
down the fermentation, 'refreshing' it the night before you
bake.

Rye Sourdough Loaf

MAKES 2 LOAVES . . . .

Olive oil, for greasing. . . . .

660g fresh rye sourdough starter . . .

400g medium rye flour . . . .

330g filtered water, at room temperature . . . .

14g fine sea salt . . . .

This recipe calls for 660g of fresh rye sourdough culture. If you're scaling up on Day 6, continue building your starter culture without disposing of any. The reason we dispose one-third of your starter culture on Days 4 and 5 is to prevent mutiny. The culture can quickly become overrun by wild yeasts and bacteria. We need to temper their enthusiasm by feeding them. Kind of like a carb coma. (Eh, that's me talking. Not the sourdough Jedi, who might have a more scientifically sound answer.) So Day 6 requires 330g rye flour and 330g warm water added to Day 5's batch. Day 7 is B-Day (Baking Day)! Just follow the method below.

If the starter has been lazing in the fridge for more than 10 days, it will need two refreshments so that you have a portfolio of wild yeasts and bacteria to offer the baking gods. If that's where you are right now, here's how you manage two feeds: given that the recipe calls for 660g of fresh sourdough culture, you'll be taking only 100g of your lazy starter and passing the rest to a mate. Refresh this 100g of starter with 100g of rye flour and 100g of warm water. Mix thoroughly and ferment for 24 hours at the usual 21–25°C. Splendiferous!

Now, the second feed will need 300g of flour and 300g of warm water just 12 hours before you plan on baking. Twelve hours is the sweet spot, when the culture smells both sweet and sour. Any remaining starter can be returned to the fridge until you fancy baking again (in which case, follow the steps to scale up or refresh).

I refresh the night before I bake. Or I refresh after breakfast, then make the sourdough before bedtime so that we have bread on the table in the morning.

May the force be with you.

Oil or line 2 x 1lb loaf tins.

Using clean hands, mix all the ingredients together in a large bowl to form a soft dough. With a wet hand, scoop out the dough and divide it between the tins. Cover the tins with a clean shower cap or damp tea towel. Place them in a warm area to rise for 2 hours. A hot press is ace.

Preheat the oven to 220°C when the dough is nearly done rising.

Bake in the oven for approximately 40 minutes. It's a good idea to spray the oven with water to help the loaves form a crust. Remove from the oven and cool for 6 hours. This bread gets better during the week as the culture continues to work. Crazy cool.

Riot Rye's Borodinsky Bread

50g molasses . . . .

25g barley malt syrup . . . .

1 teaspoon ground coriander . . . .

1–2 teaspoons coriander seeds . . . . . .

Some of Ireland's best bread is made by Joe Fitzmaurice in Tipperary. Riot Rye is Joe's bread school and bakery and his Borodinsky is vertiginously good. There are hundreds of giddy disciples celebrating his bread-making skills every day. Now you can join in too.

To make Riot Rye's Borodinsky bread, use the recipe for the 100% rye sourdough loaf but add the new ingredients.

Follow the recipe for the 100% rye sourdough, adding in the molasses, barley malt syrup and ground coriander. Before baking, sprinkle with 1–2 teaspoons of coriander seeds. Celestial stuff.

Freezer Flaxseed Focaccia, 5 Ways

⊕ Reasonable

. . . .

⏳ Store slices in the freezer to
greet busy mornings

These focaccia recipes are explosively tasty, made from pure flaxseed and brain booty. If Sudoku doesn't tickle your brain cells, this bread should sort you out. Don't forget, flax is nature's richest source of plant-based omega-3s. Body. Slam.

You can now source ground flax (also referred to as milled linseed) in your local four-letter German supermarket. It's not a problem using a flaxseed blend as long as the flax content is roughly 70% or above. The recipe will still turn out beautifully.

MAKES 1 FOCACCIA . . . .

4 tablespoons finely diced onion . . . .

5 tablespoons extra virgin olive oil .

1–2 teaspoons whole (not ground)
aniseed . . . .

240g milled flaxseed (linseed) . . . . . .

1½ teaspoons baking powder . . . .

3 eggs . . . .

185ml regular or plant milk . . . .

2 tablespoons honey, date syrup or
barley malt syrup . . . .

Flaky sea salt, to dust . . . .

Onion Focaccia with Aniseed

Onions and flaxseed are flush with flavonoids that help to fight disease. (Is ageing a disease? It feels like one.) This bread has your back.

Whack up your oven to 180°C. Line a 20cm x 25cm tin with non-stick baking paper. Size is really important – look for something a little bigger than or equal to a square brownie tin.

Start by gently sweating the onion in 1 tablespoon of the olive oil. After 3–5 minutes, add the aniseed. Stir for 2 minutes. Remove from the heat and set aside.

Let the milled flax and your baking powder get to know each other in a large bowl.

In a separate bowl, whisk the eggs, milk, preferred sweetener, cooked onion and remaining 4 tablespoons of olive oil with a fork until glossy.

Now beat the wet ingredients into the bowl of dry ingredients, then pour into your lined tin. Spread evenly and top with a flurry of flaky sea salt. Bake in the oven for about 25 minutes.

Remove from the oven and the tin. Allow to cool for 10 minutes on a wire rack. Spectacular stuff.

Rosemary, Lemon and Olive Oil Focaccia

MAKES 1 FOCACCIA . . . .

3 teaspoons dried rosemary or finely chopped fresh rosemary needles . . . .

240g milled flaxseed (linseed) . . . . . .

1½ teaspoons baking powder . . . .

3 large eggs . . . .

185ml regular or plant milk . . . .

½ unwaxed lemon, zest and juice . . . .

4 tablespoons extra virgin olive oil . .

2 tablespoons maple syrup, barley malt syrup or date syrup . . . .

Handful of golden sultanas or mulberries . . . .

Flaky sea salt, to dust . . . .

Rosemary ain't just a pretty fragrance. Its medicinal properties – appreciated by herbalists for hundreds of years – are now being confirmed by modern science. Yes, a daily round of Crossaire or brushing your teeth with your left hand will help keep brain rust at bay, but so, too, might rosemary.

This woody herb contains several groovy compounds that have been shown to inhibit the nasty breakdown of acetylcholine in the brain. Acetylcholine is a very important neurotransmitter for optimum brain function. Some of the drugs available for Alzheimer's disease work similarly by interfering with acetylcholine breakdown.

A few other racy compounds, caffeic acid and rosmarinic acid, contribute to rosemary's health-buffing reputation. These acids, along with vitamin E and assorted flavonoids from the plant, may be helpful in reducing inflammation in the body and the brain. Mother N! You clever beast!

Preheat your oven to 180°C. Line a 20cm x 25cm tin with non-stick baking paper. Size is really important – look for something a little bigger than or equal to a square brownie tin. This will look like a focaccia rather than a loaf, that's why we don't use a traditional loaf tin.

Let 2 teaspoons of the rosemary party with the milled flax and baking powder in a large bowl.

In a separate bowl, whisk the eggs, milk, lemon zest and juice, olive oil and syrup with a fork until happily glossed up. Parachute your sultanas into the mix. Dried mulberries are also awesome but are a dastardly expensive addition.

Now add the wet ingredients to the dry and immediately pour into your lined tin. Spread evenly and sprinkle the remaining teaspoon of rosemary on top along with a flurry of flaky sea salt. Bake in the oven for about 25 minutes.

Remove from the oven and the tin. Allow to cool on a wire rack. Tickle with smashed avocado, black olive tapenade or hummus. This bread freezes exceptionally well, ready to grill when there's nothing in the cupboard. I divide it into six pieces and slice each one horizontally like a bap.

Za'atar and Pistachio Focaccia

MAKES 1 FOCACCIA . . . .

3 eggs . . . .

185ml regular or plant milk . . . .

5 tablespoons extra virgin
olive oil . . . .

1 tablespoon za'atar (page 000), plus
extra to dust . . . .

240g milled flaxseed (linseed) . . . . . .

1½ teaspoons baking powder . . . .

Handful of shelled pistachios . . . .

6 dried dark unsulphured
apricots (optional) . . . .

Aside from all the nutritional yah-yah, this tastes pretty cosmic.
You can purchase good Middle Eastern za'atar in health food stores
across the country or give it a go yourself on page 206.

Boost your oven to 180°C. Line a 20cm x 25cm or 20cm square tin
with non-stick baking paper. Size is really important – look for
something a little bigger than or equal to a square brownie tin.

Start by beating your eggs into the milk and oil. Set aside.

In a separate large bowl, let the za'atar, milled flax and baking
powder get to know each other.

Now beat the wet ingredients into the dry ingredients and
tumble in your shelled pistachios. Chop the apricots finely and
stir them through the mixture (if using).

Scrape into your lined tin. Spread evenly and top with an extra
dusting of za'atar. Bake in the oven for 25 minutes.

Remove from the oven and the tin. Allow to cool for 10 minutes
on a wire rack. Beautiful served hot with hummus or sweetened
tahini.

Breastfeeding Bread

MAKES 1 FOCACCIA . . . .

1 teaspoon caraway seeds . . . .

1 teaspoon fennel seeds . . . .

1 teaspoon whole aniseed . . . .

Handful of dried dates, pitted and chopped . . . .

240g milled flaxseed (linseed) . . . . . .

1½ teaspoons baking powder . . . .

1 teaspoon ground fenugreek . . . .

3 eggs . . . .

185ml regular or plant milk . . . .

4 tablespoons extra virgin olive oil . . . .

Flaky sea salt, to dust . . . .

Some women never suffer a semi-quaver during their pregnancy. Others feel like it's a thunderous tax, short-circuiting the motherboard in their brain. Here are two things to consider if your body falls into the latter team, my friend.

For a start, swimming is an ace way to service indolent limbs and gale-force moods. It's the only part of the day you will feel like heaven's chosen fairy. No one can unexpectedly rub your bump and you can safely practise ninja moves in the event they do.

Secondly, your intake of essential fatty acids (EFAs to seasoned nerds) can provide your body with ammo to fight inflammation and Pram Brain. Omega-3s are part of the EFA tribe. They help to quench those renegade prostaglandins that cause inflammation and swelling in the body. EFAs are wondrous brain fuel too.

We now know that significant levels of EFAs make their merry way across the placenta to your hungry baba. Nice one. Scientists have also found high levels of dietary EFA present in colostrum (your first round of boob juice). EFAs have even been shown to reduce the risk of postnatal depression for mummy. So I came up with this bread to help you get your EFA game on. Flax is one of nature's richest plant sources of omega-3 and the spices I use are popular with breastfeeding mamas. Aside from the spices' avowed lactation-enhancing abilities, this bread is dastardly good for regular non-lactating specimens. That's right, bro. You too.

Whack up your oven to 180°C. Line a 20cm x 25cm tin with non-stick baking paper. Size is really important – look for something a little bigger than or equal to a square brownie tin.

Dry roast your caraway, fennel and aniseed in a hot pan for 60 seconds. Their fragrance should hit the air like a melody. Leave aside to cool.

Let the chopped dates, milled flax, baking powder and fenugreek socialise in a large bowl. Now add your roasted spices.

In a separate bowl, whisk the eggs with your preferred milk and the olive oil. Beat into the bowl of dry ingredients and scrape this gloriously gooey mix into your lined tin. Spread evenly and top with a flurry of flaky sea salt. Bake in the oven for about 25 minutes.

Remove from the oven and the tin. Allow to cool for 10 minutes on a wire rack. Magical stuff.

Rooibos, Date and Honey Focaccia

MAKES 1 FOCACCIA . . . .

3 large eggs . . . .

185ml really strong rooibos tea . . . . .

4 tablespoons extra virgin
olive oil . . . .

2 tablespoons honey . . . .

240g milled flaxseed . . . .

1½ teaspoons baking powder . . . .

Pinch of ground allspice . . . .

Large handful of dates, pitted
and chopped . . . .

¼ teaspoon flaky sea salt . . . .

This flaxseed focaccia is much sweeter than the savoury versions. We love it briefly toasted and smothered with Irish ricotta. #moonwalk

Preheat your oven to 180°C. Line a 20cm x 25cm tin with non-stick paper. A traditional 20cm square brownie tin will also work, but not a loaf tin.

In a large bowl, whisk together the eggs, tea, oil and honey until happily glossed up.

Measure out your milled flax, baking powder and allspice. Stir to combine, then tip them into the bowl of wet ingredients. Follow with your chopped dates. Give it all a thunderous mix before scraping into your lined tin. Spread evenly and sprinkle with a flurry of flaky sea salt. Bake in the oven for about 25 minutes.

Remove from the oven and the tin. Allow to cool on a wire rack before slicing and freezing in individual portions. We divide it into 6–8 pieces and slice each one horizontally like a bap.

Hallelujah Banana Bread

MAKES 1 LOAF . . . .

4 tablespoons any plant-based milk or natural soya yogurt . . . .

1 tablespoon psyllium husks . . . .

1 teaspoon good-quality vanilla bean paste or extract . . . .

170g rapadura, light muscovado, golden caster or coconut sugar . . . . .

100g extra virgin coconut oil, at room temperature (use butter if not vegan) . . . .

Roughly 320g mashed over-ripe bananas . . . .

200g buckwheat flour . . . .

1 teaspoon baking powder . . . .

Generous flurry of flaky sea salt . . . .

40g dark chocolate chips (optional) . .

Handful of whole buckwheat groats, to top (recommended) . . . .

⊕ On a budget

. . . .

⧗ Freezes well in slices

This is what to make when you don't know what to make. (Iffy guests? Picky colleagues? Neurotic rellies?) It's vegan, gluten free, egg free, lactose free and stress free.

When my nippers hound me for something trashy, I'll make this banana bread and smother it with melted dark chocolate. The result is comically hypnotic. That's because bananas and buckwheat go magically well together. They are the Amy and Brian of the breakfast table. One is naturally sweet, the other robust and burly (but very far from trashy, just to be clear!).

Preheat the oven to 180°C. Line a medium-sized loaf tin about 16cm long or a 1lb tin with non-stick baking paper.

Make your plant 'egg' by mixing the milk or yogurt, psyllium and vanilla in a cup. Leave to stand and swell for 3 minutes (or longer).

In a separate bowl, beat the sugar and fat together by hand with a fork until glossy. It's best not to do this step in a machine. Stir through the mashed banana and psyllium 'egg'. Now tumble in the flour, baking powder and sea salt. If you're using chocolate chips, add these in too. Mix well.

Scrape into your lined loaf tin. Scatter with whole buckwheat groats for an excellent crunchy topping.

Bake in the oven for 60–70 minutes. When it's finished cooking, a skewer stuck into the centre will come out 98% dry.

Remove from the oven and let the bread settle for 5 minutes before ejecting from the tin and letting it cool on a wire rack. This bread keeps really well all week in a bread basket, covered with parchment. When it gets old, a scrape of butter helps to keep each slice moist.

* See photo on page 15

Pumpkin Bread

MAKES 1 X 20CM SQUARE LOAF . . . .

Wet ingredients

1 large sweet potato (approx. 240g) . .

2 eggs. . . . .

85ml extra virgin olive oil or melted
ghee (page 194). . . . .

85ml barley malt syrup, rice malt
syrup or honey. . . . .

1 teaspoon vanilla bean paste
or extract . . . .

Dry ingredients

100g whole spelt or wheat flour or
120g sprouted spelt flour. . . . .

60g milled flaxseed . . . .

2 teaspoons baking powder . . . .

1 teaspoon ground Chinese five spice,
allspice or cinnamon . . . .

⊕ Reasonable

. . . .

⧗ Freezes perfectly in individual
slices

You want more omega-3 in your diet, right? But you'd rather eat nails? I understand. Flaxseed is designed to seduce your cranium, not your palate. I sneak flax into this recipe so that each slice boasts more than 1 tablespoon of this brain-booty.

As well as omega-3, there's a consignment of protective plant lignans and calcium inside flaxseed. Take a bow, Mother N – that's one heavyweight food you gave us! Here's a piddle-easy way of sneaking them into your diet. Imagine a cross between cake and bread – yup. Damn difficult not to throttle an entire loaf in one sitting. I call this pumpkin bread, but I actually use sweet potato in place of pumpkin – a nifty culinary hack.

Preheat your oven to 200°C. Line a 20cm square brownie tin with non-stick baking paper.

Bake your sweet potato in its skin for up to 1 hour in the oven. Do not slit the skin – sweet potatoes are different from regular potatoes and contain significantly less starch. This can be done a few days in advance. Any time I turn on my oven, I tend to chuck in a few sweet potatoes to have as snacks during the week. Remove from the oven once cooked and mash the amber flesh. You're looking for approximately 240g. Mashed pumpkin works great as well, obviously, but it's more of a hassle to cook and mash, so this is my cheat's version.

Turn the oven temperature down to 180°C. Using a food processor, or a fork and muscle, beat together your wet ingredients in a large bowl.

Now add the dry ingredients. Blend until smooth.

Scoop into your lined brownie tin. Bake in the oven for 45 minutes.

Remove from the tin after 3 minutes of cooling and discard the baking parchment. This will prevent the bread from going soggy. Dastardly good while warm with a scrape of butter or a snowstorm of icing sugar.

Onion Focaccia with Aniseed (p.64)

Pumpkin Bread (p.70)

Ricotta, Dark Chocolate and Peaches on Toast

PER PERSON . . . .

1 thick slice of sourdough bread . . . .

4 tablespoons Irish ricotta cheese . .

3 squares of dark chocolate, chopped . . . .

Mizzle of extra virgin olive oil . . . . . .

Sea salt, to taste . . . .

1 flat peach or ½ regular peach, stoned and sliced . . . .

2 fresh basil leaves (optional) . . . . . .

⊕ On a budget

. . . .

⧗ Batch prep not suitable. This is a fresh one, friends!

By golly, chocolate has a calling like an ultrasonic dog whistle. Only audible to females, of course. Ignoring these sound wave emissions is, in my experience, damaging. The longer the ear-splitting sonar pulse, the sharper the fangs. Here's a little ripper of a recipe. There's just enough chocolate to salve those fangs.

Toast the sourdough. While your bread is warming, mix together your ricotta, chocolate chunks and sea salt. Mizzle some olive oil over your slice of toast, followed by dots of chocolate chip ricotta and top with fresh peach slices. If you have a basil plant, add a few leaves and tuck in.

The Redner

MAKES 2-3 SERVINGS . . . .

5 unwaxed blood oranges . . . .

1 red pepper, deseeded . . . .

2 teaspoons grated fresh ginger . . . .

A rough cup's worth of ice . . . .

Raw honey (optional) . . . .

⊕ On a budget

. . . .

⧖ Sonic

This is for the morning after the night you worked it like a backing dancer for Beyoncé's world tour. And now you need a defibrillator for your liver and your head. No greens in sight, my friends. Fight fire with fire.

Let's get some life pumping through your veins again. You'll find a symphony of antioxidants to tap dance through your system and jazz up your bloodstream. Add ginger's natural anti-nausea and anti-inflammatory prowess and you've found yourself a Sunday morning love bug.

No peeling, please. Introduce all the ingredients to a Vitamix. That is all. We want to keep the citrus skins on the blood oranges to capture an extra net of fancy antioxidants, such as limonoids, flavonoids and polyphenols. There's all sorts of goodness in those pithy white bits. (Okay, you can peel two or three of them, go on.)

You can, if you wish, omit the ice and lightly warm the juice. Stir through some raw honey to soften the smack.

Kermit's Sonata

SERVES 2 . . . .

Handful of pitted dates . . . .

70g cashews . . . .

480ml water . . . .

½ teaspoon minced fresh ginger . . . .

½ teaspoon vanilla bean paste
or extract . . . .

25g blanched kale, leaves only . . . . . .

1–2 bananas . . . .

125g ice cubes . . . .

⊕ Reasonable

. . . .

⧗ Overnight soaking required

I've never been a smoothie sucker. Ain't no overture in my blender when the berries hit the green leafies. Generally it looks like Kermit crawled into the blender and dragged Gonzo in behind him.

The Blender Girl's version of the Green Goddess is the best I've ever tasted. It is criminally good, particularly as it contains a stash load of kale. Yes, kale, that stupid superfood I am forever trying to sneak into my diet and onto my boys' dinner plates. This is The One. If you can only find purple kale, don't fret. Add some cocoa and it will feel like an iced chocolate milkshake.

Kale has a team of nutrients like calcium and vitamin K, well-known allies for oiling your Macarena moves. Kale's potassium load can help to serenade your blood pressure and hangovers too. Expect a consignment of vitamin A for your body's defence force, iron for healthy blood, vitamin C for luminous skin and plenty of folate for growing children. Sip sip hooray!

Soak your dates and cashews overnight. In the morning, drain the dates and nuts, then belt everything except the ice, but including the fresh 480ml of water, into a blender and blitz until lusciously smooth. Add the ice and blitz again before serving.

Cold Brew Tea (p.77)

Skin Melonade (p.83)

The Kickstarter (p.87)

Cold Brew Cacao (p.76)

Kermit's Sonata (p.74)

Cold Brew Cacao

MAKES 750ML . . . .

250 raw cacao nibs . . . .

750ml cold fresh water . . . .

Feeling flush

Overnight soaking required

This cold brew cacao is peak millennial. Raw cacao wasn't even stocked in health food stores 10 years ago. Now every supermarket stocks it.

Cold brew cacao gives a blood-gurgling boost of magnesium, the mineral us fillies can crave every month. Magnesium has been shown to help alleviate circulatory problems such as varicose veins, headaches and cramps. Score.

Similar to coffee, cold brew cacao is dancing with several levels of flavour and surprising strength. You might like to soften yours with maple syrup.

Blitz the cacao nibs in a blender until they are roughly ground. You can also use your trusty pestle and mortar with some serious muscle.

Now transfer the roughly ground nibs to a large glass bowl and pour the cold water on top. Give it a good smoosh and let the flavours infuse for 16 hours (overnight).

Drain through a coffee filter, a nut milk bag or a very fine sieve to catch the residue. You can ditch or compost the solids collected in the filter. Store the cold brew cacao in your fridge and add to iced coffee or drink as is. You might like to freeze it in an ice cube tray to complement cold brew coffee over summer months.

Cold Brew Tea

SERVES 4–6 . . . .

4 teabags of black or white tea . . . . . .

1 litre cold filtered water . . . .

Nip of lemon juice (optional) . . . .

1 teaspoon maple syrup (optional) . . .

⊕ On a budget
. . . .
⧖ Soaking required

Black tea and green tea come from the very same plant. Who knew? Not my taste buds, for certain. These teas are about as similar as pugs are to poodles.

What determines whether a tea is black, green, white or just plain poncey depends on the preferred processing method of the *Camellia sinensis* leaves. Black tea is fermented. Green tea is steamed or pan-fried, then dried. And white tea is all about immaturity (no wonder I like this one best). While each processing method destroys some of the natural goodness found within the leaf, those very same methods are in fact the midwives of a new suite of protective compounds. Groovy, right?

The fermentation process beloved of black tea leaves deactivates a very important catechin called EGCG, believed to be responsible for the anti-carcinogen hype around green tea, for example. Ho hum. But wait! This very same fermentation process creates a whole new swag of burly antioxidants for the humble black tea leaves. So keep swilling!

I spend my wonga on white tea. These tea leaves are picked before ripening, before the buds of the *Camellia sinensis* have fully opened. As a result, white tea is a milder-tasting tea, but by no means a weaker-performing tea on the antioxidant league table. I get a real roast from its GABA-bombing feels. White, black and green teas are rich in theanine, thought to help improve mood. Theanine tickles the release of a neurotransmitter called GABA, responsible for calming the brain. There's also some evidence to suggest our favourite feel-good chemical, dopamine, is triggered by theanine too. So here's a recipe to help sip yourself into a shamanic frenzy.

Steep your chosen teabags in the cold filtered water for 12–24 hours. I do this overnight in the fridge. Hot water seduces tannins from the tea leaves. That's why a drop of milk gives your cuppa a smoother, sweeter finish. Cold brewing tea helps to avoid overly bitter tannins, high-jumping the need to add milk to the end result.

When your brew is ready, remove the teabags and let the lemon and maple join the party (if using). Serve over ice or chill until required.

Cold Brew Coffee

MAKES 4–8 SERVINGS . . . .

220g coffee beans . . . .

1 litre cold filtered water . . . .

1 nut milk bag or cheesecloth . . . .

⊕ On a budget
. . . .

⧗ Overnight soaking required

If Judy Garland was reincarnated, this would be it. Cold brew coffee.

Make it immediately. Today. Now. For wellness junkies, you can offset the caffeine indulgence with a field of kale later.

Cold brew is simply an easy way of making coffee concentrate. Instead of relying on heat to extract the flavour from the coffee beans, you'll be relying on an overnight moondance. I leave mine in the fridge before bed, after an interactive chorus of AC/DC's 'Thunderstruck'. In the morning, all that's left to do is strain and serve over ice. It's enough to incite poetry in a three-toed sloth.

Because the coffee beans don't socialise with intense heat, the result is a smoother, lighter, sweeter kava with an unexpected smack of hard rock.

Roughly grind your coffee beans to a super-coarse crumb.

Put the ground beans in a tall Kilner jar or French press pot and add the filtered water. I like to make a ceremony out of it. The soundtrack to *Star Wars* is not inappropriate.

Seal with a lid. If using a French press, don't push the plunger down. Leave the beans to fraternise with the filtered water in the fridge overnight or for up to 24 hours (the sweet spot).

When the brew is ready, strain twice through a nut milk bag or cheesecloth (or plunge the French press). The double filtration ensures every last scrap of silt disappears. Compost the coffee beans or use them in the shower as a body scrub mixed up with olive oil.

Refrigerate your cold brew coffee for up to six days. Serve with an audience, over ice.

Making Coffee Tonic with Your Cold Brew

PER PERSON . . . .

4 ice cubes . . . .

80ml tonic water. . . . .

1 shot of cold brew coffee or
espresso, chilled . . . .

Coffee tonic is a sparkling rocket fuel that you must try, if only for anthropological reasons. The crisp quinine in tonic water pairs really well with fruity coffees and makes me feel like Ziggy Stardust on a comet. And the bubbles help to escort caffeine into your system faster than an electric volt to your nipples.

Besides, I'm considerably kinder when I'm caffeinated.

(It's worth remembering that your body would prefer if coffee were treated as an occasional hobby and not as a full-time career. Yes, coffee is a bean and beans are plants, but you can't count it as part of your five-a-day. Nice try.)

Parachute your ice cubes into a glass of tonic water, then gently add the chilled cold brew coffee or espresso. Sip to keep you cool all summer long.

Coffee Body Scrub

MAKES ENOUGH FOR 1 USE. . . . .

Finely ground espresso coffee, for 2 (recycled) . . . .

1 tablespoon olive oil. . . . .

Squeeze of fresh lemon . . . .

⊕   Uses recycled coffee
     from the kitchen

. . . .

⧗   Bath or shower required!

Cortisol is a stress hormone released by the adrenal glands (our Call Centre for Chaos). Whenever we experience a stressful situation, we unknowingly pump cortisol into our bloodstream so that our bodies can cope with the stressor. You can carry out a short experiment by listening to Fox News and measuring your pulse with your index and middle fingers. Say hello to cortisol!

Although cortisol is our friend in many situations (e.g. freight lorry heading towards us; accidentally farting aloud in a boardroom), our systems are not designed to constantly embrace stress. Chronic stress is disease's greatest ally. Prolonged elevated cortisol levels raise blood pressure, anxiety and our risk of stroke and weaken our immune ripostes. So let's start taking self-care more seriously, my friend, and do the things you love more often. It's actually healthy!

Here's a de-stressor available to everyone: a weekly coffee scrub. Self-care is self-love. This scrub will intoxicate all five of your senses while you simultaneously morph into a nymphet with skin like marble. You can recycle your morning coffee straight from the French plunger.

Making sure your ground coffee is damp rather than soaking wet, stir through the olive oil and lemon juice. This will keep for a few days in the fridge if you don't want to use it straight away.

For your next shower, use the palm of your hand to rub the scrub over rough areas like the backs of arms, thighs and booty. Circular motions work well. Coffee can be a little strong for lower legs, face and chest, so please avoid these areas. (This is not suitable for children in case any mad ones are thinking about it.)

Wash the mess down the drain before you shampoo. Towel off and admire your buffed booty. Repeat every week.

Grapefruit and Ginger Slushie

CAN SERVE 1-4, DEPENDING
ON THIRST . . . .
250ml freshly squeezed grapefruit
juice (about 2 large pink ones). . . . . . .
1 teacup's worth of ice cubes . . . .
1 teaspoon grated fresh ginger . . . . .
4-6 fresh basil leaves, to decorate
(optional) . . . .

(+) On a budget
. . . .
⧖ A few seconds

We love citrus fruits, especially during winter. Grapefruits, oranges, limes, lemons – all contain bumptious amounts of vitamin C to resuscitate dull skin during those Baltic months. This is the vitamin celebrated for its fancy immune ripostes too. Double bonus. Beat that, Lancôme.

Put the grapefruit juice in a powerful blender like a NutriBullet with your ice cubes and ginger. Blast until icy and smooth, like a grown-up slushie. Pour into a tall glass and serve with a paper milkshake straw (regular straws are a little tricky with crushed ice). Put the optional basil leaves in the palm of your hand and spank three times before decorating each glass. This helps to release the aroma so that it dances with your nostrils.

Skin Melonade

SERVES 2-4 . . . .
300g organic watermelon, pips too . .
Juice from 1 lime . . . .
Good handful of ice . . . .
1 tablespoon extra virgin olive oil . .
Squirt of tomato purée (optional
lycopene boost) . . . .

(+) On a budget
. . . .
⧖ Spin and serve

A bonkfest for the taste buds. Lots of crazy-powerful nutrients to cartwheel towards your skin, keeping it luminous and youthful. I'll drink to that!

Belt all the ingredients into a high-powered blender and blitz until liquid. Ditch the watermelon seeds if it's not organic – seeds tend to soak up pesticides more than the flesh. Not such a good cocktail for your skin!
    Pour into chilled glasses and serve alongside factor 50 and a deck chair.

Salted Caramel and Hazelnut Cream
to serve with espresso

MAKES 250ML . . . .

70g hazelnuts . . . .

250ml fresh filtered water . . . .

1–2 Medjool dates, pitted . . . .

Good pinch of sea salt . . . .

Espresso, to serve . . . .

⊕ Feeling flush
. . . .
⧗ Overnight soaking required

I'm a nutritional Jedi. Nut for short. My crazy-assed mission is to show you how simple changes to your diet can drastically improve your mojo and your mood.

Word has it you love those caramel frappés and creamy mocha shakes. Sound, I do too. Who could blame us? They were designed to intoxicate our senses (and our liver – try counting all the chemicals … actually, never mind).

So I came up with a simple salted caramel and hazelnut cream that will tripwire your serotonin. Keep it in the office fridge to tickle your midday espresso. Or have it straight. It's just four ingredients: hazelnuts, dates, sea salt and water.

Soak the hazelnuts in water overnight.

In the morning, drain the nuts. Tumble into a powerful blender and blitz with the fresh filtered water, the Medjools and salt. Coffee nerds might prefer to blitz with 250ml of cold brew coffee (page 78).

Using a nut milk bag, muslin cloth, a clean pair of nylon tights or a fine sieve, strain the hazelnut mix into a bowl. You'll collect a luscious, smooth cream underneath the cloth, while the sieve will catch the smashed nuts and Medjools (nut milk bags make this achingly easy).

Discard the 'pulp' from the cloth (or freeze it to make the granola on page 17 another day). Prostrate before the salted caramel and hazelnut cream appearing before you. Use within two days.

Cardamom Coffee and Turmeric Milk

SERVES 1 . . . .

6 green cardamom pods . . . .

Approximately 300g freshly ground coffee . . . .

1 finger-sized piece of fresh turmeric . . . .

200ml almond or soya milk, to serve . . . .

(+) Reasonable

. . . .

⧖ A few minutes

I can upgrade your coffee. Make it seriously snazzy. Sound good? Turmeric milk has long been celebrated for its gorgeous taste as well as its medicinal benefits. And boy, has it caused much giddiness among scientists. Research has revealed several important functions of the curcumin found in turmeric. Here are some of the results so far. Firstly, curcumin has been shown to help in the reduction of amyloid plaque, a hallmark of Alzheimer's disease.

Secondly, curcumin has demonstrated antiangiogenic proprieties during extensive clinical trials on cell cultures. That's doctor speak for 'cancer-fighting ninja'.

Thirdly, curcumin can help regulate inflammation in the body. Bronchitis, arthritis, colitis, ego-itis – anything that ends in –itis. Bonkers, right?

Bash open the cardamom pods using the base of a wine bottle or pestle (being careful not to scare the bejaysus out of the budgie). Mix into your freshly ground coffee and store in the fridge until your caffeine fangs surface.

At this point, make your coffee as you would normally (espresso, short French press, Turkish pot). Prepare your golden turmeric milk by grating the fresh root into your preferred type of milk. (Fresh turmeric can stain badly, so expect your fingers to look like little Minions! I cover my fingers in olive oil before touching the root to help reduce staining.) Heat for 4 minutes over a low heat. Strain the milk to catch the fibre and add your boost of coffee.

The Kickstarter

MAKES 1 TALL GLASS OR 4 SHOTS . . . . .

2 lemons or 3 limes, juiced . . . .

1½ cups ice . . . .

Up to 2 teaspoons grated fresh
ginger (as much as you can handle) . .

1 teaspoon raw honey . . . .

½ teaspoon ground turmeric . . . .

Pinch of cayenne pepper . . . .

⊕ On a budget

. . . .

⧖ Blend and serve

Green smoothies can often look like a tall glass of sneeze. Here's what I make instead. Think of it as a powerful lemonade with more kick than a mule in heat.

Chilli is a fabulous defibrillator, making your pulse go giddy up. Its fiery sting delivers more than a tingling sensation across the lips and chest. That same sting can help to initiate a cascade of messages to the brain. It's as if a stadium of neurotransmitters gets to play with walkie-talkies. The brain responds by releasing endorphins, known as our body's natural way of relieving pain.

Our call centre for reward and pleasure in the brain also starts riffing on dopamine. This chemical messenger seems like the darling of neuroscience, involved in a myriad of important pathways, from lust to addiction. So our brain is boozing on dopamine when we eat chilli. Nice.

But that's not all! Lemons and limes contain blushing amounts of bioflavonoids and vitamin C. Both can help to heal zits and resuscitate tired skin, while a particular flavonoid called kaempferol has been indicated in the reduction of oxidative damage to our cells. You'll get even more protection from fresh ginger and turmeric, so don't leave them out! Think of them as fire extinguishers in the body. Your liver will thank you.

In a powerful blender, show these ingredients who's boss. Serve with thick paper milkshake straws or wait a few minutes for the ice to dissolve and slurp straight from the glass.

Turmeric Tonic

MAKES 850ML . . . .

750ml filtered water . . . .

2 lemons, juice only . . . .

1 orange, juice only. . . . .

4 teaspoons freshly grated ginger . . .

4 teaspoons freshly grated turmeric
(or ground organic turmeric) . . . .

2 tablespoons raw honey . . . .

A few twists of the black
pepper mill . . . .

⊕ On a budget
. . . .
⧗ 25 minutes in total

Nothing can trump the raw, authentic glow of good health. This beauty tonic is pumped with anti-inflammatory agents and scores of vitamin C. Wait until I tell my collagen!

And if you have any leftover raw honey, check out the recipe on the next page for a honey face scrub.

In a small pan, bring your water, citrus juice, ginger and turmeric to a gentle simmer, being careful not to let it bubble or boil. You're looking to heat and infuse the spices like a witch, not cook the bejaysus out of them. Warm for 20 minutes.

Remove your pan from the heat and pour through a fine cheesecloth or muslin. Catch and discard the sediment (I pop this into my freezer stock bag).

Finally, sweeten with just enough raw honey and give it some extra kick with a few twists of the black pepper mill. Drink straight away, refrigerating leftovers for up to six days or fill up a flask for a cold hike.

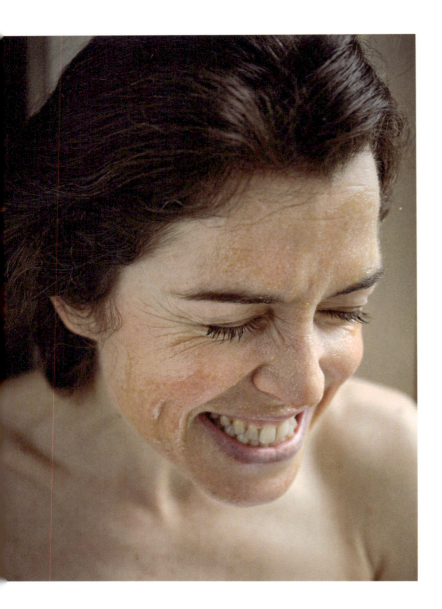

Raw Honey Exfoliator

MAKES ENOUGH FOR 1 USE . . . .

1 tablespoon ground almonds or baby
rice powder . . . .

2 tablespoons raw honey . . . .

⊕ Significantly cheaper than the
commercial stuff

. . . .

⧗ Demands some relaxation

The skin is our largest excretory organ in our body. If you're not eliminating toxins and waste products from your bowels … you've guessed it – you'll end up wearing them on your face.

Increased circulation to the face through exercise, sexing or even mortifying flushes can help with cellular renewal. Yup. Fresh blood brings new hope, especially to damaged cells.

This recipe for an all-natural face scrub should do the trick. No micro beads, just clever alternatives like baby rice or ground almonds to help slough off dull dead skin cells loitering on our cheeks. Gentle circular scrubbing increases blood flow to the area and a tidal wave of new nutrients. Double bonus! Your newly acquired 'fresh' skin will absorb serums and botanicals much quicker, whereas dead skin cells simply block it. I think that's called a hat trick.

Mash the ground almonds or baby rice powder into the honey with a fork. Lie down on your bed with a book or a podcast. Apply this honeyed love bomb to clean skin as a mask for anything between 1 and 8 minutes.

When the time's up, gently rub in circular motions to increase blood flow to the skin, helping cellular renewal. Your derrière may need some buffing during the winter months too, when it's locked up until spring. Just saying. This is best done standing in the shower with the tap turned off.

Rinse with warm water and a muslin cloth. Repeat every week.

For and From the Fridge and Freezer

Finding the time to cook nourishing meals can sometimes feel as easy as hula-hooping on a hoverboard. More often than we'd like to admit, we end up dialling in home deliveries or settling for convenience food when our bodies deserve better. The bad news is that we are overloading on cheap fat and salt by doing so, sabotaging our energy levels and our mojo. Pah!

Be good to your body. You're the one who has to live in it. Convenience foods aren't designed to keep you alive and well in the long term. What's convenient about that?

Friends often tell me they don't have time to shop and cook. You don't have to chain yourself to the cooker every evening – that would be bonkers. Developing a relationship with your freezer saves on shopping, cooking and washing up. In the longer term, you'll cash in the health benefits too. Hooo-ha.

When I keep my freezer stocked up, life flows much easier. My kitchen becomes less operatic and more playful. I find time to channel energy into other dramas life throws at me: water-pistolling magpies from our robin's nest, binge watching *The Sound of Music* or checking out Princess Charlotte's summer capsule wardrobe.

So this chapter is for readers who struggle with cooking every day. Relax. I'm here to make your life easier.

Healthy Batch Cooking Puts the Ease Back into Freeze

Benefits include:

Supporting your health and wellness goals.

. . . .

Spending significantly less time and head space in the kitchen throughout the week by removing the stress from deciding what to eat for dinner and breakfast.

. . . .

Enabling more free time for hobbies, fitness and family.

. . . .

Ensuring you have healthy meals sitting in your freezer so you won't be tempted to spend your hard-earned cash on cheap junk food or takeouts.

. . . .

Spending less time shopping and queueing in stores.

. . . .

Obliterating hanger (anger you feel when hungry) by providing swags of ever-ready snacks straight from the freezer, such as raspberry whip halva and chocolate mint freezer slice.

. . . .

Feeling like Mary Poppins.

Top Tips for Zenning the Face Off Your Kitchen

Ear candy: Find really good podcasts to keep you company while you merrily cook your way through an afternoon of batching. I love BBC radio programmes like *The Moral Maze*, *The Food Programme* and *Desert Island Discs*.

Batch Sundays: Do you work Monday to Friday outside the home? Then you'll really dig Sunday afternoons listening to your favourite Spotify list and manifesting the f%ck out of your dream batch list. Just think of all those weekdays you won't be cooking! Batching is transformational. Light some candles, clear the kitchen counter and high-five your forehead for being so deliciously organised.

Does it spark deliciousness? Take out everything in your freezer right now – if you didn't know it was in there, chances are you won't miss it. Ditch it. Your freezer space is now directly linked to your sanity. Be ruthless. Throw out most of the confusion to make way for your beautifully labelled batch cooking. These will be far more valuable to your freezer space and your sanity than the odd chicken fillet or unrecognisable mush.

Stuff I Keep in My Freezer

Bread, in slices: Including banana bread – wrap in parchment to avoid loss of moisture.

. . . . . , ...

Cakes, in slices: Quick to grab when you know you want a treat. Defrosts within the hour, just in time for your cuppa.

. . . . / . . . .

Ice cube dressings: You need only one silicone tray.

. . . .

Quirky flours: Especially ones that are near their expiry date, as freezing flour prolongs its life.

. . . .

Leftover quinoa: To add to crumpets (page 58), waffles and mashed spuds.

. . . .

Ginger: For grating into tea and yogurt.

. . . .

Red wine: Left over from the end of a party. Freeze in a silicone ice cube tray to add to Bolognese or rich stews. Pop out the cubes once frozen, then bag them and label it.

. . . .

Bones: Chicken bones can be frozen to create stock when you have enough of them. See page 160 for more.

. . . .

Frozen bananas: For ice cream or smoothies. I always have frozen strawbs at the ready too for my kombucha's second ferment or to make emergency jam (page 10).

. . . .

Frozen nuts for nut milk: And frozen pulp for the granola on page 17. By freezing soaked nuts, you have an instant supply of nut milk whenever you want. Frozen soaked nuts will defrost in 10 minutes, ready to be conjured into your favourite nut milk.

Stale breadcrumbs: For frying and topping salads or soups like the lentil minestrone on page 138. Essential for the meatball recipe on page 152.

Lentils: Lentils can freeze well in tiny portions, to add to mashed potato and to pimp up your evening meals or soups. When I cook the lentil, spinach and sweet potato curry on page 114, I make a big batch of lentils and benefit from freezing the leftovers.

Veg trimmings: Make a habit of keeping veggie trimmings such as carrot peels, wilting herbs from the fridge, fennel tops, courgette butts, onion skins and half-used garlic cloves to add to a stock bag that you've stashed in the freezer. I have two or three of these stock bags always on the go. Avoid saving kale or cabbage – they're too sulphuric for stock.

Beans: I don't like frozen beans, especially defrosted chickpeas – they taste soggy and water logged. Yeuck! It's best to freeze beans inside a curry so that they absorb the stock or curry sauce rather than freezer moisture.

Batch suppers: The vast majority of my freezer space is taken up by individual and family portion meals. The list presented above includes items that regularly come and go. I have nothing inside my freezer that is (a) anonymous or (b) over six months old. Be ruthless with your freezer space. Ditch anything that does not spark deliciousness! I can confidently say my freezer space is directly linked to my adrenal glands. When it is stocked with items we love and use regularly, life just flows much easier and I'm a nicer person because of it.

ALERT: Liquids, curries and stews expand once frozen, so always leave room in your freezable jars for expansion. You can do this by ensuring the jar is not packed to the brim before placing it in your freezer. Liquid expands once frozen, shattering the glass if the jar is particularly packed.

Where Do I Start? When Can I Start?

Right now!

1. Ditch everything in your freezer today. If there's food in there that you want to eat, defrost it this week.
....

2. Defrost your freezer, then clean it out with plain distilled vinegar and bicarbonate of soda. I just squirt in the vinegar and wipe with a clean hot cloth. Your freezer will need to be turned off. Where there are tougher stains, sprinkle on some bicarb followed with a dash of vinegar. Leave for a few minutes before wiping away with a clean, hot cloth.
....

3. Start collecting empty glass jars and lids to use as freezer containers. Recycling supermarket packaging can be useful too, although my health preference lies with glass.
....

4. Recycle BPA-free freezer bags and environmentally sound parchment paper. Paper luggage tags are nifty too. Find these in stationery shops and Flying Tiger stores nationwide.
....

5. You'll need masking tape (also called artist's tape) for name tagging everything. And a Sharpie pen. Both withstand freezer conditions and will help you feel like a worthy disciple of Marie Kondo and Mary Poppins. I write the name of the dish multiplied by the number of portions, e.g. Spanish Chickpea Stew x 4; Carrot Soup x 1. If you have a stonking big chest freezer, you might also want to put the date on it.
....

6. Invest in a good silicone ice cube tray – €10 will do the trick and it should last a lifetime. If you have little goslings, consider purchasing silicone ice pop moulds too. I fill these ice pop moulds with the butt end of smoothies instead of throwing them down the drain. We find this is much more preferable than nagging our kids to finish their smoothies!

Thawing Safely

If this is your first foray into freezing, welcome! This section is for you. Your freezer is going to help you chill out.

Thawing safely is far less dramatic than it sounds. I take a frozen curry or stew out of the freezer the night before I plan on serving it and let it defrost in the door of my fridge for 24 hours. When it's time for dinner, I heat the thawed meal over a medium heat, covered, until piping hot (and always within 48 hours of taking it out of the freezer).

Meat needs longer than vegetables to thaw. Stick to the vegan or vegetarian recipes for shorter thawing times and always make sure they reach bubbling or boiling point before plating up.

It's also worth remembering that smaller jars will thaw more quickly. Submerging the jar in tap water can also help to safely speed up the process. We often do this with soups.

The freezer dressings all thaw within 10 minutes at room temperature. Some, like the harissa butter, only contain healthy fats and spices and will therefore defrost in moments. Score.

Many of the speedy treats are eaten straight from frozen, so no thawing necessary #backflip (e.g. each of the three halva recipes, the coffee caramels, chocolate mint freezer slice, ninjabread men, ice lollies, energy bomb-bombs, BAE-sic vegan ganache, probiotic shortbread and mini Medjool Swiss rolls). Don't worry, I remind you of each recipe's seismic freezing abilities alongside the list of ingredients. You're in complete control.

What Is the Best-Sized Freezer?

A freezer with three trays is the best size. Any bigger and you'll only end up loading it with mysterious shit. You don't need an industrial freezer chest to make batch cooking work for you. Small is mighty and leaves you in complete control. Here's a pic of mine.

Rich Tofu Curry with Sweetcorn and Red Onion Salsa

SERVES 4 . . . .

3 tablespoons extra virgin coconut
oil or ghee (page 194) . . . .

2 green peppers, deseeded
and sliced . . . .

1 white onion, diced . . . .

1 stick of celery, sliced . . . .

1 fresh green chilli, deseeded and
sliced . . . .

400g firm tofu, cubed . . . .

Good twist of the salt and
pepper mill . . . .

30g curry powder . . . .

1 x 400ml tin of coconut milk . . . .

800ml veggie stock . . . .

1 tablespoon soya sauce . . . .

1 tablespoon maple syrup . . . .

6 garlic cloves, grated . . . .

1 fat thumb-sized piece of fresh
ginger, peeled and grated . . . .

**For the sweetcorn and
red onion salsa**

1 unwaxed organic lime,
zest and juice . . . .
1 small tin of sweetcorn, drained . . . .
½ red onion, diced . . . .
½ cucumber, diced . . . .
Fresh coriander leaves (optional
expense) . . . .

⊕ Double the quantity to make it
more economical

. . . .

⧗ Lasts for five days in the fridge,
or freeze until beckoned.

My husband said he's never tasted tofu before. 'I've seen you eat it!' I say, outraged. 'Yes, I have *eaten* tofu. But like I said, I've never *tasted* it.' So I set about making an indulgent, colourful, kickass tofu curry that would excite carnivores and herbivores alike. (Okay, and to prove him wrong, which is one of my favourite hobbies, you understand.)

Organic, firm tofu is rich in manganese. Athletes dig this trace mineral for its ability to help with muscle and nerve recovery. Manganese comes from the Greek word for magic. Nuff said.

In your largest stockpot or pan, gently warm 2 tablespoons of your chosen fat. Leave the final tablespoon for later.

Tip in your prepped peppers, onion, celery and chilli. Sweat the veg for 15 minutes, until fragrant and soft.

While your veg party, heat the remaining tablespoon of coconut oil or ghee in a skillet over a medium-high heat. Sear the tofu and cook until coloured on all sides, about 6–8 minutes. Season with a few turns of the salt and black pepper mill. Scrape into your medley of vegetables once cooked, along with the curry powder, and coat thoroughly. Whack up the heat.

Now pour in your coconut milk, twice filling the empty tin with stock (about 800ml). I find it handy to use the empty tin as measurement. Follow with the soya sauce and maple syrup. Cook for 20 minutes on a medium gurgle.

Taste and adjust the seasoning before adding your grated garlic and ginger. Cook for a further 5 minutes before ladling into deep bowls to serve.

Tumble all the salsa ingredients together and tickle the top of each bowl. Really great with naan bread or plain basmati rice.

Three-Bean Chilli with Avocado Sour Cream and Corn Tortillas

SERVES 10–12

10 garlic cloves . . . .

2 aubergines . . . .

2 red peppers, deseeded . . . .

1 teaspoon good-quality sea salt. . . . .

Good run of extra virgin olive oil. . . .

3 white onions, diced . . . .

2 teaspoons smoked chipotle chilli powder. . . . .

5 teaspoons ground cumin . . . .

3 teaspoons dried oregano . . . .

1 teaspoon smoked paprika. . . . .

2 x 400g tins of black beans, drained and rinsed. . . . .

2 x 400g tins of kidney beans, drained and rinsed. . . . .

1 x 400g tin of creamy white beans, such as butter beans or cannellini . . .

2 x 400g tins of whole plum tomatoes

1 mugful of vegetable or chicken stock. . . . .

Just over 1 tablespoon maple or date syrup . . . .

100g cooking chorizo (optional for carnivores), chopped . . . .

150g hard sheep's cheese, to serve (optional) . . . .

Fresh coriander leaves, to serve . . . . .

Organic corn tortillas, to serve . . . . .

Avocado sour cream (page 226) . . . . . .

⊕ On a budget

. . . .

⏳ Freezes well

I'm surviving on meals that rely on the combined forces of heat and time to do all the work. No fiddling around with spiralisers. No timer beside the frying pan. No last-minute dashes to the corner store for fresh veg. These days our pantry is the midwife for recipes, because who has the time to get fresh food every single evening? We're going big on flavour with minimum effort. This bowl of chilli comes from superstar staples in the cupboard. You can switch out the aubergine for whatever veg you find loitering in your fridge.

Fire up your oven to 200°C. You want to roast the vegetables first, so you'll need two large roasting trays.

Keep the garlic cloves whole and unpeeled in their papery shells. Dice the aubergines and peppers into postage stamp-sized pieces. Tumble the garlic and veg into your roasting tray(s), toss with the salt and give them a good lick of olive oil. Roast in the oven for 20–30 minutes, until sweet and almost collapsing. If your tray is too packed, the veg will go soggy instead of caramelising – you won't like this! Better to roast the veg across two or three trays if in any doubt.

Sweat your onions with another lick of olive oil in a large heavy-based pot for 12–15 minutes, until translucent. Shake over your dried spices halfway through. Once the onions are sweet and soft, add your platoon of drained beans and cook over a high heat for a further 3 minutes. Turn down the heat to a simmer, add the tinned tomatoes and stock and let the sauce thicken over 30 minutes. Add in a dash of maple syrup – this is needed to counter the acidity that tinned tomatoes introduce. If you fancy bowing to the carnivores in your house, you could also add some chopped cooking chorizo at this point. Irish Gubbeen is perfect.

When the tray of veg is ready, remove it from the oven. Carefully squeeze out the softened garlic from within their papery pods. It should be almost creamy. Discard the paper and add the roasted garlic to your simmering pot of beans. Tumble in the cooked veg.

To serve, spoon into bowls and grate sheep's cheese on top (if using). Parachute some fresh coriander and crisp tortillas on top, with a side of avocado sour cream.

Tamarind and Miso Butter Beans with Sweet and Salty Almonds

SERVES 6–10 AS A MAIN OR SIDE . . . . .

4 large aubergines . . . .

2 small unwaxed lemons,
zest and juice . . . .

125ml extra virgin olive oil . . . .

4 fat garlic cloves, minced . . . .

4 tablespoons sweet white miso. . . . . .

4 tablespoons tamarind paste . . . .

2 tablespoons just-boiled water . . . . .

2 x 400g tins of butter beans, drained
and rinsed . . . .

Smoky almonds (page 216),
to serve . . . .

Natural yogurt, to serve . . . .

⊕ On a budget

. . . .

⧗ Freezes well

Did you know there are crazy-tasty foods that can help your cholesterol levels? And I'm not referring to those dubious brands claiming to do the same. Nature provides plenty of help without the interference of chemistry labs, manufacturing plants and marketing campaigns.

Extra virgin olive oil has been shown to raise the 'good' HDL cholesterol in our body, resulting in a better overall cholesterol score. Doc wants our HDL levels to be high and our LDL score to be low. Think of HDL as the garbage truck of the bloodstream, ferrying bad cholesterol from the walls of our arteries back to the liver for disposal. That's why HDL is referred to as 'good' or 'protective' cholesterol. Other savvy choices include garlic, nuts and fibre-rich beans, so I've included them here.

This tamarind and miso butter bean dish makes a great vegetarian supper or breakfast with fried eggs every morning this week. It's also great with clouds of yogurt and hot basmati rice. Slices of fresh chilli and crisp tortillas are another favourite accompaniment of ours. It's even good with boiled baby potatoes and a dusting of fresh parsley.

Fire up your oven as high as it will go. Mine does 240°C.

Roast the whole aubergines on a baking tray, just as they are, for 1 hour. The flesh needs to be squishy squashy and collapsed inside. Take them out of the oven once cooked and leave to cool before handling.

In the meantime, zest and juice your lemons into the olive oil. Mix through the minced garlic and miso paste. Loosen the tamarind with the hot water before stirring it through the lemony oil.

Tumble in your drained and rinsed butter beans. Freshly cooked beans are even nicer, but tend to demand more time and patience. Now all you need to do is wait for your aubs to roast.

Once the cooked aubs are sufficiently cool enough to handle, split them in half with a very sharp knife. Scoop the flesh out into a colander and let the excess liquid drain away in the sink for 30 minutes while you do something exciting like clean the budgie cage or open a bottle of Tempranillo. Or both.

Stir the roasted aubergine flesh into your medley of butter beans. A few turns of the salt and pepper mill, followed by a handful of smoky almonds and a lick of yogurt, and it's ready to plate up.

Roasted Cauli Korma with Burnt Raisins and Pistachios

SERVES 6

1 head of cauliflower . . . .

1 head of Romanesco cauliflower (or another head of the regular variety if this is tricky to find) . . . .

4 tablespoons coconut oil or ghee (page 194), plus extra for roasting . .

3 onions, diced . . . .

8 garlic cloves, diced . . . .

1 large finger-sized piece of fresh ginger, peeled and grated . . . .

25g Indian korma dried spice mix . . .

6 ripe cooking tomatoes (e.g. Roma), chopped . . . .

1 x 400ml tin of full-fat coconut milk . . . .

1 large cup of Greek yogurt . . . .

2 tablespoons maple syrup . . . .

Handful of raisins, to serve . . . .

Shelled, smashed pistachios, to serve . . . .

Wedges of lime, to serve . . . .

⊕ On a budget

. . . .

⧖ Freezes well

This vegetarian korma is immensely satisfying. Don't get me wrong, I enjoy meat. But I find myself wondering whether future generations will look back and yack at the idea of supermarkets selling solid lumps of animal flesh. If you arrived on Earth today and saw how we dismembered other living creatures, then sold them in plastic trays, you'd think that we were greasy psychopaths.

But for now, the mass manufacturing of meat limbs seems perfectly acceptable. Strange, eh? (Come to think of it, we'd probably find our obsession with Wow Brows and golf equally disquieting.)

If society's relationship with factory meat seems disturbing, could we start buying less of it? Give sales a massive wedgie? I'd love to see footfall directed back into our butchers, where it mindfully and respectfully belongs. We'd also be doing our wallet, our health and our environment a whopping great service. Look, I'm pretty caffeinated right now, and this roasted cauli korma is making me disproportionately happy. Try it.

Fire up your oven to 220°C.

Prep your cauli pieces by removing the outer leaves from both heads of cauliflower and carefully slicing the arse off their stems. Compost these (they don't make good stock – too much sulphur). Break your cauliflower into good-sized florets – not too small, but not too monstrous either. The Romanesco variety will need more stem trimming, but you can add these pieces onto your baking tray too. They taste just as good.

Jumble your florets onto two baking trays (or one large tray) with a lick of coconut oil or ghee and roast on high for 16–20 minutes, shaking halfway through to prevent them from sticking to the tray. You're looking for a lightly charred, golden floret that still holds its shape.

While the cauli cooks, get going on your korma. Using your biggest casserole or stockpot, sweat your onions with 2 tablespoons of your preferred choice of fat for 5 minutes before adding the garlic, ginger and korma spices. Stir until the garlic starts to colour.

Now add the fresh tomatoes, coconut milk, yogurt and maple syrup. Gently putter on a low heat for 15 minutes, until the cauli florets are ready – at which point, simply rocket in the roasted cauli and cook for another 5–10 minutes.

If you have time, heat a frying pan with the remaining 1-2 tablespoons of coconut oil or ghee and add a handful of raisins. Stir until they turn chewy on the outside and are swollen on the inside. Sprinkle on top of your korma alongside some smashed pistachios and wedges of lime. Serve with brown basmati rice or steamed baby potatoes.

Lentil, Spinach and Sweet Potato Curry

ENOUGH FOR 6 . . . .

2–3 tablespoons ghee (page 194) or extra virgin coconut oil, plus extra for roasting . . . .

4 medium sweet potatoes

3 tablespoons mild curry powder . . .

1 x 400g tin of chopped tomatoes . . . .

About 160g cooked or tinned lentils (these can be taken from the freezer, see page 101) . . . .

1 x 400ml tin of coconut milk . . . .

300ml good vegetable stock, bone broth (page 160) or seasoned water . .

1 lime, juiced . . . .

1 tablespoon maple or date syrup . . .

Great big handful of baby spinach leaves, washed . . . .

For the wet paste

400–500g onions, peeled . . . .

6 garlic cloves, peeled . . . .

2 mild fresh chillies, deseeded

Good chunk of fresh ginger, peeled . .

1 finger-sized piece of fresh turmeric (optional) . . . .

⊕ On a budget

. . . .

⧖ Freezes well

Lentil curry is BAE (Beyond Anything Else). Okay, so this teenspeak is normally a reference point for Justin Bieber's abs or bare-chested members of One Direction. Grand so. Except that when you get to my age, food will excite you more.

Preheat your oven to 200°C.

Pop all the wet paste ingredients into a food processor and pulse into pieces. This saves time on chopping and also helps the veg to melt into the curry later on. Gently cook the wet paste in a large heavy-based saucepan with the ghee or coconut oil for approximately 10 minutes, until softened.

Meanwhile, peel your sweet potatoes (if they're not organic) and chop into little cubes. Roast in the hot oven with a little more ghee or coconut oil for 30 minutes, until super-soft and slightly coloured.

Add your curry powder to the pan of veg. I usually use 3 tablespoons, but it will depend on the mix you choose. As a rule, go stronger than you think you should.

Whack up the heat and stir briskly to prevent burning, then tip in the tinned toms, cooked lentils, coconut milk, stock, lime juice and syrup. Let this putt-putter away for 20 minutes.

When the sweet potato is coloured on the outside and soft on the inside, shake the pieces into the pot of curry. Both should be ready at about the same time. All that's left is to stir through your spinach leaves before plating up.

There is a range of seriously good finishing yogurts later in the book for extra jazz hands. A simple bowl of basmati rice or naan bread will help stretch the portions out to feed more mouths.

Rogan Squash with Sour Cream and Almonds

MAKES 6–8 SERVING (DOUBLE THE
RECIPE TO SERVE 12) . . . .

2 butternut squash . . . .

4 tablespoons coconut oil or ghee
(page 194) . . . .

3 red onions, roughly chopped. . . . . . .

25g rogan josh spice blend . . . .

1 fat finger-sized piece of fresh
ginger, peeled and grated. . . . .

1 x 400g tin of chopped tomatoes . . . .

250g natural yogurt . . . .

1 tablespoon maple syrup . . . .

3 garlic cloves, crushed. . . . .

1 lime, cut into wedges, to serve . . . . .

Sour cream, to serve . . . .

80g toasted flaked almonds,
to serve . . . .

⊕ On a budget
. . . .

⧗ Will happily hang out in the
freezer until beckoned

Raw garlic woofs. But golly whizzbang, I love the stuff. That sulphur honk on your breath contains a compound called allicin. The thing is, allicin is not actually found in garlic. Allicin is the prodigal child of two other special compounds in garlic, alliin and alliinase. When these hot-diggity compounds meet (say, when we crush garlic), the mighty allicin is born. Oh Allicin!

This dish is immensely flavourful. We add the garlic just before serving to maximise on allicin's dance moves. Tastes great with quinoa, poppadoms, naan bread or wholegrain sticky rice.

Clock your oven to 200°C.

Dice the flesh of your butternut into 1.4kg of bite-sized pieces, leaving the skin on if it's thin and organic. Compost the seeds and stringy insides. Roast your butternut pieces in the oven with 2 tablespoons of your coconut oil or ghee on two rimmed baking trays for 45 minutes, until slightly charred and/or soft.

Meanwhile, heat your largest and heaviest saucepan over a low heat. Add the onions and remaining 2 tablespoons of coconut oil or ghee and sweat for a few minutes. Tip in your spices and grated ginger and stir for 1 minute.

Time to tumble in your chopped tomatoes, yogurt and maple syrup. Leave to putter on your lowest setting, with the lid on, until the squash is ready from the oven.

Once the squash is cooked, add it to the pan. Stir through your raw garlic and serve immediately. A squeeze of lime is all that is needed. We love this with sour cream and toasted almonds, or loads of coriander and naan bread, or crowned with a plump poached egg and extra yogurt. But all the same, it's savage on its own – earthing and warm, like a mother's hug.

To toast the flaked almonds, pour a handful of them onto a roasting tray without any oil. Pop the tray into a preheated oven at 200°C. Toast for 4–5 minutes, watching them very carefully. You want to catch the flakes before they brown!

Black Beans, 2 Ways

⊕ Reasonable

....

⧗ Overnight soaking required.
Freezes well.

Quite apart from tasting surprisingly creamy, black beans are fibre heavyweights. Fibre is your bro. He's always looking out for you, making sure you're regular and tickety-poo. Without fibre, your personality would expire. Yep. Kiss haemorrhoids bye-bye. (That would be a feat in itself, actually. I should drop the visuals.)

About 75% of us will experience haemorrhoids (piles) at some point in our lives, although they most commonly occur between the ages of 45 and 65. Haemorrhoids also seem to like pregnant women. Jeesh. As if they aren't busy enough growing the next generation of *Homo sapiens.*

Star Anise and Cocoa Black Beans with Caramelised Bananas

SERVES 4 . . . .

200g dried turtle black beans, soaked overnight . . . .

1 litre veggie stock or bone broth (page 160) . . . .

1 star anise . . . .

2 onions. . . . .

2 garlic cloves . . . .

2 tablespoons olive oil, coconut oil or ghee (page 194) . . . .

4 Medjool dates, pitted and mashed . .

1 tablespoon cocoa powder . . . .

2 bananas or 1 plantain, cut into thin strips. . . . .

2 tablespoons butter or ghee, to fry the bananas . . . .

Coconut yogurt (page 218), to serve . .

Drain the soaked black beans, then bring to a rolling simmer with the stock and star anise. Cook for 1–1½ hours, until creamy inside, not crunchy.

While the beans are cooking, finely chop the onions and garlic or blitz them in a food processor. It only takes 5 seconds in a food processor, so I tend to do it this way.

Warm your preferred fat in a large saucepan over a confident yet gentle heat. Sweat the onion and garlic for 10 minutes. It's time to tumble in the cooked beans along with their cooking liquid, the mashed Medjools and the cocoa powder. Reduce the heat to a putt-putter on your lowest setting for 15–25 minutes to help the cooking liquid reduce.

We serve the cocoa beans with caramelised bananas on top. To do this, whack up the heat on a frying pan. Add butter or ghee (as much as you fancy, friends) and fry thin strips of banana or plantain until caramelised and gooey on the outside. Flip to do the other side. Drop them over your bowls of cocoa black beans and serve with a cooling cloud of coconut yogurt.

Mexican Black Beans with Tortillas and Smashed Avocado

SERVES 4 . . . .

200g dried turtle black beans, soaked overnight . . . .

1 litre veggie stock or bone broth (page 160) . . . .

2 onions. . . . .

2 garlic cloves . . . .

1 tablespoon olive oil, coconut oil or ghee (page 194) . . . .

100g salami sausage, cubed (we love Gubbeen Irish salami) . . . .

2 teaspoons ground chipotle chilli powder . . . .

1 teaspoon cocoa powder . . . .

2 ripe avocados . . . .

Squeeze of lemon . . . .

Good twist of the salt and pepper mill. . . . .

4 tablespoons pumpkin seeds . . . .

Organic corn tortillas, to serve . . . . .

Drain the soaked black beans, then bring to a rolling simmer with the stock. Cook for 1–1½ hours, until creamy inside, not crunchy.

While the beans are cooking, finely chop the onions and garlic or blitz them in a food processor. It only takes 5 seconds in a food processor, so I tend to do it this way.

Warm your preferred fat in a large saucepan over a confident yet gentle heat. Sweat the onion and garlic for 10–15 minutes, until soft. Now add the salami and chipotle chilli powder, cooking for another 3–4 minutes, until the oils have been released from the salami.

It's time to tumble in the cooked beans along with their cooking liquid and the cocoa powder. Reduce the heat to a putt-putter on your lowest setting for 15–25 minutes to help the cooking liquid reduce.

While your beans finish cooking, mash your avocados with a little lemon, salt and pepper. Dry-fry the pumpkin seeds in a frying pan over a high heat, until aromatic and almost popping (60 seconds will do the trick).

To plate up, scrape your cooked beans into a large bowl and top with mashed avocado and toasted pumpkin seeds. We love a side of corn tortillas too. That's it, my friends. A spicy pot of black beans for your weekend DVD nights.

Vegan Sunflower Mince

SERVES 4 (DOUBLE IT TO BATCH
COOK)..........................

35g organic sunflower mince ....
1 onion, diced....................
1 tablespoon extra virgin olive oil...
2 garlic cloves, sliced ....
1 jar of your favourite tomato pasta
sauce ....

⊕ Good value

⌛ Swift. Freezes well.

Our nine-year-old is obsessed with plant-powered mince, mainly because soccer star Héctor Bellerín is vegan. This recipe brings him one step closer to Arsenal's hero (and a man bun).

Sunflower mince is soy-free, animal-free, preservative-free and hipsteria-free. I promise it won't terrify your tonsils. There's just one ingredient: 100% sunflower seed protein. You can order sunflower mince into your nearest health food store if it's not already dancing on their shelves. Serve this meat-free mince your usual way: in cheesy jacket potatoes, with fried eggs and greens, with tacos and rice to keep it vegan, or as a simple spag Bol with giddy amounts of vegan Parmesan (see page 201).

Cover your sunflower mince in warm water (or hot stock if you have it) and allow to steep for 10 minutes. It will double in size. Drain and set aside.

Tumble your onions into a large frying pan with the olive oil over a low to medium heat. Gently cook until soft and glassy. At this point, stir through your sliced garlic and let your nostrils samba.

Whack up the heat, add the mince and fry for a few minutes, until the mince is slightly coloured. Time to tip in your tomato pasta sauce. Heat through and serve your favourite way.

Meat-Free Beluga Bolognese

SERVES 6 . . . .

3 Portobello mushrooms, diced . . . . .

2 small carrots, diced . . . .

2 small onions, diced . . . .

2 garlic cloves, diced . . . .

3 tablespoons extra virgin olive oil .

300g dried beluga lentils . . . .

500ml tomato passata or tinned
toms . . . .

250ml good homemade stock . . . .

½ teaspoon dried oregano . . . .

Pinch of ground cinnamon . . . .

Splash of balsamic vinegar . . . .

4 tinned anchovies, finely chopped
(optional) . . . .

On a budget
. . . .

Worth doubling the recipe to
fill your freezer

These are no mulchy lentils, my friend. Nah-awh. Beluga lentils are pitch-black teensy lentils that hold their girth once cooked, unlike their cousins. Why beluga? Because it looks like caviar. Oh, don't get carried away – beluga lentils are about as close to caviar as Forrest Gump is to Elon Musk.

Now, I'm not trying to trick you into Meatless Mondays, but I swear you won't notice the lack of meat in this Bolognese recipe. It's a dastardly good dish for your dinner party arsenal. There's always a surprise vegetarian who turns up to scupper your plans and maim your synapses. No more! With the number of vegans in the UK rising by 360% per annum, there's probably a secret vegan in your house already.

Gently sweat all the diced vegetables in the olive oil for 15 minutes on your lowest heat. This makes them deliciously sticky and sweet. You'll need to use your biggest pot or do this in batches.

Rinse the dried lentils, then tip them into the pot along with all the remaining ingredients. (I like to parachute in a few finely chopped anchovies at this stage, but not if vegetarians are joining us for supper.) Let them party under a lid for 1 hour, until the lentils are cooked through. They need time to socialise and get to know one another.

Taste and season if necessary. It's your Bolognese – I'm not going to tell you how to serve it! But here are some ideas on what to do with leftovers the next night.

· Snuggle onto a baked sweet potato
· Cosy it up beside tacos and softly fried eggs
· Serve with courgetti (zoodles)
· Pop on a plate smeared with smooth hummus
· Make a parsnip purée and serve with garlic yogurt
· Try rolling into a soft tortilla wrap with avocado and pickled red onions (page 234)

Yellow Split Pea Daal with Harissa Butter

SERVES 3–5 . . . .

250g dried yellow split peas or chana dal, rinsed . . . .

½ teaspoon ground or fresh turmeric . . . .

1 white onion, finely diced . . . .

3 tablespoons coconut oil, butter or ghee (page 194) . . . .

4 fat garlic cloves, crushed . . . .

1 fresh red chilli, deseeded and sliced . . . .

Chunk of fresh ginger, lightly peeled and grated . . . .

1 teaspoon cumin seeds . . . .

Generous handful of ripe plum tomatoes, halved . . . .

Squeeze of lime . . . .

Natural yogurt, to serve . . . .

Fresh coriander, to serve . . . .

Harissa butter (from the freezer, page 198), to serve . . . .

 Reasonable

. . . .

Leftovers freeze beautifully or will keep in the fridge for up to five days

During those biting autumnal weekends, daal can be a life-enriching experience. It's a form of spellbinding magic. My nostrils do an all-consuming samba as I inhale a whole load of happiness that only food chemists could explain. This is daal – noun, verb, adjective, it's much more than a bowl of hot legumes.

Food is always my first medicinal port of call. I prepare daal to soothe indolent moods and sore hearts. It's got to have lots of sizzling garlic and blood-thumping ginger. Like a hug, this is to help us feel grounded yet simultaneously lifted, something Indian cooking almost always achieves. The injection of chilli is life's defibrillator – the bigger the burn, the quicker we wake and shake.

Cook the split peas or chana dal and the turmeric in a small deep pan, covered with unsalted water. Let them putt-putter for 30–45 minutes, until you can crush the peas between your thumb and forefinger. You're looking for a soupy consistency.

While the peas gurgle away, gently colour the onions in your preferred form of fat (coconut oil, butter or ghee) over a low heat for 12 minutes. Turn up the heat and add the crushed garlic, chilli, grated ginger and cumin seeds, stirring for a few minutes to prevent charring.

Now you can add the fresh tomatoes and lime and turn the heat right down to let the flavours socialise under a lid. After 10 minutes of cooking, stir through the cooked split peas.

Serve in large bowls with some natural yogurt, freshly torn coriander leaves and a pat of harissa butter from your freezer stash.

Wondering what to do with leftovers?

· Day 1: Rice and pickled red onions (page 234).
· Day 2: Crown with a simple poached egg or crumbled tempeh.
· Day 3: Freeze leftovers in portions.

Sweet Butternut and Cardamom Red Daal

SERVES 3 AS IS OR 5 WITH RICE . . . . . .

2–3 tablespoons extra virgin coconut oil . . . .

1 red onion, chopped . . . .

1 butternut squash, peeled and diced

1 fat garlic clove, sliced . . . .

2 teaspoons black mustard seeds . . . .

1 teaspoon ground cardamom . . . .

½ teaspoon ground fenugreek . . . . . .

½ teaspoon ground turmeric . . . .

180g dried red lentils, rinsed thoroughly . . . .

1 big fresh chilli, deseeded and thinly sliced . . . .

A good handful of dried dark unsulphured apricots, halved . . . .

1 x 400ml tin of coconut milk . . . .

240ml vegetable stock or bone broth (page 160) . . . .

A few twists of the salt and pepper mill. . . . .

🙂 Reasonable

. . . .

⧖ Can be doubled to batch cook for your freezer

I often ponder whether my two boys will look back on our age and marvel at our madness. We think of child labour, Nigel Farage and kale crisps as monstrosities our species has blindly tolerated over the past decade, but I wonder how future generations will translate the indolent apathy of today.

Get past contouring and yoni incense as modern-day bewilderment. Go deeper than that. We are the generation that both permitted and fuelled the mass incarceration of animals to eat their flesh or drink their milk. Don't get me wrong, I love meat! But I'm struggling with my lunacy as I contemplate getting a family cat.

We are the generation of animal lovers. You and I pour adoration onto our family gerbil or dog, yet inflict brutal acts of suffering onto other animals as if they are incapable of feeling. This behaviour is hugely bizarre and disturbing. Each time we eat meat, we fuel the flesh factories, which in turn contribute to 60% of our greenhouse gas emissions. Yup. This crazy meat-eating habit of ours is not only pathologically bonkers, but is one of the key drivers of climate change.

I'm not dry humping my moral compass here. I still eat meat. I'm just trying to navigate my hypocrisies, and for now this recipe helps to take the 'me' out of meat.

Using your largest pan, melt the coconut oil with the onion and butternut. Sweat on a gentle heat for 10 minutes. Add the garlic and spices – your nostrils and neighbours will enjoy this. You'll need to stir frequently to prevent the garlic from charring.

When the spices start sticking, whack up the heat and add the remaining ingredients.

Once bubbling, cover with a lid and reduce the temperature to a gentle gurgle. Cook for 20 minutes, until the butternut is sufficiently fragrant and soft. If the daal looks a little dry, add a few tablespoons of water to loosen it up. If it looks too wet, remove the lid during the final few minutes of cooking so that some of the liquid will evaporate. Season with a few twists of the salt and pepper mill.

Serve in big deep bowls and freeze the rest for another evening with poached eggs or crumbled tofu.

Chicken Thighs with Fennel, Pomegranate and Parsley

SERVES 4 . . . .

1 large or 2 small fennel bulbs . . . . . .

1 large red onion, sliced . . . .

2 tablespoons olive oil. . . . .

4 chicken thighs . . . .

3 garlic cloves, sliced . . . .

1 finger-sized piece of fresh ginger, peeled and grated . . . .

2 teaspoons ground cumin . . . .

1 teaspoon smoked paprika . . . .

Pinch of dried oregano . . . .

Pinch of chilli flakes . . . .

2 tablespoons tomato purée . . . .

300ml chicken stock . . . .

2 yellow peppers, deseeded and sliced . . . .

10 whole Nocellara or green olives, stones intact . . . .

Handful of fresh parsley, to serve (optional) . . . .

Seeds from ½ pomegranate, to serve (optional) . . . .

⊕ On a budget

. . . .

⧗ Freezes well. Save the bones and add to your freezer stock bag (page 101)

Oxidation is the damage done by free radicals in our body, kind of like rusting. So it's no surprise that oxidation is a major contributor to ageing and just about every pesky disease you can imagine.

We need to recruit *anti*oxidants to help decommission these marauding free radicals! Luckily, we can source heaps of antioxidants from fresh food. Ginger and garlic are particularly talented. We need to provide our booty with plenty of nutritious foods to prevent oxidative stress in the first place. Trying to repair the damage once it is done is significantly harder.

This chicken stew is an active hub of antioxidants and ninja moves. One spoonful will have your toes singing.

Prep your fennel by slicing the bum off (chucking that bit into your freezer stock bag) and cutting the bulb in half. You can then slice each half into slices. Set aside.

In a large sauté pan or casserole pot, gently sweat the onion over a medium heat in your olive oil until glassy (5–10 minutes).

In the same pan of onions, whack up the heat and colour the chicken all over. You'll need to push the onions to the side of the pan for this.

Now tumble in the garlic, ginger and spices, stirring while your nostrils party. When the garlic starts to colour, add the tomato purée and cook for 1 minute, then pour in your stock, reducing the heat to a soft simmer. Add the peppers and olives and cook for 45 minutes with the lid on, until the chicken is cooked through.

To serve, plate up in big bowls and parachute a generous helping of parsley and pomegranate seeds on top. We love this with a side of watercress in the summer or lemony quinoa in winter. Black rice is also ace.

Pumpkin Curry with Hemp Garlic Cream

SERVES 8 . . . .

1kg pumpkin flesh (not the decorative Halloween ones) . . . .

2 large carrots . . . .

3–4 tablespoons ghee (page 194) or coconut oil . . . .

3 medium onions, peeled . . . .

4 garlic cloves, peeled . . . .

2 thumb-seized pieces of fresh ginger, peeled . . . .

25g hot curry powder (use mild if preferred) . . . .

400g ripe plum tomatoes (summer) or 1 x 400g tin of chopped tomatoes (winter) . . . .

Handful of jumbo raisins or Chilean flame raisins . . . .

1 x 400ml tin of coconut milk or 250ml good stock . . . .

½ x 400g tin of butter beans, drained and rinsed (optional) . . . .

Hemp garlic cream (page 224), to serve . . . .

😊 Reasonable
. . . .

⧖ Freezes well

I love spicy food that terrifies my tonsils. And the hotter the blaze, the bigger the appeal. Only curries and PMT truly afford me the freedom to curse like an angry otter with Tourette's.

Chillies help to increase heart rate, making it feel like coffee cantering through our veins.

Then there's capsaicin, Mother N's very own painkiller. Capsaicin is a compound found inside chillies. This recreational compound (kidding! ish) helps to alleviate aches by messing with the transmission of pain signals to the brain. The highest concentration of capsaicin can be found in the white pith in the chilli where the seeds are attached, not the seeds themselves.

I had a bunch of vegan pals around for a white-hot curry last week and stopped breathing when I realised I couldn't pair the heat with cooling clouds of dairy. A maniacal dialogue with self, and a sneaky smoke signal on Instagram, resulted in this shockingly good alternative that's 100% animal free, 0% stress. Desperation has never let me down. (Well, the 1980s don't count. For anyone.)

Fire up your oven to 200°C.

Peel and chop your pumpkin into bite-sized pieces. Do the same with your carrots, slicing on the diagonal if you're really snazzy. Tumble both veg onto two large baking trays. Dot with some of the ghee or coconut oil and roast in the oven for 30–40 minutes, shaking the tray several times throughout, until caramelised on the outside and soft on the inside. Set aside.

Roughly chop your onions and pulse with the garlic and ginger in a food processor (not a blender) for 5 seconds. You can finely chop them with a sharp knife if you prefer to practise your ninja skills. Sweat the chopped onion mix for 10 minutes over a gentle heat with the remaining ghee or coconut oil. Add the hot curry powder and stir for 1–2 minutes to coat everything thoroughly.

Tumble in the tomatoes, raisins, coconut milk or stock. If you fancy adding beans to this, now is a good time. Cook for 10 minutes before socialising with the roasted tray of pumpkin and carrots.

Stir and serve straight away or cool and store in the fridge for up to three days.

Aubergine Rendang

😊 Not cheap, but not expensive

⧖ Keeps beautifully in the fridge all week or freeze any leftovers

I have completely bastardised lamb rendang, and man, did it work. I use 75% less red meat than the traditional recipe and lob in lots of aubergine and gojis. Goji berries look like teensy chillies in the rendang and will scare the bejaysus out of your guests.

These teensy gnarled berries hide most of their beauty. Gram for gram, one serving of goji berries can deliver more vitamin C than those egotistical oranges. Gojis are a good plant source of iron and protein too. As a tonic, they've been central to Tibetan and Chinese medicine for over a thousand years. This berry's immune-boosting reputation could also stem from its specific polysaccharide permutation, just like mushrooms. Polysaccharides apparently work by influencing our immune response by stimulating certain 'fighter' cells. Fancy shmancy. But science is rarely that simple. Perhaps its impressive stash of antioxidants is responsible for all the hype? Whatever the reason, we love the result!

Start by sweating the onions on a gentle heat with 1 tablespoon of the coconut oil or ghee until glassy looking (5–10 minutes). Add the lamb, garlic, chilli, lemongrass, ginger, spices and a few twists from the salt and pepper mill. No need to brown the lamb first. Whack up the heat for a few minutes to briefly colour everything, then pour in the coconut milk and turn down to a putter. I use the lowest setting on my cooker. It needs 2–3 hours over a low-medium heat on the hob with a lid securely fastened. Any higher and the lamb will toughen. Taste after 2 hours and see if the lamb needs longer. It should be juicy and flavoursome, not tough. Leave it for longer if needed.

About 40 minutes before the end of the cooking time, preheat the oven to 200°C.

Remove the lid for the final 20–30 minutes of cooking and parachute the goji berries into the mix. This will add sweetness and nutrition while concentrating the flavours. Rendang is best when it's strong and punchy rather than soupy or saucy.

About the same time as you are adding the gojis, slice the aubergines into thick discs, then into quarters. Divide between two roasting trays. Service each tray with the remaining coconut oil or ghee and roast in the oven for 30 minutes, until soft and caramelised.

Once the aubergines are roasted, stir them through the rendang, tickle with fresh coriander leaves and holler at everyone to take their seat.

Sticky black rice is a fabulous accompaniment if you want the rendang to stretch to eight mouths. We also love chickpea poppadoms and pickled red onions (page 234) on the side.

Smoky Aubergine and Walnut Ragù

SERVES 8 WITH RICE OR POLENTA . . . .

6 aubergines . . . .

1 teaspoon fine sea salt . . . .

4 or more tablespoons extra virgin olive oil . . . .

2 large white onions, halved and sliced . . . .

5 garlic cloves, sliced . . . .

1 teaspoon whole cumin seeds . . . .

2 teaspoons ground cumin . . . .

1 teaspoon smoked paprika . . . .

1 teaspoon dried oregano . . . .

1 teaspoon maple syrup or honey (optional) . . . .

1 teaspoon pomegranate molasses (optional) . . . .

1 x 650g jar of tomato passata . . . . . .

Maple-coated walnuts (page 212) . . . .

⊕ On a budget

. . . .

⧗ Another freezer hero. Just leave out the walnuts until serving.

Check out this umami-rich aubergine and walnut dish. Even the most testosteroney, murderous, barbecuing mammal will squeal like a chipmunk in a sea of nuts.

Fire up your oven to 220°C. Take out two large roasting trays and line with non-stick baking paper.

Remove and discard the tops from your aubergines. Slice the aubs vertically down the centre, then cut each half into uniform long strips. Divide between the roasting trays, sprinkle with the sea salt and coat generously with olive oil.

Roast the aubergines for 20–30 minutes, until caramelised around the edges and squishy inside. The cooking time will vary greatly depending on what size your strips are, so it's worth checking on them every 4–5 minutes.

While your aubs are roasting, heat a frying pan or heavy-based pot with a dash of olive oil over a medium flame. Add your sliced onions and sweat for 8–12 minutes, until floppy and translucent. Add the garlic and whole cumin seeds halfway through cooking the onions. Stir to prevent burning.

When the garlic is colouring, tumble in the remaining spices, maple syrup and pomegranate molasses (if using) and the passata. Putter for 20 minutes. As soon the aubergines are caramelised, add them to the pot of passata and holler for everyone to take their places at the dinner table.

Stir a generous portion of smashed maple-coated walnuts through your aubergine ragù just before plating up. We serve this ragù alongside creamy polenta or hunks of sourdough and horseradish yogurt (page 217). It's good with poached eggs too. Leftovers can be frozen in individual portions for another night.

Beet Bourguignon with Horseradish Yogurt

SERVES 6 . . . .

4 tablespoons olive oil . . . .

1 white onion, chopped . . . .

4 garlic cloves, finely chopped . . . . . .

6 carrots, sliced into large discs . . . .

4 large beetroot, peeled and chopped

3 bay leaves. . . . .

3 sprigs of fresh thyme . . . .

3 Portobello mushrooms . . . .

2 handfuls of wild mushrooms . . . .

2 tablespoons Dijon mustard . . . .

2 tablespoons tomato purée . . . .

1 small tin of anchovies, drained, or 2 tablespoons sweet white miso (for vegetarians) . . . .

500ml red wine . . . .

500ml good stock . . . .

2 tablespoons kuzu or arrowroot (natural thickener) . . . .

2 tablespoons cold water . . . .

Horseradish yogurt (page 217), to serve . . . .

⊕ Reasonable

. . . .

⧗ Double the recipe to serve 12 or freeze half the batch

This is a delectable Scandi twist on the classic beef Bourguignon. Beets are loaded with potassium, that slavishly loyal mineral to hangovers. Potassium works by redressing the imbalance of sodium in our system. When we have too much sodium, we are vulnerable to high blood pressure, cramps, heat stroke and very stinky pee. Fresh fruit and vegetables are top sources, but some brag higher grades than others. Bananas, avocados and pumpkins are all gloating with rich potassium levels to keep your liver on speaking terms with you. But beetroot is the heavyweight champ, ringing in at a stonking 530mg of potassium for just two beets. Here's a very useful recipe for a Sunday lunch.

Heat half of the olive oil in your largest heavy-based saucepan over a gentle heat. Add the onion and garlic and sauté until glassy, then tumble in the carrots, beetroot, bay leaves and thyme and let them socialise for 5–10 minutes while you prep the mushrooms.

Slice the Portobellos across the diameter. Depending on the type of wild mushrooms you chose, chop them into bite-sized chunks or leave whole if small. Set aside for now.

Check your pot of sweating veg and stir through the mustard, tomato purée, anchovies (if using), red wine and enough stock to cover. Simmer on a low putt-putter for 90 minutes or more. Make sure you leave the lid off to let the alcohol escape. Being Irish, this step sounds counter-intuitive, but trust me. You don't want the alcohol content in the finished dish.

Heat the rest of the olive oil in a large frying pan, then lower the heat and sear the mushrooms until tender. Season to taste and parachute them into the pot as they cook.

Dissolve the kuzu or arrowroot in the cold water and add to the pot 10 minutes before the end of the cooking time to thicken the broth.

When the beets and carrots are cooked and still have a nice bite to them, remove the pot from the heat. For vegetarians who skipped the anchovies, stir through the white miso at this point to preserve its nutritional kudos and get that same umami punch.

Remember to pick out the bay leaves and thyme before serving. Bourguignon is traditionally dished up with lots of lentils, but we find mashed potato suits our Irish DNA. Either way, serve with dollops of horseradish yogurt on top.

Kale and Lentil Minestrone with Parmesan Bombs

MAKES 2–3 LITRES . . . .

2 tablespoons extra virgin olive oil .

1 large carrot, cut into circles . . . . .

1 stick of celery, sliced . . . .

1 large onion, diced . . . .

1 teaspoon flaky sea salt . . . .

A few twists of the black pepper mill . . . .

1 x 690g jar of tomato passata . . . . . .

300g dried speckled green lentils, rinsed . . . .

2 Parmesan rinds . . . .

2 bay leaves . . . .

2 teaspoons dried oregano and/or thyme . . . .

1.5 litres freezer stock (page 159) . . .

1 litre water (or more stock if you have it) . . . .

100g chopped cavolo nero . . . .

4 garlic cloves, minced or grated . . .

Wedge of Parmesan to pass around (or vegan Parmesan, page 000) . . . . . .

Stale sourdough, for croutons (optional) . . . .

⊕ Reasonable

. . . .

⏳ Freeze leftovers

Health divas have already dubbed cavolo nero, with its Italian sophistication and unlikely elegance, as sexy Tuscan kale. The cavolo may have already slammed curly kale off its number one spot (hoorah!). Instagram is imploding with giddy disciples and hashtags, while vegetarian societies are curating shrines for the stuff. One can't help but wonder whether this Dark Green Leafy was hand-harvested by Wes Anderson and blessed by Ali Wong under a full moon.

This will take 50 minutes to cook and you'll add the greens in the last 5 minutes of cooking. Let's get prepping (and pod-listening!).

Tumble your olive oil, carrot, celery, onion, salt and black pepper into your largest pot or pan. Gently cook for 15 minutes, until the onions are softened, stirring every few minutes in the process.

Now add your passata, rinsed lentils, Parmesan rinds if you have them (for extra flavour), bay leaves, oregano and stock. Bring to a rolling boil, then reduce to a gurgling simmer for 30 minutes.

Add your greens and crushed garlic at the end of the cooking time. Remove the Parmesan rinds and bay leaves. Taste and season with more salt and pepper to your preference.

Ladle into deep bowls and pass around a wedge of Parmesan at the table for grating over. The vegan Parmesan recipe on page 201 is also ace. A few fried croutons are very welcome – simply fry cubes of stale sourdough in hot olive oil for 15 seconds before parachuting over each bowl of minestrone. I keep stale sourdough in my freezer, torn up, ready to use as croutons for soups or salads or for breadcrumbs in the meatball recipe on page 152.

Winter Root Madras with Kefir Cream

SERVES 8 . . . .

6 large sweet potatoes. . . . .

2 parsnips or carrots . . . .

5 tablespoons coconut oil or ghee (page 194) . . . .

3 white onions, peeled . . . .

6 garlic cloves, peeled . . . .

3 finger-sized pieces of fresh ginger, peeled . . . .

3 finger-sized pieces of fresh turmeric, peeled (optional) . . . .

25g ground Madras curry spice blend . . . .

1 x 400g tin of tomatoes . . . .

1 x 400ml tin of coconut milk . . . .

8 pitted Medjool dates or dried figs, chopped . . . .

½ lime, zest and juice . . . .

Cheat's kefir cream (page 235) or natural yogurt, to serve . . . .

Chopped almonds, to serve . . . .

⊕ On a budget

. . . .

⧖ Freezes well

Butternut is not a nut butter. Nor is it dairy. If you think butternut is a silly name, it comes from the squash family. Who comes up with these titles? The cruciferous family has it worse. Sounds like a cross between crucifying and sulphurous. Anyway, back to the department of cooking. We totally dig one-tray dinners. Less washing up to do, especially when we lick our plates pretty. That's why this recipe is a household favourite. Roast a large tray of winter roots. Add to a pan of bubbling curry sauce. That's it.

Fire up your oven to 200°C.

Peel and chop your sweet potatoes and parsnips or carrots into reasonable bite-sized chunks (not too small, as they tend to shrink once roasted). A uniform size is important to ensure even cooking. Tumble onto a large roasting tray (or two smaller ones will do), dot with 4 tablespoons of the coconut oil or ghee and roast for 30 minutes, until deliciously soft and caramelised around the edges.

In the meantime, make the Madras sauce. I like to pulse the onions, garlic, ginger and turmeric (if using) all together in a food processor to save on chopping. Works perfectly. Tip this blitzed medley into a large deep casserole with the remaining tablespoon of your preferred fat. Gently cook for 12 minutes over a low heat, until softened. Add your Madras powder, whack up the heat and stir continuously for 60 seconds.

Now tip in the tin of tomatoes, coconut milk, Medjools or figs and lime zest and juice. Reduce to a bubbling simmer and allow to putter away for 20 minutes, half lidded, while your tray of veggies continue to roast in the oven. Feel free to use two tins of chopped tomatoes in place of the coconut milk for a change.

As soon as the root veg are done, scrape them into your pot. Serve immediately or allow the recipe to cool before distributing between glass jars designated for your freezer. I use masking tape and a Sharpie marker to label the jars. We love this with kefir cream or natural yogurt (or any of the flavoured yogurts starting on page 217) and chopped almonds. We also have a soft spot for a side of short-grain brown rice tumbled with sesame oil and flaky sea salt. This also helps to stretch the madras to more mouths.

Ratatouille

SERVES 6–8 IF SERVED WITH
POLENTA . . . .

2 red onions . . . .

6 tablespoons extra virgin olive oil .

6 garlic cloves . . . .

2 aubergines, thinly sliced
lengthways . . . .

8–10 ripe plum or Roma tomatoes . . .

2 courgettes . . . .

2 large red peppers, deseeded and
quartered . . . .

2 teaspoons dried oregano . . . .

1 teaspoon dried thyme . . . .

A few twists of the salt and pepper
mill . . . .

(+) On a budget
. . . .

⏳ Time consuming. Freeze
leftovers.

When tomato season heats up, get your mitts on the plumpest, reddest, juiciest ones swelling with value and virtue. Lycopene, a fancy carotenoid found in the red pigment of tomatoes, has heroic antioxidant properties. Good news for Sunday hangovers. This is a dish to seduce your taste buds and your liver.

A note for the cook: you're going to need patience or plenty of pans. It takes longer to cook the vegetables separately, but this method teases out each vegetable's inner diva. Instead of a homogeneous stewy slop, you'll end up with layers of flavour and complexity. Get your podcasts queuing!

Whack up the oven to 180°C.

Peel and quarter your onions. Sweat them over a gentle heat with a splash of olive oil in a heavy-based pan until soft. Slice the garlic and add to the onions as soon as they have softened. Cook until the garlic starts colouring, then transfer to the oven in a deep baking dish.

Fry the aubergine strips in a pan with more of the olive oil until lightly golden, adding more oil as necessary. You don't need to cook it through – we're looking for colour at this stage. Transfer to the oven into your dish of onions.

Slice your plum tomatoes and add to the veg in the oven.

Now for the courgettes. I find they are best sliced thickly into coins, then halved again. Lightly colour in your pan, charging up the heat and adding extra oil if required. Parachute these into your dish of veg in the oven.

Finally, you can do the same with your peppers. Once slightly softened, tumble into your oven dish of vegetables, adding the dried herbs and plenty of salt and pepper. Return to the oven, with a lid, and bake for 45 minutes, stirring gently halfway through cooking.

Once tender, serve straight away with soft creamy polenta. We also love serving this ratatouille with a poached egg and fried sourdough crumbs on top – a stealthy way to use up stale bread. The popped capers (page 214) or black olive crumb (page 210) add tiny taste explosions for the evenings you plan on defrosting this dish. On those busy evenings, a hunk of bread works beautifully on the side.

Mushroom and Merlot Stew

MAKES 7–8 SERVINGS . . . .

6 tablespoons ghee (page 194), butter or olive oil . . . .

2 large onions, diced . . . .

4 fat garlic cloves, sliced . . . .

1 celeriac, peeled and chopped into bite-sized pieces . . . .

3 bay leaves . . . .

5 sprigs of fresh thyme . . . .

2 litres really good veg stock or bone broth (page 160) . . . .

750ml Merlot or other dry red wine .

1 small tin of anchovies, drained and chopped . . . .

8 big handfuls of wild or regular mushrooms . . . .

A few twists of the salt and pepper mill . . . .

4 teaspoons grated fresh ginger (optional) . . . .

2 tablespoons kuzu or arrowroot . . .

2 tablespoons cold water . . . .

Horseradish yogurt (page 217), to serve . . . .

☺ Reasonable

. . . .

⧗ Fair bit of prep. Freezes well.

Mushrooms can make a stealthy replacement for meat, like in this recipe. Apart from their umami-fuelled, lip-dancing taste, mushrooms of all sorts like to fangirl our immune system. Especially shiitake. A polysaccharide found in shiitake – the beta-glucan – has been shown to tickle the immune system by activating cytokines and killer T-cells. Party for your bloodstream!

This mushroom and Merlot stew uses bone broth to help it sing. But this ain't no singsong. Think opera.

Heat 2 tablespoons of your preferred fat in your largest heavy-based saucepan. Add the onion and garlic. Sauté over a low-medium heat until glassy.

Tumble in the chopped celeriac, bay leaves and thyme and let them socialise for 5 minutes on a low heat while you get going on the shrooms (see below). Then pour the stock, Merlot and anchovies into the pot. Let the pot gurgle for 1 hour, until the celeriac is tender. Leave the lid off to let the alcohol escape.

To prep the shrooms while the stew merrily cooks, slice them into bite-sized chunks or leave whole if small. Heat the remaining ghee, butter or olive oil in a large frying pan, then lower the heat and cook the mushrooms until tender and caramelised. I do this in batches while the stew bubbles. Season the mushrooms and parachute them into the pot as they cook.

At this point, you can grate some ginger into the pot and let it gently simmer until the celeriac is tender. Dissolve the kuzu or arrowroot in the cold water and add to the pot 10 minutes before the end of the cooking time to thicken the broth. That's it.

Serve with fabulously spicy horseradish yogurt. Creamed potatoes or a chickpea mash are also good with this and will help to stretch the pot to 8–10 mouths.

Spanish Chickpea Stew

ENOUGH FOR 10 . . . .

450g good-quality cooking chorizo, such as Gubbeen (this can be replaced with smoked tofu sausage) . . . .

3–4 tablespoons extra virgin olive oil . . . .

300g sliced leeks . . . .

2 large white onions, diced . . . .

2 teaspoons cumin seeds . . . .

1 tablespoon of sliced garlic . . . .

6 red peppers, cut into strips . . . .

2 x 400g tins of chickpeas (reserve some of the liquid from the tins) . . . .

2 x 680g jars of tomato passata . . . . .

60g fresh flat-leaf parsley, stalks and leaves chopped . . . .

A few twists of the salt and pepper mill . . . .

Squeeze of lemon . . . .

Natural yogurt, kefir or cultured cream, to serve . . . .

Black olives, to serve . . . .

Crusty bread, to serve . . . .

⊕ Very reasonable
. . . .

⧖ Speed up prep. Freezer
rock star.

Batch cooking is about upgrading your life. It's about developing a savvy rhythm with your freezer, giving your evenings ammunition so you can spend less time cooking in the kitchen, and more time straddling Netflix. You're welcome.

Preheat your oven to 220°C.

Slice your cooking chorizo into bite-sized rounds (not too thin, but not too chunky either). If you're using smoked tofu sausage, add it along with the chickpeas later on.

Using the largest heavy-based pot you have, warm it over a medium heat, then add the chorizo and colour it all over (chorizo can burn very quickly, so keep a watchful eye). You'll need to do this in two batches to stop the pan from overcrowding and stewing the meat. Depending on your pan, you may benefit from a lick of olive oil to help the process along. The natural fat melting away from the chorizo is usually enough. Once coloured, set the chorizo aside on a large plate.

Using the same heavy-based pot, sauté the leeks in the residual fat. Give these 10 minutes. Once the leeks are soft, tip them onto the resting plate of chorizo and leave aside.

Now add the onions and cumin to the heavy-based pot. You may or may not need another lick of olive oil. Sauté until soft (another 10 minutes). Stir through your tablespoon of sliced garlic 2 minutes before the end of the cooking time. Garlic cooks swiftly compared to onions.

While the vegetables sweat in the pan, tumble the peppers with a splash of olive oil and roast on a large baking tray (or two medium trays) in your preheated oven for 20–25 minutes. You're looking for the peppers to be slightly charred at the sides. Remove from the oven and add to the plate of chorizo.

As soon as your onions are done, parachute in your tinned chickpeas along with a bit of the liquid from the tins, the medley of cooked chorizo and veg, both jars of passata and the freshly chopped parsley. If you're using smoked tofu sausage in place of chorizo, add it now. Cook over a low to medium heat for 30 minutes so that the chorizo can socialise with the chickpeas.

Taste, season and lift with lemon. Allow to cool fully before storing in individual portions designated for the freezer.

Wild Mushroom and Chestnut Lasagne

SERVES 6 . . . .

For the filling

250g cooked vacuum-packed
chestnuts . . . .

700g wild mushrooms (use regular if
preferred or shiitake for an immune
system boost) . . . .

Lick of extra virgin olive oil . . . .

A few twists of the salt and
pepper mill . . . .

3 medium white onions, diced . . . .

4 garlic cloves, sliced . . . .

2 teaspoons dried oregano . . . .

1 teaspoon chipotle chilli powder (or
a dash of chipotle Tabasco) . . . .

1 x 680g jar of tomato passata . . . . . .

For the cheese sauce

2 tablespoons ghee (page 194)
or butter . . . .

2 tablespoons buckwheat flour
or plain flour . . . .

500ml plant milk or regular milk . . .

Pinch of ground turmeric . . . .

250g good Cheddar, grated . . . .

For the pasta

9 sheets of wholemeal wheat,
wholemeal spelt or brown rice
lasagne . . . .

⊕ Use button mushrooms to reduce the expense

. . . .

⧗ Fair bit of prep involved, but
freezes beautifully in individual portions

Mushrooms have been revered throughout many cultures as far back as Ancient Egypt. These furred-up fungi were believed to bring bottomless libidos and immortality. (Eh, that must have been before the empire disappeared.) In Chinese medicine, mushrooms were celebrated for giving superhuman strength. Take that, Popeye! Today, mushrooms don't enjoy nearly the same level of prestige unless they are of the hallucinogenic kind. But many of these outrageous health claims can now be traced to a range of polysaccharides specific to mushrooms.

Lentinans and beta-glucan polysaccharides, for example, are believed to stimulate the immune system by activating hungry macrophages and combative T-cells. These white blood cells declare war on terrorism (pesky bugs and the like) and begin bombing the blood with their infantry. In laboratory studies, the polysaccharides present in shiitake extract have slowed the growth of tumours in some cell cultures – but not all cell cultures, highlighting the complexity surrounding their use. For now, I'm sufficiently excited to indulge in the fantasy of everlasting life while horsing into this lasagne.

This recipe will fit perfectly in a traditional 20cm square brownie tin. Double the recipe if you have two brownie tins and cook them side by side in the oven. That way, you can slice them up and freeze them in 12 portions, high-fiving your genius all month long.

To make your filling, dice the packet of cooked chestnuts. Set aside.

Prep your shrooms by cleaning off any grit or dirt. Depending on your mushrooms, you may need to remove and compost some stems if they're tired or growing mould. Shiitake stems are tough, so snap these off and save them in your freezer stock bag for making broth (page 159).

Chop your shrooms into bite-sized pieces. You can either pan-fry the mushrooms in batches over a gentle heat or divide them between two rimmed baking trays and roast in the oven for 10 minutes at 180°C–200°C. Whichever way you choose to cook them, they'll need a lick of olive oil and seasoning. Don't panic if they shrink to half their original size – you're on the right track!

While the shrooms cook, you can sweat down the onions in a splash of olive oil over a gentle heat for a similar timeframe (10–12 minutes). We use our largest heavy-based saucepan for this step. Add your garlic halfway through cooking your onions. Any sooner and the garlic will brown too quickly, resulting in a soapy, bitter taste. Your oregano and chipotle can go in at the same time as the garlic. (If your chipotle is in liquid form, such as Tabasco, add it at the same time as your passata instead.)

When both your onions and mushrooms are cooked through, tumble them into the same pot together with your passata and chopped chestnuts. That's your filling done!

To make the cheese sauce, heat your preferred form of fat in a small pan over a medium heat. Once melted, beat in your flour. Thoroughly. Count to 10, then pour a little milk in at a time, whisking to incorporate the milk into your smudge ball. I use a balloon beater for this step. (FYI, a balloon beater is not what you think it is. It's basically a wire whisk whose identity has been misused somewhere along the way.) I add a pinch of turmeric for a gorgeous glow.

When all the milk has been poured in and beaten through, the sauce should be thick enough to coat a spoon. Time to parachute in your grated Cheddar. Most varieties of cheese will work, in truth, but Cheddar is cheapest for maximum effect. Classier chefs will recommend Gruyère and Parmesan.

To assemble your lasagne, preheat your oven to 180°C. Sit a 20cm square loose-bottomed tin onto a large tray to catch any runaway juices while cooking.

Pour a thin layer of cheese sauce on the bottom of your tin. Layer with two full lasagne sheets. You'll need to break a third lasagne sheet to fit into the sides. Spoon over half of the shroom sauce. Now cover with more lasagne sheets, then pour over another layer of cheese sauce. Carefully top the cheese sauce with the remainder of your shroom sauce. Add a final layer of lasagne sheets, breaking to fit. Finish with the rest of the cheese sauce (and a some grated cheese if you have any left over).

Bake in the oven for 35 minutes. Remove from the oven and serve alongside fresh garden leaves dressed in freshly squeezed lemon juice. Or allow to cool before slicing into six generous portions and folding into baking parchment for the freezer.

Roasted Garlic and Butternut Gnocchi

SERVES 8 . . . .

1 whole head of garlic . . . .

1 tablespoon extra virgin olive oil . .

1 butternut squash . . . .

A few dots of butter or ghee (page 194), for roasting and frying . . . .

120g brown rice flour or all-purpose gluten-free flour, plus extra for dusting . . . .

2 handfuls of fresh tarragon leaves (sub with basil if tarragon is tricky)

Generous pinch of flaky sea salt . . . .

A few cracks of the black pepper mill . . . .

⊕ On a budget

. . . .

⧗ Freezes perfectly. Very demand-ing, but rewarding.

Butternut squash is a sweet, buttery vegetable that looks like an extraterrestrial peanut from a Roald Dahl novel. Its amber interior contains roaring amounts of beta-carotene (the stuff that morphs into vitamin A). One cup of butternut will ring in at a whopping 22,000 IUs, trumping even the most sophisticated multivitamin pills.

Why does this excite me? Because scientists agree that our immune system requires beta-carotene to kick ass, especially when the sniffles are doing their office rounds. Others swear it helps to protect the skin during summer months. Either way, I happily defer to the great Italians on this one. Italian cuisine can be a nightmare for gluten-free goslings, but it doesn't have to be. Check out this gluten-free gnocchi recipe. And if it all seems like too much trouble, date an Italian instead. Just as tasty.

Fire up your oven to 180°C.

Carefully cut the head of garlic in half horizontally and place each half on top of a square of tinfoil. Drizzle over the tablespoon of olive oil, wrap up the foil like a tent and pop onto a baking tray. Cook on the middle shelf of the oven for 30 minutes, until all the cloves of garlic are deliciously squishy and creamy in colour.

You can cook the butternut in the oven at the same time. Peel the big beast and chop its amber flesh into bite-sized chunks. Discard or compost the seeds and stringy core. Tumble onto a roasting tray with a dot of butter or ghee and cook in the oven alongside your garlic. You'll need to cover the tray with foil to prevent the squash from browning. Your butternut pieces should be soft, sweet and velvety after 30–40 minutes. Perfect.

Remove both trays from the oven, open the foil lids and allow both to cool. Drain the juices from the butternut into a bowl and refrigerate for a later date (this juice is great to use in soup, stews, gravy or curries during the week or freeze it for stock). You want the butternut to dry out as much as possible before mashing.

Measure out about 200g of your mashed butternut (if it's particularly wet, let it sit in a sieve for 20 minutes to drain further). Set the rest aside in the refrigerator for another day or another meal.

Squeeze the roasted garlic cloves into the mashed butternut. Add the flour and beat into a dough. Turn out onto a lightly floured surface. Divide into four dough balls and coat with flour to make it easier for your mitts. Roll each dough ball into a snake. Cut the snake into 2.5cm gnocchi pieces, parachuting over a little more flour if necessary to keep the dough from sticking to your hands and work surface. You can use the tines of a fork to make a gentle imprint on the top of each gnocchi piece. Let them air dry on the work surface if time permits (or even overnight), but no worries if not.

In a large frying pan, heat a good glug of olive oil or ghee and fry the tarragon leaves for 60 seconds, until crisp. Drain and set aside. (If you're subbing with fresh basil, it's best to serve this herb fresh, not fried.) Using the same olive oil in the pan, fry the gnocchi for 6 minutes, until piping hot and cooked through. Sprinkle in a flurry of sea salt and freshly cracked black pepper.

Divide between your guests' plates and crown with crisp tarragon leaves. Freeze any unused gnocchi to pan-fry another evening.

Sounds like a lot of arsing around, but honestly, it's not – especially when this version of gnocchi tastes so incredibly good. I recommend choosing a comedy podcast to keep you jiggy in the kitchen. (*The Guilty Feminist* podcast gets my first vote, but be careful, it's not suitable for younger ears!)

Korean Gochugaru Beef with Ginger, Garlic and Chilli

SERVES 6–8 WITH RICE OR MASH . . . . .

3 beef cheeks, sinews removed
(add an extra beef cheek for an
additional 3 people) . . . .

For the marinade

3–6 garlic cloves, minced . . . .

4 tablespoons tamari or soya sauce . .

3 tablespoons sesame oil . . . .

Generous flurry of Korean red
pepper flakes (chilli flakes or
gochugaru) . . . .

The rest

3 white onions, chopped . . . .

1 tablespoon extra virgin coconut oil
or ghee (page 194) . . . .

3 thumb-sized pieces of fresh ginger,
peeled . . . .

A few twists of the pepper mill . . . . .

12 Portobello mushrooms, sliced . . .

1 litre stock or bone broth . . . .

1 lime, juiced . . . .

1 tablespoon honey or a good brown
sugar . . . .

Chopped spring onions, to serve . . . .

Sliced fresh chilli, to serve . . . .

⊕ Uses off-cuts

. . . .

⧖ Use several pots at once to
speed up the prep time. Freezes
well.

Hot chillies put the super into superfood (and the hell into healthy, if you're not careful). I see them as little endorphin bombs for my body and my brain.

Keep an eye out for a Korean dried chilli combo called gochugaru. It's dastardly good. A compound found in this devious little vegetable has been shown to stimulate the release of feel-good endorphins, like a jamboree through the veins. These same endorphins help to put out internal 'fires' by blocking inflammation in the body, numbing us of our day's aches and pains (and tedious colleagues).

Historically, chillies were not merely used as an aphrodisiac – they also played a role in alleviating chronic pain and servicing circulatory problems. That's right, gentlemen. Most notably, chilli pepper fortified the chocolate drink that Montezuma the Great consumed to make his pulse dance in preparation for visits to his concubines. No need for little blue pills back then.

But back to the kitchen! Beef cheeks are meltingly tender, inexpensive off-cuts. Serve with mashed sweet potatoes or sticky brown rice and a side of kimchi (page 229) or chilli sriracha sauce (page 184) to get your pulse beating like a voodoo drum.

I get my lovely butcher to help me with the beef cheek sinew. He slices these gritty bits off for me, then divides each cheek into 10 good pieces.

When I'm home, I whisk all the marinade ingredients together and leave the cheek pieces to drink up the flavours for 1 hour (but it's fine to leave them up to one day or overnight to revel in the soya sauce).

Using a heavy-based sauté pan or casserole, sweat down the onions in your chosen fat until soft and glassy (8–10 minutes will do the trick). You'll need a gentle heat for this. While your onions are dancing, chop the peeled ginger lengthways into matchstick-sized pieces. Add to the pot of onions, then season with a few twists of the black pepper mill.

Remove the cooked onions and ginger and set aside. Using the same pan, turn up the heat and brown the beef cheeks all over. Keep the marinade, as we'll be tipping this into the pot later.

Set the browned meat aside with the onion mix. Using the same pan (less washing-up, you understand), lower the heat to medium and sauté the mushrooms for 8 minutes. This will need to be done in several batches, so get yourself a good podcast or nerd up on those physio exercises you've expertly avoided until now.

Once the mushrooms are coloured, let the meat and onions come back to the party. Pour in your stock, lime juice and honey or brown sugar and slow cook over your lowest flame for 6–8 hours. I prefer to throw a lid on and put it in the oven overnight at 120°C. In the morning, it's meltingly delicious.

Cool first before storing in the fridge for up to six days. Transfer any leftovers designated for the freezer into glass jars, and label with masking tape and a Sharpie. Don't forget to leave an inch of space at the top of the jar to give the food room to expand when frozen.

We love this with black rice, scattered with chopped spring onions and freshly sliced chilli, then as leftovers a few days later with mashed sweet potatoes and horseradish yogurt (page 217).

Sourdough Meatballs

MAKES 45 MEATBALLS . . . .

900g–1kg minced lamb or beef . . . . . .

2 onions, finely chopped . . . .

6 garlic cloves, grated . . . .

1 egg, beaten . . . .

200g crustless sourdough crumbs
(pulse stale bread in a food
processor) . . . .

100g milled pumpkin and sunflower
seed mix . . . .

2 tablespoons capers (adults only),
chopped . . . .

4 teaspoons dried oregano . . . .

2 teaspoons ground cumin . . . .

1 teaspoon flaky sea salt . . . .

  Uses less meat
. . . .

☒ Freezes well in little bags

Sometimes weird can be good. Opening a jar of pickles on a bus when you're famished. Cycling and laughing in the lashing rain. Knitting your dog a hoodie. Such experiences are better for being weird – that's half the enjoyment. And so, too, with this meatball recipe. To reduce our red meat consumption, I add milled seeds, normally a feature in my dessert recipes. When the seeds samba with meat and breadcrumbs, something beautiful happens. Try it and see.

One serving of these meatballs will gift your bod with 100% of your recommended daily intake of vitamin E. Swit swoo. I like to think of vitamin E as the Patron Saint of Sexy Skin. Vitamin E patrols the bloodstream, neutralising free radicals. What a clever beast. Vitamin E also teams up with another potent player inside the sunflower seed, called selenium. They cast their magic by working synergistically. Groovy, eh?

So let's get weird with meatballs.

One meatball, 8 ways:
· As a soup topper with any of the soups you have stored in your freezer.
· You can make cucumber ribbons by using a potato peeler and shaving strips off the length of cucumber. Gorgeous with fresh mint leaves, these meatballs and a dollop of flavoured yogurt (page 217).
· With a plate of super smooth hummus (page 43) and salsa.
· With your favourite pasta or courgetti and a Bolognese tomato sauce.
· As kebabs in kids' lunchboxes.
· One of our favourite ways to serve them is with plain tomato passata and loads of freshly grated Parmesan.
· Mould half the batch into oblong little koftas by adding 4 tablespoons of pine nuts, ½ teaspoon ground cinnamon and some freshly grated nutmeg. Roll into little torpedoes of flavour. Serve with a tahini yogurt (page 225).
· Roll into your favourite wrap with kimchi (page 229) and salad leaves.

Wash your hands thoroughly with hot soapy water, making sure every last scrap of soap has disappeared from your digits. Now mix the meat by hand with all the remaining ingredients, squishing it all together with a good Spotify list. If I don't have stale sourdough to hand (or stored in my trusty freezer), I'll just leave a few fresh slices out overnight. It will quickly turn stale. Fresh bread turns to putty inside the food processor, whereas stale bread holds more structure and crumb.

Using damp hands, roll the mince into apricot-sized balls. Set on a suite of lined baking trays and chill in the fridge until firm, or freeze half the batch. Make sure they are not touching one another inside your trusty freezer. You can bag these raw frozen meatballs into labelled containers in quantities that suit you.

To cook (or when defrosted), heat a large pan over a high heat with 3 tablespoons of your preferred form of fat (I use ghee). Fry all over for 5 minutes, until coloured and cooked through.

Serve in a Bolognese sauce or skewer a few with wooden sticks for a quick kebab. We love them with smooth hummus and alarming amounts of stinky kimchi.

Cucumber, yogurt and mint

Hummus plate

Soup topper

Kebabs

Wrap filling

Smoked Tofu, Olive and Caper Sauce for Pasta

MAKES 8 SERVINGS . . . .

2 medium onions, halved and thinly sliced . . . .

3–4 tablespoons olive oil . . . .

5 garlic cloves, sliced . . . .

2 medium-sized fresh chillies, deseeded and chopped . . . .

Small bunch of fresh flat-leaf parsley, leaves chopped . . . .

2 teaspoons dried oregano . . . .

1 x 690g jar of tomato passata . . . . . .

1 tablespoon maple or date syrup . . .

Large handful of stone-in black olives, such as Throumpa . . . .

400g smoked tofu, cubed . . . .

½ tablespoon capers per person, to serve . . . .

Your favourite pasta, to serve . . . . . .

Crème fraîche or freshly grated Pecorino cheese, to serve . . . .

⊕ Reasonable
. . . .

⧗ Lives in the freezer until beckoned

I don't expect to eat something thrilling every evening. So long as I feel I have nourished my growing family and demanding bod, I'm good. This dish has five vegetables smuggled inside – seven if you count the oregano and chilli. And because my eldest has sworn off meat, he gets to torment his dad with tofu. (In return, his dad haunts him with blue cheese.)

Fresh tomatoes would be nicer, of course, but I don't live on an organic farm in Southern Greece, so the toms here are a little despondent. Tomato passata will do just fine, especially when paired with salty capers.

Soften and colour the onions by sweating them in your largest pan with half of the olive oil over a medium heat for 8 minutes. The onions work really well when halved and thinly sliced as opposed to diced – the long, lanky strands of caramelised sweetness wrap around your pasta and fork. Add the garlic halfway through cooking the onions and stir to prevent them burning.

Sprinkle in your chillies, chopped fresh parsley leaves (keep the parsley stalks for your freezer stock bag – see page 101) and dried oregano. Add the passata and maple or date syrup. Simmer for 20 minutes, until thickened.

While the sauce gets saucy, work on destoning your olives. I think olives are much tastier when purchased with the stones intact, as the stones impart a wonderful flavour. Throumpa are my favourite variety. They are usually placed in sea salt for six months after harvesting, which draws out the bitterness and allows the olives to develop in flavour. There is no need for preservatives or additives when they are harvested this way. Drop the olives into the sauce once they're destoned.

In a frying pan, heat the remaining olive oil (or the oil from your jar of capers) and colour the cubed tofu all over. Add to the pot of sauce. Now fry the capers in the same pan over a high heat for 1 minute, until crisp. Set aside on kitchen paper to drain.

Cook your favourite pasta. Stir through enough sauce, tickle with crisp capers and serve with thick clouds of crème fraîche or a smattering of freshly grated Pecorino cheese. You can freeze the remaining sauce for another night in screw-top glass jars. I use masking tape and a Sharpie marker to label my freezer stash.

Kids' Bolognese

MAKES 12–16 KIDS' PORTIONS . . . .

250g button or shiitake mushrooms .

2 medium white onions . . . .

1 large carrot . . . .

A good glug of olive oil . . . .

400g organic lamb mince . . . .

4 garlic cloves, minced . . . .

1 x 690g jar of tomato passata . . . . . .

1 x 400g tin of chopped tomatoes . . .

1 x 400g tin of lentils, drained and
rinsed . . . .

1 small tin of anchovies, drained and
chopped . . . .

2 teaspoons dried oregano . . . .

Squirt of tomato ketchup . . . .

(+) On a budget

. . . .

Freeze in portions

Here is a recipe for children's Bolognese that freezes perfectly in empty jam jars and doubles up as a seraphic kitchen sylph. I'm batch cooking for sanity, which leaves other evenings free to sugar scrub my pins or chat to the petunias. Batch cooking has opened up a whole new world for me – a world without kitchen cuffs, wailing children, superfood sonatas or pans to scrub.

This recipe is my son Marty's favourite. Serve it on top of baked sweet potatoes, inside a lasagne, over wholewheat spaghetti or roll into buckwheat pancakes with lashings of avocado.

You'll be cooking the veg in separate batches unless you have a few heavy-based saucepans, in which case you can juggle between all three pots at once! I crank up a good Spotify list.

With your food processor, pulse the mushrooms into tiny pieces. Do the same with the onions, then the carrot, keeping them all separate. If you don't have a food processor, practise your ninja chopping skills instead. Remember, you're hiding the veg so your kids won't spot them!

Sweat the mushrooms in a large heavy-based saucepan with a good lick of olive oil for 8 minutes. A medium heat is perfect. You'll need to scrape the bottom of the pan with a wooden spoon from time to time to prevent burned bums.

Once the mushrooms are cooked through, scrape them onto a large plate. Repeat with the white onions, then with the carrot.

Finally, whack up the heat and brown the mince.

As soon as there are no pink bits left in the mince, add the minced garlic, passata, tinned toms, lentils, anchovies, oregano and ketchup. Let this all putt-putter for 2 hours on your lowest setting. After an hour, put a lid on if it's getting too thick.

Leave to cool before dividing into sterilised glass jars and labelling for the freezer. I use masking tape and a Sharpie marker, which withstand the freezer moisture.

Veg Trimmings Stock

MAKES 2 LITRES

2 litres filtered water

Freezer bag of kitchen trimmings

4 carrots, quartered

2 onions, quartered

Lump of ginger, halved

1 tablespoon apple cider vinegar

1 teaspoon flaky sea salt

 Repurposing scraps

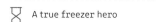 A true freezer hero

Homemade veggie broth makes everything taste better – rice, curries, stews, quinoa, soups. It's the gateway to good eating, turning everything into a richer version of itself. Without a good broth, soup tastes dispirited and lentils are lonely.

In theory, it shouldn't cost you anything if you giddily collect the kitchen scraps destined for your compost bin. Easy AF. I have a special freezer bag that I fill up with all sorts of scraps and trimmings: wilted herbs, carrot peels, turnip tops, shrivelled ginger, celery leaves, fennel butts, apple skins and even Parmesan rinds, which is a stealthy trick I learned from my local cheesemonger. Add whatever you have! (Go easy on the cabbage, kale and cauli, however.) Below is a simple guideline, but honestly, no two broths will ever taste the same.

Somewhere near you is a farm that composts as much veg as they sell. Trust me, I've seen it. Even hotels with working gardens have tons of veg for the compost heap. See if you can help them offload some of their surplus by surprising them with a tray of brownies one morning. A lifetime of vegetable broth and friendship may ensue.

Bring all the ingredients to a spitting boil for 5 minutes. Reduce the temperature to a low-grade gurgle and cook for anywhere between 1 and 4 hours. Once it tastes rich and satisfying, drain the solids and allow the stock to cool down before storing in the fridge or freezer.

Bone Broth

MAKES 3 LITRES . . . .

1 organic or higher-welfare chicken carcass or 1.5kg beef bones (free from the butcher) . . . .

3 onions, peeled and sliced in half . .

1 whole head of garlic, sliced in half . . . .

Any ends of vegetables in your bag of freezer trimmings (page 101), such as leeks, carrots, celery . . . .

Chunk of ginger, roughly chopped . .

A few bay leaves . . . .

Any fresh herbs loitering in your fridge or garden . . . .

Splash of apple cider vinegar . . . . . .

½ teaspoon flaky sea salt . . . .

⊕ Repurposing scraps and butcher carcasses

. . . .

⧖ Freezes well. Very little prep.

We use bone broth as a base for rice, stews and soups. It's a yumdinger all on its own with some Tabasco, woolly socks and your favourite mug. The glucosamine and chondroitin in bone broth is thought to stimulate the growth of new collagen in our body, reduce inflammation and repair damaged joints. And they say diamonds are a girl's best friend? Pah! Give me more collagen and better dance moves any day.

Pop everything into your largest stainless steel stockpot. Cover with fresh filtered water. Bring to a very shy simmer and cook for 8–16 hours – the longer, the better. I usually transfer my stockpot into the oven on a really low setting. Do *not* let the stock boil. Prolonged boiling can destroy the beneficial properties of the bones' natural collagen.

Strain the stock with a large kitchen sieve. Taste and see if it needs a bit of soya sauce, chipotle smoked chilli or Tabasco for oomph (these are my go-tos for quick fixes). Once you are happy with its taste, leave to cool before storing in the fridge or freezer.

Chestnut Soup

MAKES 1 LITRE . . . .

3 white onions . . . .

2 tablespoons olive oil . . . .

3 fat garlic cloves, crushed . . . .

250g cooked chestnuts (from a
vacuum pack) . . . .

1 litre bone broth (page 160) or
veggie stock . . . .

Reasonable

. . . .

A freezer buddy, ready to
service those chilly evenings

This is the perfect soup for a blusterous night by the fire. We ladle it into mugs and serve it with hunks of hot sourdough. The reverie is palpable, like a toddler with a Twix.

Really great soup relies on homemade stock. It's insanely easy and not even time-consuming because you leave it alone to bubble on the stove for hours. As soon as you spot veggies on special offer (celery, onions, peppers, ginger, carrots), load up your shopping basket and prep some stock at home. I even find bunches of parsley for 10c on their sell-by date and either parachute it into my stockpot or freeze it for next week's batch (see page 101 for more deets).

Mushrooms make a meaty, umami-rich stock if you're staying vegan. Otherwise, parachute some chicken bones or Parmesan rinds into your stockpot and cook for longer (say, 6–18 hours). You can even use the bones from Sunday's roast leg of lamb. The nourishing combo of collagen, amino acids, electrolytes and minerals from bone broth makes it a supercharged elixir for sports injuries and squeaky dance moves.

Peel and roughly chop your onions. Compost the skin.

In your largest pot, warm some olive oil over a gentle flame and tumble in the chopped onions. Sweat for 10 minutes, until the onions are translucent and sweet.

At this point, add the garlic and cook for a further 3 minutes.

Let the chestnuts and stock join the party. Fire up to a simmer and allow to putt-putter for 25 minutes.

Blitz in a blender until lusciously smooth, being careful not to scald yourself. I usually wait for the soup to cool down before using my blender.

Serve with toasted sourdough croutons (page 138) and some kickass olive oil. Leftovers can be stored in the fridge for three days or frozen in individual jars for three months. Fried mushrooms and crème fraîche are also very good friends with chestnuts.

Parsnip and Cider Soup

MAKES 1 LITRE . . . .

2 tablespoons ghee (page 194),
coconut or olive oil . . . .

2 onions or the white part of 2 leeks,
diced . . . .

500–600g parsnips, chopped . . . .

2 garlic cloves, chopped . . . .

1 bottle (300ml max.) of cider . . . . . .

1 sprig of fresh rosemary or thyme .

750ml bone broth (page 160),
vegetable stock or seasoned water . .

⊕ On a budget
. . . .

⧖ Store in the fridge until
required or freeze in clean
jam jars for a later date

We've been obsessed with this soup lately. I'm pretty sure my body mass is 40% parsnips right now.

One soup, 10 ways:

1. With kefir cream (page 235) and fresh parsley.
2. Top with some crushed vegetable crisps and crème fraîche.
3. Add watercress to your soup and blend.
4. Fried squares of halloumi and maple-coated walnuts (page 212).
5. Try caramelising slices of banana in ghee (page 194) or butter and top with a curry cream made from combing a little natural yogurt with some mild curry powder and a splash of olive oil.
6. Top with horseradish yogurt (page 217).
7. Top with chickpea croutons (page 215) and garlic yogurt (page 219).
8. Top with harissa butter (page 198) and sourdough crumbs (page 213).
9. Top with buckwheat pops (page 207).
10. Top with pistachio and kale pesto (page 192).

Heat your preferred fat in a heavy-based saucepan. Add the onions or leeks and sweat for 10 minutes.

Add your parsnips and garlic to the pan for another 10 minutes of sweating.

Tip in the cider and deglaze the sticky bits at the bottom of the pan. Let the alcohol burn off (sounds counter-intuitive if you're Irish, but alcohol tastes too boozy in soup). Pop in the rosemary or thyme. Cook for 10 minutes, then cover with broth or seasoned water and boil until the parsnips are soft.

Remove the sprig of herbs and discard. Purée the soup until smooth. Gorgeous as is, with a simple twist of the black pepper mill.

Shiitake Dashi

MAKES OVER 1 LITRE . . . .

4 dried or fresh shiitake
mushrooms . . . .

1 strip of dried Irish kombu . . . .

1.25 litres filtered water . . . .

Feeling flush

. . . .

Soaking required. A true
freezer babe.

For hundreds of years, Chinese medicine has had a serious crush on the shiitake mushroom. Shiitake compounds called lentinans and beta-glucan polysaccharides are believed to stimulate the immune system by activating certain macrophages and killer T-cells that usually declare war on foreign invaders. Nifty, eh? I like to think of shiitake as my immune system PT.

In lab studies, shiitake extract has slowed the growth of tumours in certain cell cultures. But not in all cell cultures, highlighting the complexity surrounding the use of shiitake extract. Scientists are still unsure as to why this is – some conjectures include the ability of beta-glucans to trick the immune system into thinking it's under attack. Perhaps the body reacts by releasing its finest ninja stars into the bloodstream or sending armed drones to survey the entire area. Who knows? More clinical trials are underway to understand which compounds in shiitake may be effective for which immunological disorders. But given that shiitake are so damned delicious, I'm happy to horse into them while scientists work it out. Maybe it's time to start offering laureates to vegetables?

This dashi is terrific in vegetarian stews where the depth of bone broth or chicken stock is noticeably missing. You can find packets of dried kombu or dried shiitake in delis and health food stores across the country. Both will last for years in the cupboard.

Soak the shiitakes and kombu in your filtered water first thing in the morning. After a good soak – anywhere from 4 to 12 hours – remove the shiitake mushrooms. Discard the stems. Slice the meaty caps and return to the soaking water.

Pour into a large pot and bring to a gentle simmer with the kombu. Cook for 8–10 minutes. Strain and keep the chopped shiitake and kombu for a later date in your freezer stock bag (page 101).

What you're left with is a delicate, umami-infused broth. Store in the fridge for up to seven days and use as a gorgeous broth with chopped spring onions and tofu or add to rice when cooking.

Simple Pumpkin Soup with Maple-Coated Walnuts

MAKES APPROX. 2 LITRES . . . .

2 white onions . . . .

1 small organic pumpkin, like
Hokkaido or red kuri squash . . . .

3–4 tablespoons olive oil . . . .

1 teaspoon flaky sea salt . . . .

1–1.5 litres water or vegetable stock .

Fresh nutmeg, to grate (optional) . . .

Maple-coated walnuts (page 212), to
serve . . . .

⊕ On a budget

. . . .

⧗ Freezes well

This is not just a bowl of soup. This is a stab at eternity, my friend, with swags of beta-carotene, vitamin C and antioxidants to keep your skin peachy and your immune system jiggy. Oxidation is the damage done by free radicals. Down with free radicals! Picture it as a type of a rusting. Oxidative stress is a major part of ageing and just about every degenerative disease you can imagine. Even DNA corruption. Pah! Antioxidants can help to fight the damage done by these renegade free radicals.

We can pump up on artillery and quash those marauding geezers with good homemade soup like this pumpkin one. It's practically crooning with antioxidants. Serve with maple-coated walnuts for extra giddiness.

One soup, 6 ways:

1. You can grate ginger straight from frozen, which results in a finer ginger zest than the stringy fresh alternative. A bit of orange zest is magical too.
2. Add leftover lentils (I freeze these in ice cube moulds, ready to pop into mashed potato for my boys or soup for me). Any of the freezer dressings from page 183 onwards are also ace.
3. Crown with fresh or pickled red onions (page 234) and finely diced apple.
4. Use coconut milk instead of water or stock.
5. Swirl on chimichurri (page 183) and cheat's kefir (page 235).
6. Sprinkle over crumbled feta, pumpkin seeds and slices of fresh chilli.

Fire up the oven to 220°C.

Prep your veggies by peeling the onions (compost their skins) and slicing into wedges. Tumble these wedges between two or three large roasting trays.

Cut your pumpkin open with a very sharp knife and careful concentration. Compost the seeds and remove the outer skin if it's a touch too tough. Chop the amber flesh into 4cm cubes and scatter among the onion wedges. Give everything a good lick of olive oil and sea salt. Shake the tray until the veg are well coated with the oil and roast in the oven for about 25 minutes, until the onions and pumpkin are soft and caramelised around the edges. You might need to use two roasting trays to prevent overcrowding and steaming the veg.

Remove from the oven and transfer to a free-standing blender with your water or stock. You'll need to do this in three or four brief batches. Pulse until smooth and creamy. You can make it thick or thin – whatever your taste buddies decide. I find 1 litre of stock plenty.

Heat the soup again before serving or store in clean glass jars for up to three days in the fridge and 12 weeks in the freezer. We serve this with great dollops of crème fraîche, a scrape of nutmeg across the grater and some crunch from the maple-coated walnuts.

Caramelised Carrot Soup

MAKES 1.5 LITRES . . . .

2 medium white onions, peeled and quartered . . . .

700g carrots, chopped . . . .

4 tablespoons olive or coconut oil . . .

Good shake of flaky sea salt . . . .

2 pinches of whole cumin seeds (optional) . . . .

1–1.5 litres water . . . .

⊕   Budget days

. . . .

⧗   Freezes well. Works in Thermos flasks for kids' lunches.

Yes, once again this soup is vegan, but for no major reason other than it tastes really good. (Calm down. I still wear leather pants and drink honey straight from the jar.) Just double the recipe if you want to feed more mouths, or satisfy your freezer.

One soup, 12 ways:

1. Top with avocado sour cream (page 226). Fry a handful of fresh sage leaves in oil for 2 minutes over a high heat until fragrant and crisp and scatter on top.
2. The recipe for pistachio dust on page 213 will serve you well.
3. Harissa butter (page 198). Drop into a bowl of hot carrot soup, straight from the freezer.
4. Toasted pumpkin seeds and crème fraîche. Dry-fry the seeds in a frying pan over your highest heat setting, until swollen and crisp.
5. Burnt raisins and caraway seed – see the method for burnt raisins on page 113 and simply add a pinch of whole caraway seeds while frying the raisins.
6. Top with garlic yogurt (page 219).
7. Sriracha chilli sauce (page 184).
8. Add black sesame salt and fried cubes of halloumi.
9. Grate over ginger from the freezer. Organic orange zest is also ace.
10. This soup can be often used as a pasta sauce with fusilli for kids.
11. Try some refried beans, like black beans in coconut oil, and chilli flakes with kefir cream (page 235).
12. Swirl through vegan cream, like the hemp garlic cream on page 224 or coconut yogurt on page 218, and sprinkle over lightly roasted slivers of almonds.

Fire up your oven to 190°C. Find your two largest roasting trays. You can even use three trays, if necessary.

Tumble the onion wedges and chopped carrots into one tray, gloss with plenty of olive or coconut oil and sea salt, then divide between one or two additional roasting trays. You want your veg to have plenty of space between each other and room to caramelise. If the veg are packed beside one another, they will sweat and stew instead of caramelise. Shake over the cumin seeds (if using).

Roast in the oven for 30 minutes, until soft, sweet and sticky around the edges. Take the trays out of the oven to briefly cool. A few onion pieces will be burned – ditch these.

Pulse in a free-standing blender with your water until smooth. I do this in two batches.

Store in the fridge until required or freeze in clean jam jars for a later date. I label the soup using masking tape and a black marker – both survive extreme freezer conditions!

Celeriac and Butter Bean Soup

MAKES 1 LITRE . . . .

2 tablespoons butter, olive oil or
ghee (page 194) . . . .

2 leeks, white part only . . . .

3 garlic cloves, roughly sliced . . . . . .

1 large celeriac, peeled and
trimmed . . . .

1 x 400g tin of butter beans, rinsed
and drained . . . .

800ml chicken or vegetable stock . . .

(+) Reasonable

. . . .

⧖ Freezes well

Not so pretty, these celeriac things. They look like a cross between
the butt of a matted yak and a swede with dermatitis. But damn, are
they delicious.

Like Stephen Fry, you'll find treasure beneath that exterior. There
is a smooth, understated elegance to a celeriac. And a faint nutty
aroma.

One soup, 8 ways:

1. Crisp chorizo.
2. Crumbled feta and pumpkin seeds.
3. Cured egg yolk, grated (page 208)
4. Brown bread croutons.
5. Black olive crumb (page 210) and sour cream.
6. Chickpea croutons (page 215).
7. Romesco sauce (page 187) from your swag of freezer bags.
8. Salsa verde (page 186), straight from frozen.

In a large heavy-based casserole or sauté pan, gently heat your
preferred fat over a low heat. Wash and slice the white part of
the leek and sauté in the pan with the warm fat for 8 minutes,
until softened (but not coloured). Now add your garlic and
cook for 3–5 minutes, stirring regularly to prevent it sticking or
burning. Garlic tastes soapy and bitter if it burns.

In the meantime, while your pan is busy, chop the celeriac
flesh into rough 3cm cubes.

When the leek and garlic are ready, add the celeriac, butter
beans and stock, whacking up the heat to a playful simmer. Cook
for 30 minutes, until the celeriac has softened into the stock.

Blitz in batches with a hand-held soup gun or in a free-standing
blender. I like mine silky smooth and thick, but add more
seasoned water if you prefer a thinner soup. Store in the fridge for
three days or in individual portions in the freezer for up to three
months.

Five-Spice Apple and Ginger Lentil Soup

MAKES 1 LITRE . . . .

2 white onions . . . .

2 tablespoons extra virgin coconut
oil or ghee (page 194) . . . .

1 tablespoon Chinese five-spice
powder . . . .

1 large apple, peeled and cored . . . . .

Thumb-sized piece of fresh ginger,
peeled . . . .

225g dried red lentils, rinsed . . . . . .

900ml good stock or seasoned
water . . . .

1 tablespoon tomato purée . . . .

2 garlic cloves . . . .

½ large tub of natural yogurt . . . .

⊕ On a budget
. . . .

⧗ Store in the fridge until required or freeze in clean jam
jars for a later date

Five-spice powder is a magnificent blend of star anise, cloves, cinnamon, fennel seeds and black pepper that helps to ramp up this soup's flavour and nutritional purchase.

Serve with woolly socks, an open fire and good company.

Start by sweating the onions to bring out their natural sweetness. To do this, peel and dice the onions. Tumble into a warm pan with the oil or ghee on a low heat. As the onions gently cook, they will turn translucent and sweet. After 5 or 6 minutes, add the five-spice. Dice the apple and ginger and let them join the party. As soon as the onions look glassy, tip in the lentils, stock and tomato purée. Whack up the heat to get it pumping, then turn it down to a gentle putter for 15 minutes.

Meanwhile, get going on the garlic yogurt. Mince the cloves using the finest part of your grater (the one usually reserved for lemon zest). Add the minced garlic to the yogurt and grab any herbs you may have loitering in the fridge. Allow the flavours to infuse while you wait for your lentils to yell.

As soon as the lentils are done, whizz into a smooth soup using a hand-held blender. Pour into great big mugs and dot with garlic yogurt.

White Gazpacho and Iced Grapes

MAKES 8 PORTIONS . . . .

Handful of green grapes . . . .

650g cucumber, peeled . . . .

200g natural yogurt . . . .

6 spring onions . . . .

4 garlic cloves, peeled . . . .

Handful of stale sourdough bread . .

Handful of walnuts . . . .

Handful of fresh mint leaves . . . .

Handful of fresh dill sprigs . . . .

250ml strong chicken or veggie
stock . . . .

150ml olive oil . . . .

Squeeze of lemon . . . .

A few twists of the salt and pepper
mill . . . .

 Reasonable

. . . .

Lasts for four days in the fridge

Chances are you've been munching on a cucumber at some stage over the past 48 hours. After tomatoes, cucumbers are the bestselling vegetable in Europe. (I blame Hendricks.) As well as being 92% water, cucumbers even have a thirst-quenching fragrance. One sniff of a fridge-cold cucumber on a muggy day can feel as refreshing as skipping through a water sprinkler. So I've made it into a beautiful white gazpacho for hot summer days, using frozen grapes in place of ice. Diana Henry, one of my absolute favourite cooks, is responsible for the inspiration and kitchen sorcery.

Halve and deseed the grapes. If they happen to be seedless, leave them whole. Freeze for at least 2 hours.

Using a powerful blender, pulverise the rest of the ingredients into a smooth, creamy soup. Taste. Decide whether you need to season it with salt and pepper or maybe a splash more lemon or olive oil.

Chill in the fridge along with some shallow soup bowls. To serve, pour into your chilled bowls and top with frozen grapes.

One-Tray Roasted Red Pepper Soup

MAKES 1.25 LITRES.................

3 red peppers, deseeded and
chopped ....

2 red onions, chopped ....

4 whole garlic cloves, unpeeled .....

3 tablespoons extra virgin olive oil .

A few twists of the salt mill ....

500ml bone broth (page 160), veggie
stock or seasoned water ....

500ml tomato passata ....

(+) On a budget
....

⧖ Lasts all week in the fridge,
waiting to play dress-up, or
freezes well

This is a deliciously simple soup, one that kids also seem to like. No faffing around on the hob – just chop, roast and purée. The only difficulty is deciding which way to serve it.

Peppers are another superfood the Gooperatti are genuflecting to. Why so? I'm guessing it's their vital amounts of antioxidants and vitamin C. Antioxidants seem pretty pivotal in the battle against skin damage. That's because oxidants can damage cells and promote inflammation.

Dermatologists (aka swanky skin specialists) stress the importance of providing our skin with the necessary nutrients it needs from our diet to prevent oxidative stress in the first place. Trying to repair the damage once it's done is so much harder. This soup should help.

One soup, 8 ways:

1. Grated Parmesan and chickpea croutons (page 215).
2. For a Mexican vibe, serve with crisp tortillas on top, chopped avocado and lime juice.
3. Sautéed salami and fresh parsley.
4. Black olive crumb (page 210) and basil yogurt (finely chop some fresh basil leaves and stir through natural dairy yogurt or almond yogurt).
5. Cheat's kefir cream (page 235) and BBQ salt (page 201).
6. Furikake seasoning (page 202) and a poached egg dropped into a deep bowl of the steaming soup.
7. A gorgeous blob of burrata and a teaspoon of good pesto, like the pistachio and kale one on page 192.
8. Serve any remaining soup as a pasta sauce with buckwheat fusilli and vegan Parmesan (page 201). →

Preheat the oven to 200°C.

Arrange the chunks of peppers, onions and the whole garlic cloves on one large tray or two medium-sized trays. It helps if the onions and peppers are approximately uniform in size so that they all cook at the same time. Drizzle generously with olive oil and sea salt, then bake in the oven for 25 minutes.

Allow the tray of veggies to cool before squeezing the roasted garlic from their papery pods. Blitz all your roasted veg and garlic in a blender with your bone broth, stock or water and the passata. It's important to blitz to a lusciously smooth texture to pulverise the pepper skins.

Freeze in individual portions or keep in the fridge for up to five days.

Chilled Beetroot and Yogurt Soup

MAKES 5–6 SERVINGS . . . .

150g cooked beet (vacuum packed are perfect, free from vinegar) . . . .

1 garlic clove, peeled . . . .

Small pot of natural yogurt . . . .

700ml dashi (page 165), vegetable stock, seasoned water or cold-pressed carrot juice . . . .

⊕ On a budget

. . . .

⧗ Lasts all week in the fridge, waiting to be pimped up

Beetroot is surely the favourite veg at Hogwarts. It makes your tongue turn purple and your pee turn pink. Plus, beetroot is deliciously sweet and earthy, like a snuggle with a pug (a puggle?). Magic.

Beetroot has long filled the cells of mankind with burly antioxidants and enough iron to make Popeye quake. But the real magic lies in its plant pigment. That glorious crimson colour holds a clever compound called betacyanin. This marvellous show-off is commissioned by our inner intelligence to do all sorts of fancy ripostes in our bloodstream. Let's hear it for betacyanin!

One soup, 6 ways:

1. Dry-fry ½ teaspoon of caraway for 2 minutes on a hot pan and parachute on top with a dot of crème fraîche.
2. Crunchy buckwheat pops (page 207) and horseradish yogurt (page 217). Add a pinch of ground turmeric to turn the yogurt bright yellow.
3. Try some smoked mackerel flaked on top and freshly chopped dill.
4. A chilled, grated boiled egg goes wonderfully well.
5. Fry up some stale sourdough crumbs, stored in a freezer bag for just such occasions.
6. Chimichurri (page 183) with extra chilli.

Belt all the ingredients into a blender or use a soup gun if you have one. Chill in the fridge until hunger hollers.

Part Three Other Really Fast Things You Need to Know About

These recipes are so much more than flavoured yogurts, dressings and sides. They are ammo.

We are taking unrefined ingredients and celebrating them for their fresh flavour and sass, in contrast to society's reliance on conveyor belts and chemicals. And we are doing it with speed and style. Ultimately, you will be spending less money and time in the kitchen throughout the week, all while supporting your health and wellness goals.

There are freezer dressings like salsa verde to last you months in the freezer, ready to dance with a simple piece of fish, bowl of soup or avocado toast. Just when you think you have nothing in the house to eat, a freezer dressing or flavour grenade will reignite your appetite and give a plain poached egg or a shy salad a makeover. These recipes are designed to help you spend more time with your family and less time stressing about what to put on the table.

The section on flavoured yogurt is simple and helps remove the stress of keeping mealtimes exciting. You can knock up a simple yogurt dressing in less than 3 minutes and improve any meal three-fold. Our favourite is the horseradish yogurt, which we let fox trot with tortillas, boiled potatoes, soup, slow-cooked meats, smoked mackerel, boiled eggs and bad moods. This yogurt is magical – enough to impress Hermione Granger.

Want to do your body and your wallet a favour? Get going on some simple gut grooves. The fermentation section will introduce you to a whole new level of health and wellness. Your bowel movements will be practically Instagrammable.

Freezer Dressings

I'm freezing all my dressings now in a nifty ice cube tray, making my kitchen a beatific mecca after 6 p.m. I just grab a flavoured cube from one of my labelled freezer bags and leave it to defrost within minutes. It's super fancy on top of plain soups, rice, fish, toast, waffles, roasted veg or despondent-looking salads. No mess. No washing up. Just yumdingers in an ice cube.

No freezer? No problem. Many of these dressings store beautifully for up to three weeks in a fridge. Sayonara, stress.

Chimichurri
for vegetables, eggs, fish and meat

MAKES ENOUGH FOR 1 JAR . . . .

1 red onion, finely diced . . . .

4 garlic cloves, crushed . . . .

1 fresh green chilli, deseeded and diced (optional) . . . .

2 bunches of fresh parsley, roughly chopped . . . .

125ml extra virgin olive oil . . . .

1 lemon, juiced . . . .

4 tablespoons sherry vinegar or red wine vinegar . . . .

2 teaspoons finely chopped fresh oregano or thyme . . . .

⊕ Budget babe

. . . .

⧖ Freeze in ice cube trays

In truth, a forgotten dishcloth would taste good in chimichurri. It just needs its own hashtag now, for celebrity benediction. Serve with fried eggs, falafel, meat, fish, hummus, roasted veg. Anything, actually.

I prefer stirring all the ingredients together. You can, of course, use a food processor to break it all up and marry the flavours, but the end result looks different – greener and thicker than if you were to stir the listed ingredients separately.

Mizzle over plain veg or excite an unsuspecting bowl of rice.

Sriracha Chilli Sauce

10 medium-sized fresh red chillies, topped . . . .

2 red peppers, deseeded and topped .

3 garlic cloves, sliced . . . .

1 generous lime, juiced . . . .

Thumb-sized piece of fresh ginger, peeled and sliced . . . .

1 tablespoon nam pla (fish sauce) . . . .

⊕ Reasonable

. . . .

⧗ Blend and freeze in ice cube trays

Sriracha has become quite the tickle in certain postcodes across Ireland. It's the cheapest legal high on the market right now, second to icy morning swims and slo-mos of Daniel Leavy.

A hot, fermented chilli sauce, sriracha ramps up sufficient voltage in my bloodstream to power a rural village. If you're lucky enough to try it, expect your heart to feel like a propeller taking off through your chest.

Here's the science. A devious compound found inside the chilli stimulates a carnival of feel-good endorphins. These clever compounds belong to the capsaicin family, also thought to be responsible for some impressive Mr Miyagi moves against inflammation in the body.

Then there's the delicious sting you get from a chilli, suspiciously like smoking a cigarette the wrong way around. That explosive heat ironically carries pain relief properties (the chilli, not the cigarette) while simultaneously igniting your toes and your tonsils. Watt's not to love?! (Boom boom.) You'll even find over-the-counter capsaicin cream for sprains and strains. Groovy, eh?

Traditional sriracha is carefully cooked, strained and lacto-fermented, but I can't be bothered with so many steps for a simple high, so I make this copycat version. The trick is to freeze fresh sriracha in a small ice cube tray as soon as it's made. Now you'll have it on tap whenever you fancy spicing up your life.

Place all your prepped ingredients in a high-speed blender and pulverise until smooth. I prefer to leave in the chilli seeds for extra flames. Pour into a silicone ice cube tray and freeze until, eh, frozen.

Pop them out of your tray and transfer them into a recycled freezer bag marked 'hot and spicy sriracha'. When you want to ignite a boring supper or guest, pop one of these into your dish from frozen. Or defrost thoroughly for 1 hour if serving chilled with avocado toast, for example. Namaste.

Sriracha Chilli Sauce (p.184)

Ghee (p.194)

Pistachio and Kale Pesto (p.192)

Mustard and Mulberry
Salad Dressing (p.196)

Anti-Inflammatory
Salad Dressing (p.191)

Salsa Verde (p.186)

Romesco Sauce (p.187)

Salsa Verde
for soup, lentils, fish, quinoa, eggs

MAKES ENOUGH FOR 1 X 150ML JAR . . .

1 big bunch of fresh flat-leaf
parsley . . . .

5 tinned anchovy fillets, drained . . . .

4 spring onions, chopped . . . .

½ lemon, zest and juice . . . .

Handful of fresh mint leaves . . . .

6 tablespoons extra virgin olive oil .

1 tablespoon capers . . . .

⊕ Reasonable
. . . .
⧗ Freeze in ice cube trays

I top my soup with a cube of frozen salsa verde, which defrosts within seconds. It will also disproportionately excite a bowl of lentils or quinoa. During summer months, we toss it through spiralised carrots and apples and bring it to barbecues. Your brilliance might piss everyone off, but that's a pleasure in itself.

Roughly pull off the leaves from the parsley stalks and drop them into a food processor. Transfer the tougher stems to your freezer stock bag (page 101). Add the remaining ingredients and pulse briefly until it looks like a chunky salsa. If you don't have a food processor, don't panic. Finely chop it all and tumble together with clean fingers.

Serve on crostini with ricotta or crown a bowl of plain quinoa with this salsa verde. Always great on toast with eggs and avocado.

Romesco Sauce
for chicken, meat, pasta, quinoa, eggs, anything!

MAKES 12 SERVINGS . . . .

3 red peppers . . . .

6 tablespoons extra virgin
olive oil . . . .

4 ripe plum tomatoes . . . .

A few twists of the salt and pepper
mill . . . .

1 head of garlic . . . .

50g ground almonds . . . .

30g stale sourdough crumbs (or more
ground almonds) . . . .

1 tablespoon sweet sherry vinegar . .

1 teaspoon smoked paprika . . . .

🙂 Pretty reasonable
. . . .
⌛ A true freezer hero.

We tumble this Romesco sauce through big bowls of courgetti (courgette spaghetti). Expect a cavalry of antioxidants to canter through your veins.

Feel free to parachute some pan-fried chorizo or creamy clouds of goat's cheese on top. The sauce stores beautifully in the freezer and also loves lazy weekend eggs or waffles.

Start by firing up the oven to 220°C.

Cut the peppers into chunks, discarding the seeds and the stems. Tumble onto your largest roasting tray with a lick of the olive oil and roast in the oven for 20 minutes.

Meanwhile, cut your tomatoes in half, season and put on another large tray. Cut the head of garlic in half horizontally and place cut side down on the tray of tomatoes. They will steam beautifully in their own paper pods in the same tray as the toms. Anoint with another splash of olive oil. Roast for 20 minutes, until the tomatoes are charred and the garlic is squishy. Turn off the oven and leave the trays inside for a further 10 minutes of gentle cooking (if the peppers are blackening around the sides, let some heat out of the oven).

In a food processor, whizz the ground almonds and slices of sourdough (if using) into fine breadcrumbs. Add the contents of both roasting trays, scraping out all the juices and transferring every garlic clove carefully with a sharp knife. You don't want the garlic paper. Add the vinegar, paprika and a few twists of the salt and pepper mill. Blitz until sumptuous, but not smooth. Stir through the remaining olive oil.

Serve alongside your Sunday roast, French toast, fried eggs or massive bowls of courgetti.

Black Garlic Cream (p.189)

Harissa Butter (p.198)

Black Garlic Cream
for roasted aubergines, rice, asparagus, fish and hummus

MAKES 10–12 SERVINGS . . . .

50g peeled black garlic cloves . . . . . .

1 small lemon, juice only . . . .

3 tablespoons extra virgin olive oil .

1 tablespoon almond butter . . . .

1 tablespoon cacao powder . . . .

1 tablespoon barley malt syrup
(optional) . . . .

 Feeling flush

. . . .

 Another freezer babe

Black garlic cloves are chewy, zany flavour bombs used in Korean cooking and health circles. I'm necking tubs of the stuff and feel like I'm going to live forever. And if I don't? I'll die trying.

Black garlic starts off as white garlic. Nothing is added except several weeks of heat to kick-start the alchemy. It is this gentle excitement that prompts the transformation of the cloves' natural sugars and amino acids into something so fundamentally different from the original raw clove. If vegetables did opera, this would be it.

In the smallest bowl of your food processor, blitz all the ingredients until smooth. That's it, my friend.

We often serve this tumbled into strips of roasted aubergine topped with pistachio and pomegranate. It's BAE (Beyond Anything Else, in Twitter speak) and comes with an assurance to transform despondent lentils or leftover quinoa. This dressing also responds well to kimcheese toasties (page 47) or delicately roasted cauliflower. Think of it as a superhero cape for bored and lazy vegetables. Spoon on top of toasted sourdough and let it socialise with avocado, toasted walnuts and Netflix.

Miso and Almond Dressing
for broccoli, and other cruciferous veggies

SERVES 2-4 . . . .

2 tablespoons white miso . . . .

2 tablespoons almond butter . . . .

2 tablespoons warm water . . . .

1 tablespoon extra virgin olive oil . .

⊕ Reasonable per portion

. . . .

⊠ Beat and serve

I know – sometimes it's really hard to get those Dark Green Leafy veg into your schedule. But you'll find loads of goodness balled up into their bouncing florets and slinky stalks. While broccoli can't promise to banish cellulite, it sure does like to tickle dull skin. Check these out for jazz hands: beauty vitamins A and C, blood-strengthening iron, riotous antioxidants and award-winning phytonutrients. (Okay, I made that last bit up. But there's lots of research on the cancer-fighting compounds found in cruciferous veg, y'all.) Think Navy SEALS in the bloodstream.

Let me introduce you to this miso and almond dressing. It will transform your relationship with DGLs (Dark Green Leafies).

Whisk the miso, your nut butter, a splash of warm water and the oil together to make a sumptuous creamy sauce. Mizzle across your favourite veg (or your not-so-favourite veg to pimp its appeal).

Anti-Inflammatory Salad Dressing

MAKES 1 X 250ML BOTTLE . . . .

1 thumb-sized piece of fresh ginger, peeled if necessary . . . .

1 finger-sized piece of fresh turmeric, peeled if necessary . . . . . .

1 fresh chilli, stalk removed . . . .

1 garlic clove, peeled . . . .

1 small orange, juiced . . . .

1 small lemon, juiced . . . .

125ml extra virgin olive oil . . . .

Pinch of sea salt and twist of black pepper . . . .

😊 Reasonable

⧗ Freezer hero

I eat chilli with the kind of mindful reverie others reserve for yoga or religion. There's nothing quite like a delicious sting chased by that all-star dopamine riff. I start to vaporise with happiness.

Fresh chilli and ginger is a potent duo. Quite aside from their flavour and fireworks, these devious little dudes service our body parts in more ways than I ever imagined. A special compound particular to chilli stimulates the release of feel-good endorphins. Think of it as 'La Cucaracha' through the veins. These same endorphins help to block local inflammation, numbing us of our day's aches and painful dinner companions. We like.

Slice the fresh ginger and turmeric. Fresh turmeric can stain badly, so skip the peeling if it's organic. Pop into a blender with the remaining ingredients. Whizz into a glossy cream.

Pour into an ice cube tray and freeze until required. These frozen cubes of yum will defrost at room temperature in just 10 minutes. Super fancy on top of plain soups and despondent salads.

Pistachio and Kale Pesto
for soups, lentils, rice, avocado, fish, chicken

MAKES 8 PORTIONS . . . .

200g Irish kale, Russian kale or cavolo nero . . . .

Small bunch of fresh flat-leaf parsley . . . .

2 good-quality (tinned) anchovies, drained of oil . . . .

2 garlic cloves, roughly chopped . . .

Good fistful of freshly grated Parmesan or Pecorino cheese . . . .

Handful of shelled pistachios . . . . . .

4 tablespoons extra virgin olive oil . . . .

Very reasonable
. . . .

Bit of fiddling required.
Another freezer babe.

This pesto is a paean to Dark Green Leafies and wholefood punks. Bring it into the office with some cult sourdough and let everyone rub your halo.

Wash the kale well and strip the leaves from the tough stalks. Toss the stems onto the compost or juice them with apples and lemon for a 'detox grenade'. Stop sniggering, I'm almost serious.

Bring a large pot of water to the boil, drop the leaves in and cook for 2 minutes. Transfer the cooked kale to an ice bath to keep its neon green glow and stop it cooking any further. Drain well in a salad spinner.

Put the blanched kale into a food processor with the remaining ingredients. Briefly pulse for 5–10 seconds, until you reach your desired consistency. You don't want a purée, so go easy on the buttons. You're aiming for little flecks of kale and anchovy. Taste, and air punch.

Freeze in ice cube trays and store for another day in portions that suit you. Once frozen, the pesto cubes can be stored in re-usable glass jars.

Nori Paste
for eggs, avocado toast, brown rice bowls, fish and grains

MAKES 1 SMALL JAR OF 8-10

SERVINGS . . . .

10 sheets of nori . . . .

2 tablespoons coconut sugar or palm
sugar . . . .

1–2 tablespoons brown rice vinegar
(or a squirt of lemon in a pinch) . . . .

1 tablespoon soya sauce . . . .

150ml water . . . .

⊕ On a budget

. . . .

⧗ Freezes well

Ocean vegetables are the Biggest Thing since Ron Burgundy's sideburns. Calling them ocean veg is, of course, diplomatic speak for seaweed.

Nori, and its brothers and sisters in the ocean veg world, deliver a cargo of calcium for strong bones. Go nori! Not worried about your bones? You should be, especially if you're female. One in four Irish women will suffer an osteoporotic fracture in their lifetime. That number jumps to one in every two women over fifty.

This nori paste will have your synapses doing somersaults. I now bestow this recipe upon you with deference to my food crush, Katie Sanderson. Hallowed be thy paste.

Using a scissors, roughly chomp the nori sheets into bite-sized pieces. Migrate to a saucepan and add your choice of natural sugar, some brown rice vinegar and the soya sauce. If you are coeliac, you can find wheat-free soya sauce, called tamari. Leave everything to chillax for 20 minutes.

Add the water and cook on a gentle heat. Remove from the heat after 10 minutes or when the nori collapses into a paste.

Store in an airtight jar once cooled and keep for up to seven days in the fridge. Indecently tasty stuff.

Ghee
for frying, sweating and baking

MAKES 1 LARGE JAR . . . .

500g unsalted Irish, grass-fed or
organic butter . . . .

50g patience . . . .

⊕ On a budget
. . . .

⧗ Needs a watchful eye. Lasts
longer than butter.

Ghee is a first cousin of butter. It is rich in fat-soluble vitamins A and D, without which some nutrients, like calcium, cannot be synthesised in the body. Interesting, eh?

Why not just use butter? I hear you! The milk solids (proteins and natural sugars) bring butter's smoke point down to 150°C. In the process of making ghee, these milk solids, including lactose, are removed, leaving only liquid gold (and a house smelling like freshly baked shortbread). Removing the milk solids markedly raises its smoke point and 'stability' when heated in a frying pan. Go ghee! A smoke point refers to the point at which the fat begins to decompose and make free radicals. As soon as any fat reaches its smoke point the fat will lose any nutritional purchase it once had. Free radicals are those nasty carcinogenic compounds that act like evil Power Rangers in our system. Not the sort of thing you want to serve your family.

You can find ghee in Middle Eastern stores or health food shops across Ireland, but you can also make it in your own kitchen today.

Ideally, use a small heavy-based saucepan. Bring the butter to a gentle putter on a low to medium heat. Let it burp and rumble for 20–40 minutes.

During this time, expect a foam to coat the top. Just scoop this off and throw it away. We are interested in the next layer – the liquid gold. After 20 minutes, the lighter-coloured milk solids will drop to the bottom of the saucepan, underneath the layer of fabulously golden butterfat.

Watch carefully. When the smell of freshly baked croissants fills the air, it's done. You'll also notice the milk solids changing colour on the bottom. Remove from the heat.

I use scrupulously clean jam jars and line each one with muslin or cheesecloth. Pour your hot clarified butter into each jar, straining it first through the muslin cloth. This will catch the milk solids, which in turn will prevent the ghee from spoiling.

Leave to cool at room temperature before storing in the fridge. Expect ghee to last for many months in the fridge or six to eight weeks at room temperature. This will be your frying pan's new BF.

Mustard and Mulberry Salad Dressing

MAKES 1 MEDIUM JAR . . . .

80g dried mulberries . . . .

2 apples, freshly pressed (yields 250ml juice) . . . .

100g fresh flat-leaf parsley . . . .

2 tablespoons smooth Dijon mustard . . . .

Splash of extra virgin olive oil . . . . .

Feeling flush

. . . .

Blend and serve, or freeze

Only half as sweet as other dried fruit, mulberries offer an interesting crunch to lentils and curries. These teeny berries will sneak a good dose of vitamin C and iron into your family's mealtime. Or you can smuggle them into bags of granola. But keep it away from smoothies or it will taste like an intrepid snail found your blender.

First, let the dried mulberries, apple juice and Dijon party together. Set aside to soak for 10 minutes.

Using a very sharp knife, roughly chop the parsley, keeping the larger stalky parts for your freezer stock bag (page 101). Blitz with the dressing ingredients that have been resting to the side and a splash of oil using a hand-held blender. Namaste.

Green Veg Hero
for all members of the veggie kingdom

MAKES 6–8 SERVINGS . . . .

4 tablespoons barley malt extract . .

4 tablespoons toasted sesame oil . . .

2 tablespoons brown miso paste . . . .

1 fresh hot red chilli . . . .

1 big lime, juiced . . . .

Feeling flush

Blend and freeze

The trick to eating more greens is not buying more greens. It's finding a range of kickass sauces to dunk broccoli into, to straddle kale or to tango with a platter of green beans. That's what all these freezer dressings are for. With the right sauce, you can easily turn a dreaded Dark Green Leafy into a firm family favourite.

This green veg sauce should do the trick. It's a licky-sticky yumdinger. All manner of greens are served at the table and dunked in a sprightly fashion. Nothing gets spared, so bring in the heavies (spinach, cauli, asparagus, sprouts).

I've been stalking (bad pun, sorry) leading researchers in the field of bone disease and apparently dark green leafies are your bones' BF. Yes, they contain calcium, but more importantly, green veg facilitate the absorption of calcium from food. So we should all be mainlining more green veg into us. It's the cheapest way to better bone health and killer yoga moves.

Using a blender, belt all the ingredients together. The fresh chilli seeds are seriously hot, so decide whether you want to include them.

Serve in a bowl for dunking broccoli into or mizzle over steamed greens for a flavour bomb.

Harissa Butter
for eggs, grain, curries, yogurt, roasted veg, greens

MAKES 8–10 SERVINGS . . . .

1 tablespoon coriander seeds . . . . . .

1 tablespoon cumin seeds . . . .

1 tablespoon caraway seeds . . . .

1 garlic clove, peeled and minced . . . .

6 tablespoons butter or ghee (page 194), softened . . . .

1 tablespoon ground paprika . . . .

1 tablespoon extra virgin olive oil . .

Squeeze of lemon . . . .

Pinch of fine sea salt . . . .

Pinch of chipotle chilli or cayenne pepper . . . .

Feeling flush

Another freezer hero

One blast of this butter will have you trotting like a fiesty showhorse. There is electrifying happiness to be found inside cayenne pepper. It's not simply the mild heat hot-wiring your dimples. It is, in fact, the active compounds within the pepper that tickle our feel-good endorphins.

Special Agent Capsaicin is responsible for this biochemical effect. Surprisingly, capsaicin's real prowess does not lie within its antioxidant taekwondo moves. Capsaicin is a brilliant agitator. As we freak out to cope with the blaze of a hot chilli, for example, our body releases an armada of natural painkillers in direct response to the capsaicin content. These endorphins canter through our bloodstream like nectar in our veins. Is it any wonder why that Friday night vindaloo is so damn popular?

Fire up a frying pan and dry-toast the coriander, cumin and caraway seeds until your nostrils start to party. Stir continuously with a wooden spoon to avoid scorching.

Transfer to a pestle and mortar or a coffee grinder and pulverise to a powder. Now beat in the remaining ingredients.

Spoon into a silicone ice cube tray, freeze until firm and transfer to a marked freezer bag. It's a thing of beauty.

When the mood beckons, pop a frozen cube of harissa butter on top of toast with eggs or you can snazzjazzle a boring soup.

White Miso and Garlic Butter
for everything

FOR 2 . . . .

3 tablespoons ghee (page 194)
or butter . . . .

1 tablespoon white miso paste . . . . . .

1 garlic clove, crushed . . . .

(+) Reasonable

. . . .

Triple the quantity and freeze
the leftovers

Hot melted butter, smashed garlic and a few teaspoons of sweet white miso paste will transform any tired vegetable into a sultan of seduction. Hell, even a tired flip-flop would taste damn good with this!

Gently warm your ghee or butter until it's runny. Whisk in your miso paste and crushed garlic. Mizzle over veg or crisp Cos leaves.

Flavour Grenades

These small but mighty recipes pump flavour where you need it most. Parachute on top of eggs or over a dull soup, jazz up some roasted spuds or resuscitate that leftover rice with any of these flavour grenades to crank up any dish's appeal. They will sit on your kitchen shelf until your hour of need over the coming months. Each has its own unique melody and can turn a despondent supper into a Pinterest-perfect feast.

Sesame Snaps

SERVES 1–5, DEPENDING ON USE . . . . .

5 tablespoons sesame seeds . . . .

1 tablespoon rice malt syrup or maple syrup . . . .

Pinch of fine sea salt . . . .

⊕ On a budget

. . . .

⧖ Easy to knock up and store on your kitchen shelf

Simple but sensational. Think of it as a superhero confetti for bored and lazy vegetables.

Preheat your oven to 220°C. Line a baking tray with non-stick baking paper.

Mash all the ingredients together in a cup with a fork. Spread the mixture over the lined baking tray in a single layer as best as you can. It's outrageously sticky, but don't worry. The heat will help the mixture to collapse.

Turn the oven down to 200°C. Bake for 5 minutes, until bubbly. You want moisture to evaporate from the mixture, which will give it its crunch.

Allow to solidify once cooled, then smash. Sprinkle over soups and salads or store in an airtight container and munch within the week.

Vegan Parmesan

MAKES 1 SMALL JAR . . . .

120g cashew nuts . . . .

3 tablespoons nutritional yeast
flakes . . . .

1–2 teaspoons flaky sea salt . . . .

⊕ Reasonable

. . . .

⧗ Keeps for four months in the
fridge

For our vegan pals and dairy-free darlings.

Pulse everything in a food processor or coffee grinder for 30 seconds, until it resembles fine breadcrumbs. Store in an airtight container in the fridge and use within four months. Sprinkle liberally on mash, pasta and pizza.

BBQ Salt

MAKES 1 SMALL JAR . . . .

1 teaspoon flaky sea salt . . . .

1 teaspoon smoked paprika or
chipotle chilli powder . . . .

1 teaspoon ground cumin . . . .

½ teaspoon cayenne pepper . . . .

⊕ On a budget

. . . .

⧗ Lasts for six months at room
temperature

Expect a chorus of tiny little taste explosions. Sprinkle over sweet potato wedges, chicken wings or charred cauliflower for maximum giddiness.

Shake it all up in a scrupulously clean jam jar. Label with masking tape and a marker.

Furikake Seasoning

MAKES 1 SMALL JAR . . . .

10g dried Irish dulse flakes or
strips . . . .

6 sheets of roasted nori . . . .

6 tablespoons sesame seeds . . . .

1 tablespoon coconut (or other)
sugar . . . .

Sprinkle of fine sea salt . . . .

⊕ Reasonable

. . . .

⧖ Lasts for months in a tightly
sealed jar

Umami is our fifth taste sensation. Scientists refer to this often-neglected taste bud as the lip-smacking point. Think of the deep, rich roast you get from garlic, Parmesan, meat, miso and mushrooms. Oh, and seaweed. Yes, 'sea veg' is a stellar source of umami flavour bombs. And this furikake recipe is crammed with sea veg.

Sea veg are truly beguiling. For such a slimy beach toy, they are also an ace source of nutrition. There's an impressive stash of calcium for burly bones and fulsome smiles. Loads of cancer-kicking lignans. And gram for gram, nori has even more iron than spinach. Bad luck, Popeye!

So here's a recipe for furikake seasoning. Furikake is to kitchens what conversation is to suppertime – endless little avenues of interest filled with warmth, fun and nourishment.

Blitz your dulse in a clean coffee mill or spice grinder. Set aside on a large plate.

Using a sharp scissors, shred the nori into thin strips. Now snip the strips like chives over the plate of dulse. Many health food stores sell flaked nori, which works equally well.

Now toast the sesame seeds in a hot, dry pan until the smell hits your nostrils. Add the sugar and sea salt, stirring without taking your eye off it. When the seeds start to colour, quickly take the pan off the heat and allow to cool before socialising with the plate of seaweed.

This can be stored in an airtight jar for many weeks. Excellent on top of scrambled eggs and any manner of greens.

Za'atar (p.206)

Pistachio Dust (p.213)

Buckwheat Pops (p.207)

BBQ Salt (p.201)

Black Olive Crumb (p.210)

Sugared Pecans (p.211)

Vegan Parmesan (p.201)

Sesame Snaps (p.200)

Sourdough Crumbs (p.213)

Za'atar

MAKES 1 SMALL JAR . . . .

1 tablespoon sesame seeds . . . .

4 teaspoons cumin seeds . . . .

1 teaspoon fine sea salt . . . .

2 tablespoons ground sumac
(optional) . . . .

4 teaspoons dried thyme . . . .

4 teaspoons dried oregano . . . .

2 teaspoons dried marjoram . . . .

⊕ Reasonable
. . . .
⧗ Freezes well

Za'atar is a deliciously pleasing Eastern Mediterranean spice blend. There are as many recipes for za'atar as there are grannies along the Med. This version is easy to make in Ireland given that supplies of fresh marjoram and wild thyme are close to nil.

It's used as a nifty condiment on tables to excite bread, hummus, yogurt dressings, roast chicken or plain ricotta. Za'atar is brilliant for BBQ season too, used as a marinade with olive oil.

We seal and store our za'atar in the fridge for those moments we don't know what to serve with our breakfast eggs or when we're wondering how to resuscitate yesterday's leftovers. Or just to show off. You can freeze the spice mix too and shake it straight from frozen. Persian poetry on a plate. Eat your heart out, Hafiz!

Dry toast your sesame and cumin seeds in a very hot frying pan until a nutty aroma makes your nostrils samba. Add the salt, stir the party for 20 seconds, then transfer to a plate to cool.

In a clean coffee grinder, a spice grinder or pestle and mortar, blend the sumac (if using), dried thyme, oregano and marjoram with your cooled sesame and cumin seeds. You're looking for a few seconds of blitzing or pummelling.

Store in a clean, airtight glass jar on your kitchen shelf and use within two weeks. It will keep in the fridge for six weeks or the freezer for six months. Sprinkle over your Sunday roast veg or add to a small bowl of olive oil for enthusiastic bread dippers.

Buckwheat Pops

MAKES 4 PORTIONS ....

4 tablespoons whole buckwheat
groats ....

⊕   On a budget
....

⏳   Ready in 15 minutes

Want to know how to hammer herpes? Confuse it. Yup. Cold sores have been shown to thrive on arginine, an amino acid commonly found in daily food choices like peanuts, lentils and red meat. We can trick the virus by feeding it a different amino acid called lysine, a second cousin of arginine. Lysine won't kill the virus, but it could help to prevent the symptoms. So stocking up on lysine-rich foods might successfully confuse the virus and compromise its main source of fuel. Fist. Bump.

Where can you find lysine, you shout? Buckwheat! This gluten-free grain is dead tasty. You'll love its rustic, grassy tones. The Russians and Japanese eat it regularly. Let me show you why.

Preheat the oven to 170°C.

Roast the buckwheat in the oven for a maximum of 15 minutes on a lipped roasting tin, taking care the groats don't misbehave and burn. They should give a crisp crunch when ready.

Set aside to cool and store in a screw-top jar for up to two weeks. This doesn't keep as long as the other 'salts', so use straight away if you fancy and stick to small batches.

Cured Egg Yolks
for grating over veg or pasta

MAKES 2 CURED YOLKS . . . .

50g fine sea salt . . . .

50g caster sugar . . . .

2 organic egg yolks . . . .

⊕ On a budget

. . . .

⧖ Lasts for one month in the fridge. Can be frozen.

Here's an indecently good way to treat an egg yolk. It may sound fussy, but you'd be devastatingly wrong. Cured egg yolks are like buttery, salty umami grenades. Using a lemon zester, grate the cured yolk over soup and plain pasta. It resuscitates leftover greens within nanoseconds.

Toss the fine sea salt (not flaky salt) and your caster sugar together.

Using two paper muffin cases – one for each yolk – layer the bottom with lots of the salt/sugar mix. In each, create a little depression for your egg yolk to sit inside, then very gently top each yolk with the remaining salt/sugar mix. You can pop these onto a snug dish and cover with cling film or beeswax wrap. Ta-dah!

Allow to sit and 'cure' for two to three days at room temperature, until the yolks are as firm as a Gruyère cheese. The salt will end up looking like wet sand, so don't panic, my fellow gastronaut!

When cured, the yolks will be bright and translucent. Run each cured egg yolk under a gentle tap to get rid of the excess salt and sugar glued to the surface. Pat dry and refrigerate in a glass jar until a plate of pasta hollers.

Black Olive Crumb

MAKES 1 X 330G JAR . . . .

400g good-quality Kalamata olives . .

⊕ Reasonable

. . . .

⧗ Lasts for four weeks in the fridge

Olives can help to vaporise cholesterol levels. Their monounsaturated fat has been shown to boost the 'good' HDL cholesterol in our body, resulting in a better overall cholesterol score. But you'll need to watch out for cheeky imposters that can't boast such cardiac superpowers. Traditionally prepared olives taste much better because they are naturally cured or fermented. Time is the most important ingredient here. You'll find the canned varieties of olives are often hastened on conveyor belts with the aid of caustic chemicals. Not so swell.

Traditionally prepared olives, on the other hand, are practically belching with superhero compounds. The first, oleocanthal, holds anti-inflammatory properties thought to help alleviate symptoms of high blood pressure. The second includes a suite of active polyphenols, helping to reduce the risk of heart disease. This black olive crumb reads like a love letter to your ticker.

Preheat your oven to 50°C. Line a baking tray with non-stick baking paper.

Roughly chop each olive in half and remove the stones. You can compost the stones or bin them.

Tumble the halves onto your lined baking tray, spacing them out nicely. Cook in a low oven overnight or for 5–10 hours. It all depends on how juicy the olives are. But don't panic, as it's hard to overcook olives at this temperature. They are done when they crunch.

Remove from the oven and allow to cool for a few hours before belting into a food processor and blitzing until it resembles chocolate soil (this usually takes 7–10 seconds) or leave chunky.

Store in an airtight container and use within three months. We use this as an umami-rich finishing salt on top of almost everything – avocado toast, hummus plates, curries, lentils, plain fish. We've even paired it with white chocolate and Netflix.

Sugared Pecans

MAKES 1 JAR . . . .

110g pecans . . . .

2 tablespoons rice malt syrup . . . . . .

Generous pinch of fine sea salt . . . . .

Feeling flush

. . . .

Lasts for weeks on your kitchen shelf, in theory

These candied nuts use a low-glycemic syrup for those concerned about blood sugar levels. If you have fresh rosemary, you could finely chop some into the syrup before coating your pecans. Candied nuts are ace in salads and on top of soup.

Find rice malt syrup in savvy delis and health food stores. Glorious stuff.

Whack up the oven to 150ºC.

Spread the pecans across a roasting tray lined with non-stick baking paper. Roast in the oven for 12 minutes.

Remove from the oven and let the rice malt syrup and the sea salt join the party. Coat thoroughly. Pop the tray back into your oven for a further 5–10 minutes.

Remove from the oven and give the pecans a decent chance of cooling down before plundering. Store in a jar, away from thirsty fingers, and sprinkle onto instant mango ice-cream (page 289) whenever the need arises.

Superhero Walnuts

Find the best walnuts in health food shops or your local four-letter German store

So swift to make and the benefits last all month

Walnuts, particularly black walnuts, are rich in L-arginine (erm, scientists, look away while I mutilate your language). Arginine is an amino acid necessary to make a molecule called nitric oxide, which has been found to relax constricted blood vessels and ease blood flow. Think of it as the Bach of the blood. This might indeed help to explain why nuts are applauded for their potential role in nourishing arterial walls, making the walls more pliable and less susceptible to damage. Good news for health insurers!

Here are two simple ways of dusting some extra flavour and nutrition over your plates.

Maple-Coated Walnuts

MAKES 250G

250g walnut halves

5 tablespoons maple syrup

Pinch of fine sea salt

Preheat your oven to 190°C. Line a baking tray with non-stick baking paper.

Tumble your walnuts onto the lined tray. Using your fingers, coat with the maple syrup and sea salt. Roast in the oven for 14–16 minutes, but watch they don't burn. An oven thermometer is really useful to make sure your oven is telling you the truth! They cost around €5, last a decade and will save you many a kitchen strop.

Remove from the oven and allow to cool down entirely before tasting. The maple will set once cooled. Break up and store in a clean, airtight jam jar until summoned for service.

Sprouted Walnuts

MAKES 400G

400g walnut halves

1 teaspoon fine sea salt

Soak the walnuts overnight in fresh filtered water with your sea salt (you can also soak them first thing in the morning if you prefer and cook them when you return home from work).

In the morning (or evening, depending), drain the walnuts and tumble them onto a roasting tray. Pop in the oven on your lowest setting, about 50°C, and roast for 8–12 hours, until crisp. If you have a fancy dehydrator, you can set the timer. If you want to use pecans instead, take them out after 8 hours, as they are slimmer than walnuts and will crisp quicker.

Allow to cool completely before storing in an airtight glass jar for up to six weeks. They taste amazing.

Pistachio Dust

MAKES 1 SMALL JAR . . . .
1 packet of salted and roasted
pistachios . . . .

⊕ On a budget
. . . .
⧖ Lasts for weeks

Little comets of deliciousness. Store in an airtight jam jar somewhere visible in the kitchen so that you can sprinkle this over porridge, soups, suppers and eggs.

Shell your pistachios. In a pestle and mortar, pound the nuts into small pieces. You can also do this by wrapping the shelled nuts inside a clean tea towel and use a rolling pin to smash them up. Their glorious green colour will shine through.

Sourdough Crumbs

ENOUGH FOR 2 . . . .
Dot of ghee (page 194) or coconut oil
Handful of crustless rye sourdough .

⊕ On a budget
. . . .
⧖ 60 seconds

On eggs, salads, roasted veg, soup, stews, guacamole, meat, fish – fried sourdough crumbs are always a yumdinger. We keep stale sourdough pieces bagged in our freezer, nifty for croutons, meatballs and crispy crumbs like this recipe.

Heat a frying pan with your chosen fat. Ghee and coconut oil have high smoking points and therefore are a healthier choice for frying at high temperatures. Olive oil tends to disfigure at a high heat, while the sugars and proteins in butter will blacken quickly.

Tear up your pieces of bread if you want to make croutons or pulse in a food processor. Fry until golden on all sides – this is easier with crumbs, of course. Remove from heat and rain the crispy crumbs over your dish.

Pomegranate Bombs

1 pomegranate . . . .

⊕ On a budget
. . . .
⧖ They live in your freezer, ready to party

I love these little crimson grenades. Each seed is practically swaggering with anthocyanins. Why should you care? Anthocyanins have attracted attention in medical circles because of their nifty ability to help decommission free radicals. Home run! This in turn may help to interrupt the cycle of inflammation in the body.

Up to 70% of an average GP's waiting room involves inflammation in one form or another (e.g. asthma, psoriasis, arthritis, haemorrhoids, cancers). While munching on pomegranate seeds is not going to clear the waiting room, these salubrious seeds are certainly your ally in the battle for better health.

Bashing the seeds from a juicy pomegranate can be comically messy. Half the craic is redecorating your kitchen walls. You could always slice the pomegranate into quarters and peel the rind in a bowl of water. The undesirable white pith floats to the top and the ruby red seeds will sink to the bottom.

Spread your pomegranate seeds in a single layer over parchment paper. Freeze. Once frozen, you can shuffle the seeds into a marked jar or freezer bag. Sprinkle over dishes or a flavoured yogurt that needs more excitement.

Popped Capers

PER PERSON . . . .
Up to 1 tablespoon medium capers . .

⊕ On a budget
. . . .
⧖ Takes a mere minute or two

Little cannonballs of flavour.

Heat a frying pan over a high heat. Carefully lower the capers into the pan, expecting some fireworks (capers have a high water content). Fry until crisp (2 minutes).

Allow to drain briefly on kitchen paper before parachuting over fish, lentils or soup.

Chickpea Croutons

SERVES 6 . . . .

1 x 400g tin of chickpeas . . . .

1 tablespoon olive oil . . . .

2 teaspoons garam masala . . . .

Sprinkle of fine sea salt . . . .

⊕ On a budget

. . . .

⧖ Needs to be made fresh –
doesn't store well

Chickpeas are mighty talented. I love them for their swag of magnesium. This mineral has the magical ability to help relieve cramps by encouraging our blood vessels to take some R&R. Good news for headaches and marriages.

We like to rain these croutons over soup and salads. You can change up the spice blend with mild curry powder, za'atar or the BBQ salt page 000. Little flavour bombs.

Fire up your oven to 200°C. Line a baking tray with non-stick baking paper.

Drain and rinse your chickpeas under cool running water. Dry thoroughly so that no moisture remains. A salad spinner is useful, or kitchen paper. If you can, let them air-dry for 5 minutes too. The drier they are, the easier it is for them to drink in flavour.

Mix the olive oil and spice together. Toss with the chickpeas, coating really well. I use my fingers for this. Tumble your glossy chickpeas onto your lined baking tray, shaking the tray so that they don't stick to one another. The chickpeas need plenty of space to crisp up in the oven.

Roast in the oven for 20–30 minutes (depending on how small or large your chickpeas are). They are done when they have deepened in colour a little and seem significantly lighter.

Toss with fine sea salt. Tumble onto soups and suppers.

Smoky Almonds

MAKES 125G

125g almonds . . . .

2 tablespoons rice malt syrup or
maple syrup . . . .

½ teaspoon smoked paprika or
chipotle chilli powder . . . .

Generous pinch of fine sea salt . . . . .

 Reasonable

. . . .

Will keep for three weeks until
summoned

Turns out our body has its own hairdressing salon. We 'bleach' our hair grey from the inside, says dermatologist and author Dr Jessica Wu. We now know that an enzyme called catalase might help to stall this pesky bleaching. So can we hamper grey hair by eating foods rich in catalase? Perhaps, says Wu.

Almonds have been shown to naturally increase the level of catalase in the bloodstream. The science behind it seems tentative and young, but crikey, I'm happy to volunteer myself for research when almonds can taste this good! My greys are cantering onto my head like iron filings to a magnet.

Preheat your oven to 150°C. Line a roasting tray with non-stick baking paper.

Spread the almonds in a single layer across your lined roasting tray. Roast in the oven for 12 minutes.

Remove from the oven and let the rice malt syrup or maple syrup, ground spice and sea salt join the party. Coat thoroughly. Pop the tray back into your oven for a further 5–10 minutes, spreading the almonds out so they don't touch each other.

Remove from the oven and give the nuts a decent chance of cooling down before breaking up and looting. After 4 hours of cooling, store in an airtight container.

Flavoured Yogurts

When the ratio of good bacteria to bad bacteria is out of kilter, your body will start to tell you. I'm talking about evil-smelling gas, The Bloat, candida, hell-raising constipation and general discomfort in the Department of Bowels. Does any of this sound familiar?

You need to start pimping your flora. The good bacteria found in natural unsweetened yogurt have been shown to stimulate our immune response and to carjack pesky gut invaders. I like to think of good bacteria as my body's little army, complete with anti-aircraft artillery.

There's an estimated 2kg of helpful little microbes loitering in your system today. That's right. You are hosting an opera in your pipes. As scientists are discovering more about our microbial ecosystems (officially called our microbiome), this army of freeloaders may be quietly controlling us. Even Steven Spielberg failed to predict this. We now know that our human genes are likely outnumbered by our microbial genes. Yes, it appears we've been colonised by these beneficial microbes for some time now and I'm enjoying a honking episode of Stockholm syndrome.

Our gut is regarded as our second brain by many cultures (except ours). The vast majority of our happy hormone, serotonin, is manufactured in our gut, for instance, and not in our head as previously presumed. Microbiome research is still young. Many of our nifty little microbes cannot survive outside the body, so it's difficult to study their behaviour in labs. Professor Tim Spencer at King's College London is confident that we can tell more about a patient's health by a detailed screening of her microbes than by screening her genes.

According to leading microbiologists behind the American Gut Report, peak gut health corresponds with eating an exciting and varied diet that includes over 30 different plant foods each week. Variety seems key, so get something new (and fresh) into you today. Preferably fermented. This section should help. (And no, fermented grape juice won't count. Nice try.)

Horseradish Yogurt

MAKES 1 LARGE TUB . . . .

1 large tub of natural yogurt . . . .

1 small lemon, zest only . . . .

4 tablespoons freshly grated horseradish, finely chopped . . . .

⊕ On a budget

. . . .

⧖ This will keep in the fridge for one week, ready to excite any supper

Fresh horseradish will make your tonsils and your toes dance.

Stir the natural yogurt, lemon zest and finely chopped horseradish together. That's it!

Coconut Yogurt

MAKES 400–500ML. . . . .

1 x 200g block of creamed coconut . .

300–400ml warmed coconut water (or filtered water) . . . .

¼ teaspoon vanilla bean extract (optional dessert mode) . . . .

1 capsule of live probiotics . . . .

⊕ Reasonable

. . . .

⧗ Fermentation required

Here's a recipe to feed that teeming metropolis in your microbiome. It will bring your Friday night curry to another cosmology.

Chop the coconut cream into small chunks. Tip into a high-speed blender along with the warmed coconut water and optional vanilla. Blend until sumptuously smooth.

Pour into a scrupulously clean glass bowl. Open and add the contents of your probiotic capsule. Stir with a wooden spoon.

Cover with kitchen paper and an elastic band. We keep ours on the warm kitchen counter for 24 hours, which does the trick. If your kitchen is not warm, you could try the hot press to achieve similar results – you're aiming for around 26°C. If it's particularly warm, 18 hours should be plenty of time to let the culture multiply. It should taste refreshingly tart. Every 6 hours, or when I remember, I whisk it to ensure a smooth consistency and to prevent the mixture splitting.

After 18–30 hours (when you have achieved your preferred level of tartness), refrigerate and gobble within seven days. We love serving cool creamy clouds of this yogurt alongside granola. It's also great as a natural icing on kids' cupcakes or dolloped on top of spicy curries.

Roasted Garlic Finishing Yogurt

MAKES 8 SERVINGS . . . .

1 head of garlic . . . .

3 tablespoons olive oil . . . .

1 large tub of natural yogurt . . . .

⊕ On a budget

. . . .

⧖ Keeps in the fridge for up to
10 days

Can't stand raw garlic? Nuff said, sista. Start with this easy recipe for roasted garlic. Creamy, subtle and luscious, it's an excellent substitute for mayonnaise in sambos. Use roasted garlic paste as a kitchen Band-Aid any time something needs a lift. Mashed potato? A despondent bowl of pasta? A timid soup? All benefit from frolicking with a dollop of roasted garlic paste.

Boost your oven to 200°C.

Chop the garlic head in half horizontally across the bulb rather than top to toe. Splash a small roasting tray with 1 tablespoon of the olive oil. Sit the bulb halves directly on the oil, cut side down.

Roast in the oven on the middle shelf for 20–25 minutes, until soft and mushy. You can check by gently lifting one of the garlic heads to reveal lots of soft cloves of garlic in their papery pods. Taste one. It should be creamy. If the garlic head is browning too quickly, place some foil over the tray.

Once cooked, allow the garlic cloves to cool on the tray inside their tiny pods. As soon as they're cool enough to handle, remove the cloves with a fork and mash with the remaining 2 tablespoons of olive oil. This paste will keep in the fridge for one week, to use whenever and wherever you deem delightful.

To make the finishing yogurt, stir a little roasted garlic paste through the tub of natural yogurt. Taste and see if it requires more garlic. You can also freeze the remaining roasted garlic paste for another day.

Coconut Yogurt (p.218)

Avocado Sour Cream (p.226)

Tahini Yogurt Sauce (p.225)

Black Garlic Cream (p.189)

Coriander and Cress Yogurt (p.224)

Horseradish Yogurt (p.217)

Cumin and Black Pepper Yogurt

PER PERSON . . . .

100g plain live yogurt . . . .

1 teaspoon extra virgin olive oil . . . .

Big pinch of ground cumin . . . .

A good twist of the salt and black
pepper mill . . . .

⊕ On a budget

. . . .

⧗ Keeps in the fridge for several
days, but it's easiest to make
this yogurt fresh as and when
you need it

Given that the vast majority of our happy hormone, serotonin, is made in the gut, it's probably a good idea to keep our pipes in good shape. The central idea surrounding the use of cultured food, like natural yogurt, is to kick-start a massive party in our pipes. This party stokes the natural flora of our gut's internal ecosystem. I do like a party.

Mix everything together with a fork. Serve straight away or rest in the fridge until later. Great with curries, beetroot salads, soups and sweet potato wedges. If the yogurt is very mild, you might find that a squeeze of lemon can lift the flavours.

Ginger, Sesame and Garlic Yogurt

PER PERSON . . . .

½ garlic clove . . . .

100g plain live yogurt or nut milk
yogurt . . . .

1 organic unwaxed lemon (optional),
zest only . . . .

1 small piece of fresh ginger,
peeled . . . .

A good twist of the salt and black
pepper mill . . . .

Big pinch of sesame seeds . . . .

⊕ Kind on the wallet

. . . .

⧗ Swift and easy

This finishing yogurt is a little flavour jamboree. Any time I eat ginger, sesame and garlic together, I feel particularly marvellous. I wonder if these foods commission my body to party and smile? It certainly feels like it.

Grate the garlic into your yogurt using the finest side of your box grater, the one normally reserved for lemon zest.

Follow with the lemon – a little zest is all that is required per serving.

Finely grate enough fresh ginger into the yogurt to meet your desired level of heat. I use an awful lot because my brain trips on the stuff.

Finish with salt and pepper, then scatter a big pinch of sesame seeds over the top. Black sesame seeds look extra snazzy.

Orange Blossom and Pistachio Yogurt

PER PERSON . . . .

Handful of salted pistachios . . . .

100g plain live yogurt . . . .

A few drops (or sprays) of orange
blossom water . . . .

Feeling flush
. . . .

60 seconds to make

This finishing yogurt is cheap to make, but the initial purchase of orange blossom water will set you back a tenner. It should contain just one ingredient: distilled orange blossom. Don't go near the many imposters! Find it in Fallon & Byrne in Dublin and other seriously savvy delis across the country.

As an added bonus, you can decant orange blossom water into a clean spray bottle and store it in the fridge to use as a refreshing spritz on thirsty skin with your favourite face oil.

Shell your pistachios, smashing a few if you have a pestle and mortar handy.

Mix everything together and serve straight away. Orange blossom is a delicate flavour, so it's best paired with mild-tasting soups and dishes.

This also makes a beautiful dessert yogurt alongside cakes or the pear and ginger muffins on page 252. Just add a smidgeon of icing sugar to the recipe.

Coriander and Cress Yogurt

MAKES 2 SERVINGS . . . .

Nip of fresh watercress . . . .

200g plain live yogurt . . . .

Handful of fresh coriander, leaves
and stems finely chopped . . . .

2 teaspoons extra virgin olive oil . . .

⊕ Reasonable

. . . .

⧖ Natural yogurt will last for
weeks in your fridge

Watercress is off-the-Richter shamazing. Citrus fruits have monopolised the vitamin C bonanza long enough. Now we know that a modest little green called watercress holds way more vitamin C than the egotistical orange. Wait until I tell my collagen.

Pick the delicate watercress leaves from their thicker stems. Compost the stems or add them to your special stock bag (page 101).
   Mix with the remaining ingredients, season and serve. This is one of our favourite cooling partners with midweek curries.

Hemp Garlic Cream

MAKES 200ML . . . .

125ml water . . . .

75g hulled hemp hearts (hemp
seeds) . . . .

1 garlic clove, crushed . . . .

Juice of 1 small lemon . . . .

Pinch of flaky sea salt . . . .

⊕ Feeling flush

. . . .

⧖ Hulled hemp hearts last for
12 months in your kitchen
cupboard

This makes a wonderful dairy-free pouring cream that's excellent with curries, stews and ragù. Yes, hemp seeds come from the same plant species as marijuana, but it is entirely legal and non-psychoactive, I'm afraid. Hemp seeds are very tasty things, so it's a welcome bonus that they're healthy too.

Blitz all the ingredients in a high-powered blender until sumptuously smooth. You're looking for the familiar consistency of pouring cream. Add an extra pinch of flaky salt if you think it needs a lift. Best served within 48 hours.

Tahini Yogurt Sauce

MAKES 2–4 SERVINGS

1 small garlic clove, finely grated

2 tablespoons tahini

1 tablespoon extra virgin olive oil

1 tablespoon lemon or lime juice

1 teaspoon any miso paste

4 tablespoons water or natural yogurt

 On a budget

. . . .

 3 minutes

It's obvious that sesame seeds are stupendously talented. These little meteors of crunch and deliciousness are just so yummy. Plus all that calcium, iron, magnesium and rampaging goodness? Yahtzee!

Flavour and health are a sexy little duo. It's my mantra for everything I make in the kitchen. I don't want health without flavour (who does?!) and flavour alone will not nourish or sustain my daily brain burps and high-watt mothering. So this recipe is a ballad to sesame.

Here at Healthy HQ, we love our antioxidants (or indeed, anything that helps to disarm the renegade little feckers wreaking havoc in our system). There are enough star antioxidants in sesame to keep Gwyneth blogging for decades. Its stash of vitamin E, for example, cartwheels through our system, helping to neutralise pesky free radicals that will otherwise rust our cells.

There's also top-grade plant lignans, such as sesaminol and sesamin. We're told that these chaps help to enhance the absorption of vitamin E in a synergistic way for the body to maximise its nutritional cargo. Those very same lignans have demonstrated an appetite for role-playing as phytoestrogens in the body. This is useful, of course, for the womenopause. Let's hear it for the lignans!

You're going to love this sauce. It's one great big licky-sticky sesame orgy.

Beat together the garlic, tahini and olive oil with a fork into a thick, glossy beast.

Stir in your citrus and miso paste and beat until smooth. Now add the water or yogurt a spoonful at a time, whisking between each addition. By the third spoonful, the paste will begin to thin out and pour like double cream.

Serve over brown rice Buddha bowls, white fish, avocado toast or any misbehaving salad.

Avocado Sour Cream

SERVES 4–6 . . . .

3 ripe avocados, halved, stoned and flesh scooped out . . . .

Trickle of fresh water . . . .

Squeeze of fresh lemon . . . .

Freshly cracked black pepper . . . . . .

Generous pinch of flaky sea salt . . . .

⊕ Feeling flush

. . . .

⧗ Ready in 60 seconds

For a good dose of healthy bacteria, you can simply serve sour cream or natural yogurt with your Friday night curry. But I love the sound of avocado sour cream – it's like a muezzin for cranky vegan teens.

In a Vitamix or high-speed blender, pelt the avocado flesh, splash of water and a dash of lemon together until lusciously silky and smooth. Season to your preferred taste (I go heavy on the flaky salt, but if serving this to kids, it won't need any seasoning). Serve alongside curries, with your favourite fish, smothered on toast or offer to your teens with tortillas and a smug giggle (a smuggle?). Namaste.

Cashew and Chive Sour Cream

FOR 1 MEDIUM JAR . . . .

110g unsalted, raw cashew nuts

1 small lemon, juiced . . . .

1 tablespoon extra virgin olive oil . .

Good twist of the salt and black pepper mill . . . .

A few tablespoons of fresh filtered water . . . .

Small handful of fresh chives, snipped . . . .

⊕ Feeling flush

. . . .

⧗ Soaking required

One for our dairy-free friends. You'll need an excellent high-speed blender, such as a Vitamix, for this.

Soak the cashews in cool filtered water for 6 hours or overnight. Drain and rinse.

Tumble the soaked cashews into a high-speed blender and blitz for 1–2 minutes with the lemon juice, oil and a good twist of the salt and pepper mill.

After 2 minutes, slowly add a few tablespoons of fresh filtered water while the motor is running. You are looking for a consistency like pouring cream. Stop the motor once you have reached the thickness or thinness you want, then stir through the chives.

Serve with curries or store in a clean bottle for up to three days in the fridge.

Fermentation

These funky foods will sit in your fridge for weeks, servicing those crazed dashes to put something on the table.

What's It All About?

Chances are you've had a course of antibiotics in the last few years. Although a precious resource, antibiotics can wipe out many useful strains of good bacteria in our inner ecosystem as well as the villainous ones. These are unintended consequences – 'collateral damage' in military speak. Restoring our microbial balance is really important to function well. Time to pimp your pipes.

As our understanding of health shifts towards the world of micro-organisms, it isn't impossible to imagine our bodies as prime real estate for microbes. At any one time, your gut can contain 1.5kg of bacteria. This is our microbiota – a gut dynasty where the good guys are constantly trying to crowd out the nasty challengers. Maybe you are already on first-name terms with a few of them, like Lactobacillus acidophilus and L-casei? Terribly friendly chaps.

Scientists can now confirm that our happy hormone, serotonin, is predominantly made in the gut and not in the brain. There is a lot more happening within our pipes than simple waste disposal. We are literally at the frontier of a new medical understanding. Microbiome research is a hot new thing in academia all around the world. The Human Microbiome Project run by America's National Institute for Health, alongside many other international laboratories, including University College Cork, has revealed that we are utterly dependent on our microbes for health and happiness. Let's help those microbes party.

Kimchi

MAKES 1 X 500ML JAR . . . .

500g Napa (Chinese leaf) cabbage, cored and shredded . . . .

Just over 1 tablespoon fine sea salt . . . .

1 carrot, peeled . . . .

2 spring onions, trimmed . . . .

2 garlic cloves, minced . . . .

Bit of fresh ginger, peeled and minced . . . .

1 tablespoon nam pla (fish sauce) . . .

½ tablespoon Korean chilli flakes . . .

Splash of fresh filtered water . . . . . .

⊕   On a budget
. . . .

⧗   Ferment for five days

Nobody wants to live forever, especially if you're in pain or if your husband has halitosis. Could we possibly enjoy both health and longevity as scientists continue to make huge advances in our understanding of human biology? I think even Disney would be doubtful. Few of us will see our ninth decade. And those of us who do will be burdened with arthritic shopping rounds, or worse still, bad conversation.

Making your own food with unprocessed, fresh ingredients is the ultimate ammo against ageing. We can't fight off the ageing process, but we can certainly engage in battle. Every cookery class I give around the country, I'm always asked for my Number One kitchen tip. Here it is: eat a little salad before your supper. Not during. Not after. Just before. This will ensure you mainline a suite of antioxidants and essential minerals into your system before you fill up on other stuff. If you do this every day, you will cash in the benefits of 365 bowls of goodness each year to help your skin glow and your limbs ignite. Here's one to get you started. Kale free.

Put the cabbage in a bowl and sprinkle over the salt. Massage the salt into the cabbage leaves until nicely softened. Cover with cold water, weigh it down with something heavy and leave for 1 hour. Rinse under cold running water and leave to dry. A salad spinner is useful.

Using a sharp potato peeler, slice long thin ribbons of carrot into a large bowl. Halve the trimmed spring onions and add them to the bowl too.

Now blitz the garlic, ginger, fish sauce and chilli with a little filtered water to form a paste. Add to the bowl.

Squeeze any excess water from your cabbage leaves before adding to the bowl of all the other ingredients. Coat everything really well and transfer to a 500ml glass jar, pressing down firmly so the brine rises to cover the veg. Add a weight, such as a clean stone or espresso cup, and seal the jar at room temperature for five days. Ta-da! I like to stand mine in a bowl to catch any adventurous brine going AWOL. Transfer to your fridge and enjoy within six weeks.

Pickled Turmeric

MAKES 1 SMALL JAR . . . .

80g fresh turmeric . . . .

110ml filtered water . . . .

Good squeeze of lemon . . . .

¼ teaspoon caster sugar or raw honey . . . .

¼ teaspoon sea salt . . . .

A few twists of the black pepper mill . . . .

⊕ On a budget

. . . .

⧗ Refrigerate for four weeks

From curcumin capsules to golden milk lattes, seems like everyone is swilling from the fount of turmeric. That bodacious yellow pigment? Curcumin. And boy, has it caused much giddiness among scientists and doctors.

Curcumin has been shown to help quell inflammation in our body by interrupting the production of odious leukotrienes. These chaps usually like to cartwheel through our veins, causing swelling and inflammation along their merry way. Inflammatory problems include conditions ending in –itis, such as bronchitis, diverticulitis, arthritis and other pesky ailments such as sprains, eczema and asthma. Chances are you're already familiar with the scourge of inflammation.

So what to do? Try this recipe to service your system. Before your fresh turmeric goes limp, either freeze it and grate it into soups straight from frozen or try this pickle to preserve it for longer. Pickled turmeric root is excellent with any curry and magically pimps up plain yogurt with its neon glow.

And get this. A radical compound in black pepper called piperine has been shown to improve the absorption rate of curcumin in the body. Piperine sounds like our very own store of sticky flypaper. Nifty, eh?

Gently scrape away the skin from your turmeric and compost it. The skin is very thin, so you can do this with a blunt knife in a downward motion. Rubber gloves can be useful here unless you want your fingers to look like little Minions, as fresh turmeric stains. Grate your peeled turmeric or slice it as thinly as you possibly can.

Mix with the fresh water, lemon juice, your sugar or honey, some sea salt and black pepper. Transfer to a sterilised jar and store in the fridge for up to four weeks. Raid whenever the mood hollers.

Homemade Cream Cheese

MAKES 400G . . . .

500g full-fat Greek yogurt . . . .

Patience . . . .

⊕ On a budget

. . . .

⧖ Patience required

People are sick of consuming products. We want experiences. Full-fat, authentic, soul-nourishing, heart-thumping, life-affirming experiences. What's missing in many of our lives is something intrinsically satisfying. Products rarely deliver the true nourishment we crave.

Cooking for yourself and for those you love is a deeply meaningful experience. What makes food truly satisfying is not just the physical hunger-squashing sensation of mainlining food into an empty stomach. It's the adoration poured into the preparation of ingredients and the fulfilment of receiving someone's time and attention. Nothing beats the magic of homemade food. High-vibing wholefoods always feel like they can burst into your engine room with an emergency toolbox and remedy your mood slump or longing to be cared for.

So let's get you dosed up. This is a dynamo recipe for homemade cream cheese. No faffing around with curdled milk, thermometers and Valium.

First, get a nut milk bag or cheesecloth. Both can be purchased in health food stores or online.

Pour the entire tub of Greek yogurt into your special cloth or bag and allow the whey to run off the yogurt for 12–16 hours. I tie my yogurt-filled nut milk bag onto a wooden spoon over my blender jug and leave it overnight.

You're left with a stellar probiotic cream cheese to enjoy as a spread or as icing on a cupcake. Store in a clean lidded jar inside the fridge for up to one week. The liquid whey collected in the jug can be sneakily added into smoothies all week.

Cream Cheese Step 1

Cream Cheese Step 2

Pickled Red Onions

MAKES 1 X 1-LITRE JAR . . . .

5 medium red onions . . . .

1 tablespoon fine sea salt . . . .

Fresh filtered water . . . .

⊕ On a budget

. . . .

⌛ Lasts for months in the fridge

I quickly learned that with just a bit of mental parkour, you can turn any vegetable into a thundering drama queen and steal the show. Meet these pickled red onions. You're going to be the best of friends.

Peel and thinly slice your onions. A mandolin or food processor is pretty nifty here. Massage lightly with the salt (don't wear mascara for this step!).

Transfer to a half-litre glass jar and top with enough fresh filtered water to submerge the onions. Place a weight on top to keep the onions covered – I use a clean beach stone or espresso cup. Keep 3cm of space free at the top to allow for fizzy fireworks.

Store at room temperature for four weeks, tasting occasionally. Refrigerate when the desired tang is achieved. Your funky onions will keep for six months in the fridge.

Milk Kefir

MAKES 500ML . . . .

2–3 tablespoons milk kefir grains . . .

500ml full-fat milk . . . .

⊕ On a budget

. . . .

⏳ Ferment for two to three days

Kefir is not another cranky health food reserved for the Birkenstock brigade. Nope. Kefir is yogurt's low-maintenance, tarty cousin. When can you meet? Today! Find kefir grains in the refrigerated section at your local health food store.

The grains burp and feed on whole milk, gobbling up the natural milk sugars and lactose. All those gorgeous bacteria multiply faster than grass through a goose. What you're left with is a funky ferment more potent than natural yogurt.

Use organic milk, raw milk, goat's milk, even coconut milk. I drink kefir straight up on ice, but yogi types like to flavour their kefir with second ferments using honey and vanilla pods. Kefir is also really great with spicy curries to help your taste buds and mascara weather the heat. It makes a rather brilliant marinade for meat, replaces buttermilk in baking recipes and sings with soft cheese as a last-minute mash-up for spreads.

Using a clean 500ml glass jar, pop the kefir grains in with your preferred type of milk.

Cover the top of the jar with kitchen paper, secure with a rubber band and leave on your kitchen counter for 24–36 hours to ferment.

When the desired tang is achieved, remove the kefir grains with a plastic sieve and pop into another 500ml of fresh milk to start the process all over again. Your kefir can be refrigerated or guzzled straight away to boot up your flora.

If you aren't reusing the kefir grains straight away, they can be stored in a little whole milk for one week in the fridge. The milk will be perfectly good to use – chilled temperatures merely slow down the fermentation process. It's okay to keep extra kefir grains in the freezer too.

Cheat's Kefir

Get your mitts on some really good sour cream. Find some store-bought milk kefir in the refrigerated drinks section (usually alongside smoothies or kombucha, for example). Then loosen up the chilled sour cream by pouring in a little kefir. Leave overnight to ferment (or serve straight away, as it's bloody gorgeous with curries). Fist. Bump.

Sweetheart Sauerkraut

MAKES 25 SERVINGS . . . .

1 large head sweetheart cabbage
(Napa is also great, Savoy a bit
trickier), cored and shredded . . . .

1 tablespoon fine sea salt . . . .

Pinch of whole coriander seeds
(optional) . . . .

2 small carrots (optional) . . . .

1 large finger-sized piece of fresh
ginger . . . .

⊕ On a budget
. . . .

⧗ Lasts for three to four weeks in
the fridge

You can't choose your DNA, but you can choose your microbiota. Your health's 'mood board' is not a simple picture of genes and environment. There's a third element that we now know of – let's just call them nifty dudes. Nature, nurture and nifty dudes.

At any one time, your gut can contain 1–2kg of nifty dudes. This bacteria metropolis is our microbiota, and each strain has its very own biological function within our body. Mind blowing, eh?

So where can we find them? Fermented foods such as natural yogurt, sour cream, kimchi and this sexy sauerkraut. Over to you!

In your largest ceramic or glass bowl, tumble the shredded cabbage with the fine sea salt and coriander seeds (if using). Leave for 1 hour while you prep the remaining gear.

Chop the heads off both your carrots, if using. With a potato peeler, skim long strips of carrot into your bowl of shredded cabbage.

Finely chop your ginger into matchstick-sized pieces. If your ginger is organic, you can keep the skin on. Add to the bowl.

By now the cabbage will be considerably softer and juicier. Massage all your ingredients together for 5 minutes before decanting into a very large glass jar. Sweetheart cabbage is the easiest type to massage into submission. Other cabbages, such as the white Irish one, can be ornery.

Press the veg down firmly inside your jar until the natural juices reach the top, leaving a little space for it all to expand under the lid (4cm or so).

Now place a weight on top of the cabbage to keep it submerged in its juices. I use a clean beach stone or an empty espresso cup. Seal the jar loosely (in case of possible but improbable explosions) and keep at room temperature for three to five days, where it will fizz, gurgle and burp. Two days is loads during hot summer spells. I find it helpful to label the date (e.g. Kraut 1/5 for the first of May) using masking tape and a black marker. This way I'll know how long it's been gurgling on my countertop.

Taste and decide whether it hits the spot. If yes, transfer to the fridge, where it will happily keep for weeks and weeks, submerged in its own funky juice. If it's not quite ready, keep it on the kitchen counter for another 12 hours.

Purple Cumin Kraut

MAKES 1 LARGE JAR . . . .

1 red cabbage, rinsed and cored . . . .

1 tablespoon fine Celtic sea salt or
Himalayan pink salt . . . .

1 teaspoon cumin seeds . . . .

⊕ On a budget

. . . .

⧗ Lasts for three to four weeks in
the fridge

Ever massaged a cabbage leaf into a deliciously dopey torpor? You'd be forgiven if it wasn't on your to-do list this afternoon. I'm here to tell you that it should be.

Pickling and fermenting have caused witchy hysteria from Berlin to Bantry. Every hipster café has dedicated a section of their kitchen to these bubbling beauties: kimchi, sauerkraut, pickles, cheese, vinegar, kombucha and sourdough. All these funky ferments send your flavour radar into another stratosphere. But that's not the best part. Fermenting your own fresh produce means less food waste, less shopping and more trips to the loo. Yup. Let's get to that last point swiftly.

Your gut is a jungle of microbiota who love a good party. These disco dudes feed on fructooligosaccharides (FOS), fibre and lacto-fermented foods like this kraut. The trick to keeping your digestive health all tickety-poo (sorry) is to crowd out the nasty challengers and the gate-crashing pathogens.

The good news? It's much easier than it sounds. Try making this purple party kraut.

Shred the cabbage in whatever way you fancy. I use a nifty blade on my food processor, which probably bruises the edges a little but I'm no kitchen angel. If you download a good podcast, shredding finely with a sharp knife won't feel so laborious. The finer the shredding, the better the result.

In your largest ceramic bowl, tumble the shredded cabbage with the salt and cumin seeds. I find that any more than 1 teaspoon of cumin seeds leads to a soapy finish. Leave for 30 minutes.

When you return, the cabbage will be a little softer and a little juicier. Red cabbage takes longer to submit than, say, Napa cabbage (aka Chinese leaf cabbage). Feel free to do a combination of cabbages. Massage the salt into the cabbage for 10 minutes before decanting into a very large glass jar (or several jars).

Press the cabbage down firmly inside your jar, encouraging the natural fresh salty juices to come to the top of the cabbage. Now place a weight on top of the cabbage to keep it submerged in its juices. I use a clean stone, which works theatrically well. My kids love this and anoint it with a spell.

Seal the jar loosely and keep at room temperature for three days, where it will fizz, gurgle and burp. Two days is loads during hot summer spells.

Taste and decide whether it hits the spot. If yes, transfer to the fridge, where it will happily keep for months. If not, keep it on the kitchen counter for another 12 hours.

Kombucha

MAKES 1.5 LITRES. . . . .

80g organic cane sugar . . . .

3 bags of black, green, white or pu-
erh tea . . . .

1 litre filtered water . . . .

125ml starter kombucha (or artisan
kombucha from the store) . . . .

1 kombucha scoby . . . .

Booch (a yogi's pet name for kombucha) has had a stellar year. From flat anonymity a few years back to becoming a household name today, kombucha is the Shawn Mendes of fizzy pop.

So what is it? Kombucha is a naturally bubbly drink made by fermenting sweetened tea. A symbiotic culture of bacteria and yeast (scoby) basically burps and pees its way through your sweetened tea to produce a cultured, microbiome-loving soda. What's not to love?!

Here's a recipe to get you started on your own sparkling journey. First step, find a large scoby or save the little rubbery sneeze you find in a bottle of artisan kombucha (such as Synerchi, KO Kombucha or Holo). You can get your mitts on a free scoby from any deli or café that serves its own-brew kombucha. Failing that, Instagram can now solve most bourgeois dilemmas.

Add the sugar and teabags to 1 litre of just-boiled filtered water and stir to dissolve. I do this in two batches with my teapot. Allow to steep and cool for 4 hours before pouring into a tall glass jar with your starter kombucha and scoby. Discard and compost the teabags.

Cover the top of your jar with a piece of cheesecloth (or a new J-cloth) and a rubber band. Leave to ferment and burp for three to six days at room temperature, out of direct sunlight. If your kitchen is cold, consider placing the kombucha in your hot press with an ambient temperature of between 20°C and 24°C.

Taste the kombucha each day to familiarise your palate with the speed of your own kombucha. If the scoby fits your jar perfectly, it will ferment and bubble faster. When you think it hits the spot between sweetness and tartness that's right for you, bottle three-quarters of your brew and refrigerate in a jar with a tight-fitting lid. Or neck it straight away with ice and a deliciously smug halo.

With the remaining one-quarter booch, start another fresh batch (go back to step 1). Summer months, my booch is ready in three days. Winter, it takes four to five days. You'll get to know yours too.

Second Ferments

Giving kombucha a second ferment takes anywhere between one to six days and guarantees extra fizz and sweetness. You'll get to know your mother scoby and her cadence. Here are some of my favourite second ferments. I hate cleaning narrow bottles, so I avoid messy purées and pastes.

Choose one of the following and leave your kombucha at room temperature to ferment a second time. You'll need a 1-litre bottle with a fliptop lid. As the bubbles mount inside the bottle, you may need to burp it each day to prevent explosions. Expect a similar sound to opening a bottle of Prosecco. If this doesn't happen, simply leave your booch to sculk a little longer. This is where the fizz gets frisky!

· Splash of raspberry cordial.
· Freshly grated ginger and 1 tablespoon of caster sugar.
· Frozen strawberries, popped straight into the bottle alongside 2 teaspoons of golden caster sugar. Apart from strawberries, I'm not mad on berries as a second ferment – it reminds me of medicine.
· I drop around to my local cold-pressed juice store and bring home pressed turmeric to add to my sencha booch for a second ferment alongside a nip of raw honey. You could also add 4 tablespoons of the turmeric tonic on page 88 for a second ferment.
· Slices of pear and ginger are gorgeous with 1 tablespoon of golden caster sugar.
· Green rooibos tea as a first ferment works beautifully with raw honey as a second ferment. Green coffee also makes a good first ferment alongside the usual green tea.

Vegan Mayo

MAKES 12 SERVINGS . . . .

6 tablespoons kimchi vinegar (or
other ferment juice) . . . .

3 tablespoons sweet white miso . . . . .

1 tablespoon finely chopped spring
onion, white part only . . . .

1 teaspoon tamari or soya sauce . . . .

1 teaspoon mirin . . . .

1 small garlic clove, minced . . . .

125ml extra virgin olive oil . . . .

Feeling flush

Lasts in the fridge all week

Glutathione has been dubbed the body's maestro antioxidant – in other words, the conductor of a large orchestra of antioxidants. For this reason, glutathione is considered one of the most important molecules our body needs to slay disease and ageing. (I say *considered* because science is always evolving. Glutathione is the current sweetheart.) Our levels of glutathione appear rather critical to the speed at which we age and how quickly we might succumb to illness.

To boost glutathione levels, we need to get to know our alliums. Onions, such as the sprightly variety found in this recipe, are ace. This is an exceptional recipe for a vegan mayo, adapted slightly from NYC's most talented vegetarian chef, Amy Chaplin. It is sheer brilliance, with a delicious encore of its own!

In a blender, whizz everything except the olive oil for 30 seconds or until seriously smooth. You might have to stop the motor and scrape down the sides once or twice.

With the motor still running, gently pour in the olive oil drop by drop until the mayo thickens beautifully. You can then progress to a steady stream of oil.

Stop the motor. Spoon the mayo into a clean jam jar and screw on the top. It will thicken once chilled. Refrigerate until required. This mayo may separate if left at room temperature – don't panic. Just knock it up with a fork.

Part Four Speedy Treats

I'm not interested in taxing my taste buds just to stick to a diet plan or put something healthy in my mouth. No thanks. Misery is not an ingredient in my pantry. When I need a sweet hit, I want something satisfying without compromising my mojo and my mood. That's what hooked me on wholefoods – the pleasure and energy it brings to everyday life. It just made sense to me that eating foods as close to their natural state as possible was going to deliver the best result possible.

What I work with now is a massive library of ingredients unrestricted to boring white flour and one-dimensional white sugar. My shelves are filled with ground almonds, milled chia seed, lentil flours, sumptuous plant oils like olive and hazelnut and spices like turmeric, ginger and cardamom. Combined in the right ratios, these are some badass ingredients. Ingredients that rock my body and my palate.

I'm not saying you shouldn't tuck into a packet of Tim Tams when the mood yodels. Penance is not my vibe. I'm all for feeling good – the food we eat should be full of whoopee! It's really that simple. I care about my body and my mind. The thrill of them both feeling ace when I wake up is really very special. I used to feel like I had woken up underneath a lawnmower. I hate feeling like shit. Being consistently under par is not good for me (or for, erm, society). Nah-aw. I can't be a good human on a diet of processed junk. It's just not possible. I deserve to feel amazing – and so do you – and have learned just how easy it is to maintain.

The first step is to start lovebombing your kitchen space. Pick some podcasts to make your dimples hurt with laughter. Own that zone. This is where the magic happens. So much of our diet is contingent on mood and convenience. If we curate both of these in our very own kitchen, then we stand a chance of giving our body the grub it so desperately needs.

The second step is to ditch diets. Anyone notice that dieting doesn't seem to be a terribly effective route to losing excess weight? An industry does not grow into a $60 billion bonanza by permanently solving the problem it is designed to address. Pah! **If you're going to count something, count nutrients, not calories.**

Salted Coffee Caramels

MAKES AROUND 50 . . . .

25 Medjool dates . . . .

1x 185g jar of roasted cashew nut
butter . . . .

120ml strong hot coffee . . . .

Squeeze of lemon . . . .

Smattering of flaky sea salt . . . .

150g dark chocolate . . . .

Feeling flush

. . . .

Lasts for months in the freezer

These coffee caramels fill my toes with magic and pinball me around the house with happiness. No white sugar, butter or thermometers required. Instead we use licky-sticky Medjools and roasted cashew butter, whipped into submission.

And if you're vegan? This could be a transcendental moment. Dating a vegan? Jackpot.

The secret to creating these salted coffee caramels is in pouring just enough hot coffee into the mix, facilitating a creamy, luscious whip that doesn't set when frozen. Then we store them in the freezer behind the fish fingers where no one will find them.

Soak the Medjools in boiling water for 5 minutes.

While the dates soak, warm the jar of cashew nut butter by carefully placing the jar in a bowl of hot water.

Drain the soaked dates, discarding the soaking liquid. Remove and compost the date stones. Blitz the fleshy dates with your warmed cashew butter, hot coffee, a squeeze of lemon and the flaky salt in a food processor or blender until smooth. If your kitchen is cold, the mixture might seize up. You can fix this by adding a little extra hot coffee or a splash of hot water. Taste the mixture and decide if it needs a touch more salt.

Scrape the sticky ball of caramel into silicone ice cube moulds to set. I do this in several batches because I have only one silicone tray. You could also use two teaspoons and lots of patience, rolling the mixture into beautiful little bonbons and dropping onto a lined tray to freeze until set (as pictured).

When the caramels are frozen, pop them out of their silicone ice cube mould and collect them in a ziplock freezer bag.

As soon as all the caramels have been formed, frozen and collected, melt the chocolate over a *bain marie*. This is basically a pot of simmering water, 2.5cm in depth, with a heatproof bowl sitting on top where a lid might otherwise have gone. The contents of the bowl will gently melt from the steam of the water underneath. The trick is not to let the water violently boil or let the bottom of the bowl touch the water underneath.

Briefly and briskly tumble each caramel into the melted

chocolate directly from their frozen state. I find a fork handy for this step. Let the chocolate-coated caramels set on non-stick baking paper before popping back into your reusable freezer bag. Store them in the freezer, ready to plunder at will.

White Chocolate and Strawberry Caramels

To make a white chocolate and strawberry version of the salted coffee caramels, follow the same recipe as above but with the following amendments:

You will need to swap out the hot coffee for just-boiled water from the kettle.

Swap the dark chocolate for good white chocolate, such as Green & Blacks Organic. I also like to add 2–3 tablespoons of melted cacao butter to the white chocolate in the *bain marie*. This facilitates easier caramel coating and fewer tantrums.

You'll need to source freeze-dried strawberries. It's practically powder. Once you coat the caramels in the white chocolate, sprinkle some freeze-dried strawbs and their powder over the top of each caramel.

Pear and Ginger Muffins

MAKES 12 VEGANS VERY HAPPY . . . . . .

1 firm (not soft) pear . . . .

350ml plant milk . . . .

100ml extra virgin olive oil . . . .

Squeeze of fresh lemon juice . . . .

2 tablespoons psyllium husks . . . .

2 teaspoons vanilla bean paste or
good-quality extract . . . .

½ teaspoon flaky sea salt . . . .

130g brown rice flour (sub with
all-purpose gluten-free flour in a
pinch) . . . .

110g chickpea flour . . . .

140g light muscovado sugar or
golden caster sugar . . . .

2 teaspoons baking powder . . . .

2 teaspoons ground ginger . . . .

50g crystallised ginger . . . .

Melted dark chocolate, to drizzle
(optional) . . . .

⊕ Reasonable

. . . .

⧗ Can be individually wrapped and
stored in the freezer

My personality would expire without muffins. I'm only kind to my brethren when I'm doped up on the warm, pillowy ones with molten centres. Muffins, as Henry David Thoreau almost said, are the very marrow of life.

When those very same muffins happen to be stuffed with nutritionally packed ingredients such as pear, olive oil, psyllium husk, brown rice, ginger and chickpeas, my brain starts to breakdance. It's like an update being installed in my body.

Preheat the oven to 190°C. Line a 12-mould cupcake tin with paper cases.

Roughly grate your pear, leaving the skin on. Compost the core. Whisk 130g of grated pear with your plant milk, olive oil, squeeze of lemon, psyllium, vanilla and sea salt with a fork. Set aside. If you make these often and have a stash of caffeine-free chai teabags from recipes such as the granola (page 17) and chai lollipops (page 301), feel free to tear two open and add the contents of the teabag in here. This will help to change the flavours up a bit and keep your family interested!

In a large bowl, let the flours, sugar, baking powder and ground ginger party. Combine the wet and dry ingredients together and beat until smooth. Avoid tasting the batter – wet chickpea flour tastes and smells like cat pee. The cooked result is peerless, though, so do persist!

Pour the runny batter into the 12 paper cases. Pop one or two pieces of crystallised ginger into each muffin and bake in the oven for 30 minutes.

Remove from the oven, turn the muffins out of the tin and let them cool on a wire rack. Feel free to mizzle across some melted dark chocolate like a giddy orchestra conductor, or tickle with coconut yogurt, dried pear and a hot cup of chai.

3-Ingredient Party Torte

SERVES 16 . . . .

1 x 154g packet of (vegan) Oreos
(possibly more, for the sides) . . . .

300g good-quality dark chocolate . .

300ml nut milk . . . .

⊕ Price depends on the chocolate
you purchase

. . . .

⧗ Takes minutes to make. Freezes
in secret slices wrapped in
parchment.

Children just love magic. Holly wands aside, your kitchen is their Hogwarts.

Take something basic like a spud and let your nippers watch you transform it with heat, ninja knives, spices or patience. (Incantation can be fun, but try not to mess with their heads too much.) Even when I burn things to within a millimetre of their lives, there is thunderous awe from my little wizards.

Home-cooking is where magic meets love – the slow and gentle conjuring of ingredients; the alchemy of belly-bombing deliciousness; the enchantment of familiar and unfamiliar scents; the instinctive pleasure of feeding friends and family. Yes, where magic meets love. I think they call this science.

This 3-ingredient torte is so bewitching that we often serve it as a birthday cake. You're about to find out why.

You'll need a springform tin to make this. Most sizes will work, but I find a 20cm one to be just right. Lightly grease the bottom with your fingers and a dab of oil.

Using a food processor, blitz the Oreos into crumbs. Add a tiny splash of tap water to bring it all together. Press into an even layer over the base of your greased springform tin and freeze while you make the ganache filling.

Chop your dark chocolate into tiny pieces. Place in a ceramic bowl on the kitchen counter.

Heat your nut milk until you can see steam rising from the surface – almost scalding, but not boiling.

Pour the hot milk over your chocolate chunks and quickly stir with a spatula (not a whisk or fork). I do a figure eight with my spatula around the bowl, which works well. It will come together fairly quickly. As soon as it's dark and smooth, stop stirring to prevent overagitation.

Pour on top of your Oreo base and leave to set in a cool place for 20 minutes. Transfer to the fridge or freezer to set further.

Once properly chilled, gently remove from the springform tin. I do this by sitting it on top of a pint glass and snapping the sides first. The sides of the tin will fall away from the torte, down the pint glass. You're free to lift the centre up without getting your fingers chocolaty. All you need to do now is to remove the base of the tin from the torte by loosening it with a sharp knife in one fell swoop.

It's ready to serve, with birthday candles! Feel free to make extra Oreo crumbs and bring it up the sides of the torte with your fingers. It will stick to the chocolate and look very snazzy.

BAE-sic Vegan Ganache, 3 Ways

SERVES 8–12 . . . .

For a glaze or sauce:

200g 70% dark chocolate . . . .

400ml hazelnut milk . . . .

For a pot of ganache or tart filling:

200g 70% dark chocolate . . . .

200ml hazelnut milk . . . .

For frosting:

200g 70% dark chocolate . . . .

100ml hazelnut milk . . . .

⊕ Cost will depend on what chocolate you use

. . . .

⧖ Ganache tarts can be frozen in secret slices, wrapped in parchment

Everybody needs a basic vegan recipe up their sleeve these days. Whether it's to impress your daughter's friends, that hottie in yogalates or simply to rile colleagues at work with your brilliance, this recipe is for you.

Chocolate ganache is traditionally made from blending chocolate with hot cream. No Paul Hollywood moves are required, so making a dairy-free version is piddle easy. Just use dark chocolate and nut milk. The trick is to make sure your ratio is right.

You have three ratios to play with: a thin chocolate sauce, a thick frosting or a smooth pot of ganache. Regardless of the version you choose, all salve itchy tempers (but may cause brain atrophy – I think this is called enlightenment).

Chop your dark chocolate into tiny pieces. Place in a ceramic bowl on the kitchen counter.

Heat your nut milk until you can see steam rise from the surface – almost scalding, but not boiling.

Pour the hot milk over your chocolate chunks and stir with a spatula (not a whisk or fork). I do a figure eight with my spatula around the bowl, which works well. It will come together fairly quickly. As soon as it's dark and smooth, stop stirring to prevent overagitation.

If you're making little pots of ganache, now is the time to pour into eight empty espresso cups and chill in the fridge until set. Serve with teaspoons. You can also pour the ganache filling while warm over a pre-made pastry shell or an 18cm tart base, and chill until set. You'll get 12 slices this way. For a chocolate glaze or sauce, use straight away over waffles and pancakes or store at room temperature for up to 24 hours. And finally, the frosting is more malleable when chilled a little in the fridge before piping onto cakes or smoothing over cupcakes.

Malted Rye Chocolate Cake

MAKES 1 LARGE CAKE . . . .

200g dark chocolate . . . .

200g ghee (page 194) (butter or
coconut oil will not work) . . . .

3 eggs . . . .

100g rapadura, muscovado or coconut
sugar . . . .

100ml barley malt syrup . . . .

1 teaspoon vanilla bean paste or
good-quality extract . . . .

100g whole rye flour . . . .

1 teaspoon baking powder . . . .

½ teaspoon flaky sea salt . . . .

Nip of lemon juice . . . .

Coconut sugar bumps up the
price

. . . .

Freezes in secret slices wrapped
in parchment

When I am poofing my final breath and my life flashes before my eyes, there is no doubt that this chocolate cake will loom large, like an illicit peep show portal. You're about to find out why.

Whack up your oven to 150°C. Line a 23cm circular springform tin (or something similar) with non-stick baking paper to prevent tantrums and sticking.

Now let the chocolate and ghee party over a pot of simmering water (this is called a *bain marie*) until gorgeously glossy.

Measure the eggs, sugar, barley malt syrup and vanilla into a bowl and beat until bubbly. Whisk in the melted chocolate and ghee. Now add your flour, baking powder, salt and lemon juice.

Pour the cake mixture into the lined tin and bake in the oven for 30 minutes. Let it cool completely before looting.

Red Wine Prunes with Cold Cream

MAKES 8 SERVINGS . . . .

200g dried organic prunes, pitted . .

400ml red wine . . . .

1 unwaxed orange, zest only . . . .

2 cloves . . . .

5 tablespoons coconut, muscovado or golden caster sugar . . . .

½ teaspoon ground cinnamon . . . . . .

For the cold 'cream':

1 vanilla pod or 1 teaspoon good-quality vanilla bean extract . . . .

800g Greek yogurt, cultured coconut yogurt, milk kefir (page 235) or crème fraîche . . . .

1 unwaxed orange, zest only . . . .

⊕ On a budget, although choosing coconut sugar will pump up the price

. . . .

⧗ Lasts all week in the fridge

Reincarnated plums are the new superfood. Your gran was spot on.

Yes, the humble prune is packed with soluble and insoluble fibre, giving them the nifty ability to samba along our canals. These wrinkled fruits are what Californian Jedi call their BF (best friend). Prunes work by spring-cleaning the gut with a fervour normally reserved for a visit from the president. So they are great for all things dermal and duodenal. Except what's this got to do with our skin? Here's the theory. If we're not eliminating waste from our pipes, our skin can inevitably become an elimination route for the build-up of toxins. The skin is one of our body's largest excretory organs. Frightening, right?

If the image in the mirror startles you every morning, then maybe it's time to give these underrated fruits a go. Aside from their seismic fibre content, prunes contain modest amounts of beautifying vitamins C and A. Vitamin C is an important ageing ally, with a star role in the creation of collagen. Yes, please, I hear you screech. And if spots are interfering with your usual luminous glow, then vitamin A can help to reduce excess sebum on the surface of the skin. One for the teens.

Prunes also carry a consignment of anthocyanins. These useful compounds have been shown to reduce inflammation in the body, which sounds good to me. Especially on a Sunday morning. Here's a dish to get your glow on. Bring it up an octave with the buckwheat pops on page 207.

Tumble all the ingredients into a small saucepan and bring to a gurgling simmer for 30 minutes, until the wine has reduced by half and the alcohol has boiled off. Remove from the heat and leave the prunes to cool in their cooking liquid for 1 hour. You'll notice that they'll plump up beautifully while they absorb the licky-sticky juices. Refrigerate for up to seven days and tuck in whenever the calling comes.

To make the 'cream', carefully split the vanilla pod lengthways into two long strips. Using a teaspoon, scrape out the seeds inside. Mix into your chosen 'cream' along with the orange zest. Chill until relatively 'clotted'. Some folks like to sweeten Greek yogurt, but I prefer the contrast of sticky, sweet prunes against cold, uncomplicated clouds of cooling yogurt. Coconut yogurt will work beautifully here. If you don't have a good organic crème fraîche available in your area, use 125ml organic double cream and 1 tablespoon milk kefir or buttermilk. Shake together really well in a clean jar for 60 seconds. Leave to ferment at room temperature for 8 hours, then refrigerate for up to two weeks and use whenever the mood yodels.

Serve great clouds of this vanilla 'cream' beside a sticky tower of red wine prunes.

Unicorn Bonbons

MAKES 20–30 . . . .

120g desiccated coconut . . . .

60ml raw honey (or rice malt syrup
for vegans) . . . .

45ml extra virgin coconut oil . . . .

2 tablespoons coconut flour . . . .

1 teaspoon plant-powered colouring
(see the options below) . . . .

Squeeze of lemon . . . .

Pinch of fine sea salt . . . .

Feeling flush

. . . .

No soaking, just rolling. Freezes
well for little lunchboxes.

Unicorn bonbons sound like something a softly spoken nanny makes for children after completing their origami homework and positive affirmation piñata. Right?

Wrong. It's for spoiled brats living in LA and bonked-up adults like me. Unicorns are still scorching hashtags all over the world and accessing the deepest of crazy childhood recesses. Our synapses are tripping on the stuff and our eyes are beating like voodoo drums. We. Can't. Get. Enough.

Unicorn toast was one of the biggest food trends of this decade. It's just some bread, cream cheese (see page 231 for my homemade version) and food colouring. Breathe – I haven't completely lost my mind. Wholefood junkies have thankfully hijacked the movement with Mother Nature's library of colours: yellow turmeric, red raspberry, pink strawbs and green matcha powder. And guess who won the dance-off? Let's hear it for the plant-powered hippies!

These bonbons are the perfect snack size for little lunchboxes or after-school treats. You don't need to stock up on 12 different plant colours. Stress gives you inflammation. Even I'm not that unreasonable. Just start by choosing two unicorn shades from the following freeze-dried fruits:

· Pink raspberry powder
· Blueberry powder
· Orange goji berry powder
· Green barley grass or wheatgrass powder
· Red strawberry powder
· Crimson cherry powder
· Purple beetroot powder
· Yellow turmeric*
· Pastel green matcha green tea powder*

(*You'll need only ½ teaspoon for the two colours in this recipe.)

Using a food processor, blitz all the ingredients into a soft snowball. My food processor usually takes 20 seconds to do this.

Pinch off a piece of dough and roll into a smooth bonbon. Repeat until all the dough has been used up. Chill in the fridge until set.

You can repeat the recipe with lots of different colours. These unicorn bonbons freeze really well if you run out of refrigerator storage or stomach space.

Strawberry and Olive Oil Ice Lollies

MAKES 6 . . . .

3 handfuls of fresh strawberries . . .

4 bananas . . . .

4 tablespoons extra virgin olive oil .

Slice of watermelon, seeds removed
(optional) . . . .

⊕ On a budget
. . . .

⧗ Needs freezing

These pops are so damn fine, they'll fabulise your life. Strawberries and olive oil may sound like an odd combination, but like Harry Potter and a holly wand, they are destined to be together. Olive oil gives a magical, creamy mouthfeel to the frozen pops. Your taste buds will freak out.

We already love strawbs for their ammunition of vitamins and anti-oxidants. But did you know that some of the nutrients in strawberries are fat soluble, and demand to be escorted by healthy fats such as olive oil? Otherwise there ain't no party for all those gorgeous carotenoids. I know! Crazy, right?

Those wily Italians have known this since forever (and that's how long they tend to live for too). That's probably why they're never far from a bottle of olive oil. Lycopene is considered the King Kong carotenoid in red fruit like tomatoes, watermelon and strawberries. By socialising these fruits with olive oil, we significantly increase the absorption of carotenoids. Light. Bulb. Moment.

Start by removing the green strawberry stems and peeling each banana. Compost these and blitz the flesh into a smoothie using a high-powered blender. Add your olive oil and optional slice of watermelon and blitz again.

Pour into your ice lolly moulds and freeze for 6 hours (if your Instagram account can wait that long).

Watermelon Kid Pops

MAKES 8–12 . . . .

1 small watermelon . . . .

8–12 wooden lolly popsicle sticks . . .

⊕ On a budget

. . . .

⧗ Needs freezing

With one flicker of the summer sun, my little thugs will feign heatstroke and demand clinical amounts of ice pops. I derive great satisfaction from sneaking vitamins into their food. Lentils in Bolognese, puréed avocado with pasta, ground sea veg in pancakes – I'm more Mary Poppins than Mary Berry.

This recipe is The Snazz. Great hunks of frozen watermelon to gnaw on and to help with hydration in the sun.

Slice across the circumference of your watermelon with a very sharp bread knife and even sharper concentration. You're looking for two thick circular slices that look a little bigger than a side plate.

Cut each circle into quarters. If you landed a massive watermelon, you will need to cut each quarter in half again. Mine usually looks like a bloodbath.

Pop a wooden lolly stick into the skin of each triangular piece of watermelon, to resemble an ice pop. It's easier if you make an insert with a sharp knife first.

Put your lollies on a non-stick baking tray and freeze for 4 hours before looting.

You could also use a cookie cutter to make funky-shaped watermelon bites for toddlers from each slice. Dinky, huh?

Homemade Cola Cordial

MAKES 500ML . . . .

5 medium unwaxed oranges . . . .

4 small unwaxed lemons . . . .

270–300g light muscovado sugar . . . .

600ml water . . . .

6 cloves . . . .

1 large cinnamon stick . . . .

1 vanilla pod . . . .

½ teaspoon ground allspice . . . .

Sparkling water, to top up . . . .

Reasonable

. . . .

Needs 45 minutes of bubbling

A long list of Ayurvedic spices and celestial goodness? Yup. It's homemade cola.

Prepare your cordial by juicing and zesting the oranges and lemons. Put into a saucepan and bring to a gurgling boil, then add the sugar, water, cloves and cinnamon stick. Now split the vanilla pod lengthways down the centre. Using a sharp knife, scrape out the sticky black seeds (which look like black sap). Add this, and the empty vanilla pod, to your bubbling pot. Sprinkle in the ground allspice – don't panic if you can't find this because you can swap it out for 2 bay leaves, a little ground coriander seed and ground nutmeg.

Boil for 45 minutes, until dark and viscous.

Strain into an airtight sterilised bottle and store in the fridge for up to six weeks.

To serve as cola, use ¼ cordial to ¾ sparking water in each glass and add some ice to the party. If it's too sweet, add as much fizz as you fancy.

Salted Almond Butter Brownies with Espresso Syrup

MAKES 20 . . . .

200g dark chocolate, roughly broken . . . .

1 x 200g block of creamed coconut (not coconut cream) . . . .

4 eggs . . . .

200–220g coconut sugar (€€€) or golden caster sugar (€) . . . .

1 teaspoon baking powder . . . .

1 teaspoon vanilla bean paste or good-quality extract . . . .

Generous flurry of flaky sea salt . . .

1 tablespoon nut milk . . . .

30g dark chocolate chips or chunks .

3–4 tablespoons almond butter . . . . .

For the espresso syrup

250ml freshly brewed dark roast French press coffee . . . .

3 tablespoons golden caster sugar . .

⊕ Coconut sugar bumps up the price

. . . .

⧖ Freeze in sneaky slices and mark as 'stinky cheese' so no one else takes it

It's amazing to watch my seven-year-old make these brownies with the kind of shamanistic frenzy customarily associated with a COS mid-season sale. Adults will appreciate the espresso syrup, but for God's sake keep it away from the childer.

Coconut sugar is not just another hipsteria colonising Ireland's fashionable cafés. This curious brown sugar actually makes sense. For a start, coconut sugar has a modest mineral content, which helps to explain why health nuts go cross-eyed and slack-jawed for it.

Then there's the taste. Even though it comes from the coconut tree, it is positively not coconutty. Think crunchy caramel crumbs without that sickly-sweet kick of regular sugar.

And my favourite bit? It won't make your heart beat like a bodhrán. Don't freak out – it's still a sugar, dear friends! Just a little less bossy with your blood sugar levels.

To make the brownies, crank up your oven to 170°C. Line a 20cm square springform brownie tin with non-stick baking paper and set aside. If you don't have one, they cost about €10 and will last a lifetime of cake binges. Another option is just to raid your brother's kitchen storage and borrow his for a lifetime.

Slowly melt your chocolate with the creamed coconut in a *bain marie*. This is just a fancy term for a saucepan filled with 2cm of water simmering away and a shallow bowl fitted snugly on top in place of a lid. The shallow bowl is where you'll melt the coconut with the chocolate. If the bowl gets too hot the chocolate will go lumpy, so take the pan off its heat source as soon as you see the ingredients melding together. Stir until smooth.

While the chocolate is melting, beat together the eggs and sugar with an electric mixer until creamy. The mixture will aerate and change colour slightly, so don't be overly alarmed. Add the baking powder, vanilla and sea salt. Whisk until well socialised.

Stir in the nut milk followed by the melted chocolate and coconut, then scatter in your chocolate chips.

Using a spatula, scrape the batter into your lined brownie tin. Decorate the top with giddiness and almond butter. Blobs

are delicious, as are creative swirls. (No one's going to know if the spoon finds your mouth by accident.) Bake in the oven for 30 minutes.

Once the salted almond butter brownies are done – they should still be a bit wobbly in the centre – allow to cool overnight in a locked room. Then refrigerate until chilled – this is not one of those desserts that tastes better while hot. If you get this far in the recipe, I think it's probably fair to lock it back in the room and tell no one. Theoretically this is not selfish, as you are looking after their teeth.

To make the optional espresso syrup, boil the coffee and sugar for approximately 20 minutes. It should just about coat the back of a spoon when ready. Best used on the same day or stored at room temperature for two days. Serve beside hunks of brownies and a side of Louis Armstrong. (Inside the locked room. Obvs.)

Superhero Halva, 3 Ways

⊕ Makes 25 servings, so the cost per serving is low

⧖ Needs freezing

My recipe for halva is a healthy-assed treat, working undercover as a sinful snack. Sesame paste is criminally healthy, stuffed with plant lignans, battery-charging B vitamins and calcium. This halva is practically quivering with superfoods you can afford. Add to that the benefits of raw honey, in place of sugared-up caramel, and you've got yourself a fancy defibrillator on a plate. If this library of halva recipes doesn't ignite your inner tango toes, nothing will.

Sour Cherry, Honey and Vanilla Bean Halva

MAKES 25–30 SERVINGS . . . .

3 tablespoons extra virgin coconut oil . . . .

125ml good honey (preferably raw) .

2 tablespoons beetroot powder . . . . .

1 teaspoon vanilla bean paste or the seeds from 1 vanilla pod . . . .

Pinch of flaky sea salt . . . .

1 x 340g jar of light tahini . . . .

4 tablespoons dried Morello sour cherries . . . .

This cold, creamy, sweet halva is nothing short of bewitching. It is at once indulgent yet deeply nourishing. Your little ones will levitate under its spell.

Prep a small rectangular container by lining it with cling film. Lunchboxes are perfect or find a groovy silicone bread tin that will save on cling film. Set aside.

Melt the coconut in a small saucepan on a very timid heat. Gently whisk in the honey, beetroot powder, vanilla and flaky sea salt with a fork. Keep going with the jar of tahini, working at speed so the mixture doesn't seize. Lastly, tumble through the sour cherries, reserving a couple to scatter along the top.

Scrape into your prepped dish and freeze for 6 hours. If you want to melt some dark chocolate and drizzle on top, I'm not going to stop you. Just like ice-cream, this halva must be stored in the freezer. You can slice delicious shards from the block once frozen and serve on a platter to pass around the party. Celestial stuff.

Raspberry Whip Halva

MAKES 20 SERVINGS . . . .

3 tablespoons extra virgin
coconut oil . . . .

85ml maple syrup or coconut nectar

1 teaspoon rosewater (optional) . . . . .

Flurry of flaky sea salt . . . .

280g light tahini . . . .

3–4 tablespoons freeze-dried
raspberries . . . .

Freeze-dried raspberries are fantastically strong. They taste like stoked-up raspberries on overtime with double pay. These roaring red berries house all the stuff that cancer researchers wildly applaud. There's ellagic acid, antioxidants and vitamin C. Ellagic acid has been shown to help fight cancer cells by initiating apoptosis (natural cell death). Sweet. No one is saying raspberries can cure cancer, but it sure is promising to see such interesting results in science labs. I rather like the idea of being prescribed raspberry whip halva to service my future. Maybe this is where I get to put my underpants over my tights and fly...

Line a small lunchbox with cling film.

Melt the coconut in a small saucepan on a very timid heat. Let your preferred choice of syrup, the optional rosewater and the flaky sea salt join the party. Beat through the tahini with a fork, then carefully fold through the freeze-dried raspberries. You can, at any stage, adjust the sweetness to your preference.

Scrape into your prepped container and freeze for 4–12 hours. Once frozen solid, remove from the lined container and wrap in parchment paper. Return to the freezer and store there until a craving hollers. I cut off wedges of halva to have with my tea most days. Indecently good stuff.

Pecan Swirl Halva

MAKES 50 SERVINGS . . . .

Sugared pecans (page 211) . . . .

5 tablespoons melted cacao butter or extra virgin coconut oil . . . .

160ml maple syrup . . . .

2 teaspoons vanilla bean paste . . . . . .

Pinch of flaky sea salt . . . .

2 x 280g jars of light tahini . . . .

2 tablespoons cocoa or cacao powder . . . .

2 tablespoons cacao nibs (optional) .

This sesame-rich recipe is not just another gift to the Gods of Immortality. (Although I do like to keep them regularly assuaged.) It's a gift to your body's battery, to your wallet and to your weeknights.

Baking or cooking for one can sometimes feel as easy as felling an elephant with wet lettuce – in other words, dastardly difficult, demanding a surplus of effort for very little return. Pah! What you need is something to stash in the freezer, servicing your munchies when the mood arrests you.

This halva can be frozen into individual portions, freeing you up on those frantically busy evenings when you have *Sherlock* reruns to satisfy. I'm fairly confident it will send your biochemical algorithm wild. And if you're vegan? This could be an ethereal moment.

Start by prepping your sugared pecans from page 211. Keep in mind that you can replace the rice malt syrup with maple syrup in that recipe.

Once you have the pecans prepped, get going on the halva. First, line a large lunchbox with cling film. Set aside.

Heat your cacao butter or coconut oil over a medium heat. As soon as it's warm and runny, add the maple syrup, vanilla and a generous smattering of flaky sea salt.

Mash in both jars of tahini, keeping the mixture over a gentle heat. Once it's glossy and smooth, remove from the heat and parachute in your sugared pecans. Scrape half the mixture into your lined lunchbox.

With the other half still in the saucepan, stir through your cocoa or cacao powder and optional cacao nibs. Pour this over the light tahini mix in your lunchbox. Using a knife, make three brief swirls without incorporating the two colours together. You want them to barely kiss. Set in the freezer for 6 hours.

When the mood yodels, remove your halva from the lunchbox, carefully peel off the cling film and store it wrapped in parchment paper. This beaut is happy to loiter in your freezer for several months, waiting to service your munchies or feed a massive tea party.

Spelt Chocolate Chip Cookies

MAKES 18 BIG-ASS COOKIES . . . .

480g finely milled whole spelt (or sprouted) flour . . . .

1½ teaspoons baking powder . . . .

1 teaspoon flaky sea salt . . . .

1¼ teaspoons bicarbonate of soda . .

380g rapadura sugar or golden caster sugar (granulated sugar and coconut sugar won't work) . . . .

280g butter, at room temperature (ghee won't work) . . . .

1 teaspoon vanilla bean paste . . . . . .

2 eggs . . . .

180g 70% dark chocolate, roughly chopped into chunks . . . .

⊕ On a budget

. . . .

⧗ Needs to chill for 24–72 hours. Dough can be frozen.

These cookies are utterly inspired by Helen James, fellow kitchen sorcerer. I like to think of them as a bespoke service to help resuscitate indolent limbs. And children.

The key to this recipe is leaving the flour, sugar and butter to fraternise for 24–48 hours. Wonderfully witchy. You can freeze the dough balls too for those pesky unexpected guests. Just defrost at room temperature for 2 hours before baking into oblivion. Our favourite version uses organic sprouted spelt, giving these cookies a crazy good crumb. If that's a trot too far, plain all-purpose flour works brilliantly. I won't mind. Much.

Measure your flour, baking powder, salt and bicarb into a massive bowl. You'll need lots of space for beating in the remaining ingredients (I do this in my biggest saucepan for ease). Set aside.

In another large bowl, cream together the sugar, butter and vanilla. Some snazzy readers can use their standing mixer for 3 minutes, but I do this by hand. When my arm starts killing me, I take a break and let loose with Beyoncé on the airwaves.

Now add the eggs into the butter mix one at a time, mixing well between each addition, then add the chocolate chunks. Scoop into your bowl (or pan) of flour and mix well.

Fashion 18 large golf balls of dough between your palms. Collect the dough balls in a bowl, cover and chill for 24–72 hours. The longer, the better.

When you are ready to bake, bring the dough balls to room temperature – 30 minutes is grand, but 1 hour is best if your kitchen is cool. Line a tray with non-stick baking paper and fire up your oven to 180°C.

I find that four to five dough balls per large tray is the sweet spot. Bake in the oven for 20–22 minutes without flattening the cookies (leave them in dough ball form). Repeat with the remaining dough balls (or keep them refrigerated for up to five days and bake cookies at a later time).

Remove from the oven and resist touching them for 25 minutes so they can solidify (sorry!). Then sink your teeth into them and telepathically tickle Helen James.

Brown Sugar Meringue with Vanilla Crème Fraîche

MAKES 16 NESTS OR 1 LARGE
MERINGUE . . . .

180g light muscovado sugar . . . .

4 egg whites, at room temperature . .

1 teaspoon cornflour . . . .

1 teaspoon lemon juice . . . .

1 tablespoon vanilla bean paste . . . . .

250g crème fraîche . . . .

1 large handful of salted pistachios,
shelled . . . .

⊕ On a budget
. . . .

⧗ Lengthy session in the oven

Sixteen trays later, and a teeny tinnitus of glee, I have finally succeeded in slaying the traditional sugar content of meringues. I've done this without mutilating the form and shape. Much.

I also switched up its flavour profile to give a delectably chewy, deep, caramel smack. This can only be achieved with freshly opened light muscovado sugar. Dark muscovado makes a flat eggy cushion that looks closer to a cowpat than an Italian meringue. I've tried combinations of caster and coconut sugar, jaggery and Demerara. All are most unlovely, leaving the meringue (and me) weeping on the baking tray.

But don't be fooled by my dulcet warblings – these are still sugar bombs! I find that plain crème fraîche is a brilliant shock absorber for a meringue's explosive sweetness. Let's be honest – cream is not exactly overburdened by charm or personality. Is it any wonder people lob in another cargo of sugar? If you start with exciting ingredients, you won't need to compensate with sweetness. You're about to find out why.

Fire up the oven to 200°C. Line two large baking trays with non-stick baking paper.

Dust your sugar over one tray and warm in the oven for a couple of minutes. This step is really important for brown sugar.

While your sugar is warming, place the egg whites into a scrupulously clean, dry bowl and start beating with an electric hand whisk. Continue until you can see the tracks from the beaters on the surface.

Add the cornflour and lemon juice. Whip.

Remove your sugar from the oven after a few minutes and reduce the oven temperature to 140°C. Slowly rain in your warmed sugar to your whipped egg whites. Beat until the mixture can stand in stiff, shiny, voluptuous peaks, not too unlike a bowl of shaving cream.

Divide between your baking trays, making two gorgeous glossy Frisbees of equal size. Or dollop eight marshmallow-hearted nests onto each lined tray. I make mine the size of an egg.

Bake in the oven at 140°C for 1½–2 hours if making nests and 2½–3 hours for meringues, depending on their size. In either case, the meringue should peel off the parchment perfectly and feel light to touch. Turn off the oven. Allow to cool for at least 2 hours before serving (they need longer than white meringues). You can cool them in the oven with the door ajar if you fancy perfection. This will help prevent cracking, but personally I love those bits.

Stir your glossy vanilla bean paste through the crème fraîche.

Serve the brown sugar nests alongside a cloud of vanilla crème fraîche and a smattering of roasted pistachios if you have them. To assemble meringue pies, sandwich a layer of vanilla crème fraîche between the tiers and slather the remaining lot on top with a dusting of crushed pistachios.

Pimped-Up Popcorn, 3 Ways

⊕ On a budget

⧗ Fairly instant

SERVES 2–5 ....

3 tablespoons ghee (page 194) or coconut oil ....

70g organic popcorn kernels ....

2 tablespoons sesame seeds ....

1 teaspoon fennel seeds ....

25g jaggery powder or coconut sugar ....

Pinch of chilli flakes ....

These popcorn flavour combos are more than enough to override my brain's limbic system and combust with excitement.

Jaggery, Fennel and Chilli Popcorn

When you quit relying on industrially processed foods, you're basically quitting Junk. The less Junk you eat, the less toxins damage your body and your battery. So you not only benefit from eliminating rubbish from your diet, but you also profit from nutrient-rich replacements like this homemade popcorn. Double points! Add to that the praise thundered upon you by your housemates and you've bagged yourself a hat trick.

To pop the kernels, heat 2 tablespoons of your preferred fat in a deep pan on a medium to high heat. Try not to let the oil smoke – this is crappy health-wise and taste-wise. Tip in your kernels and secure with a lid. Let the kernels heat and pop. They are ready when the popping slows down to one every 3 seconds. Remove from the heat while you get going on your topping.

Dry-fry the sesame and fennel seeds in a pan on a high heat until their scent plays with your nostrils. Remove and grind in a pestle and mortar.

Return to the pan along with the remaining tablespoon of ghee or coconut oil, your jaggery powder or coconut sugar and some chilli flakes. Let them party. Mizzle over your cooled popcorn and tuck in while you can.

Black Pepper, Turmeric and Honey Popcorn

SERVES 2–5 . . . .

3 tablespoons butter, ghee (page 194)
or coconut oil . . . .

70g organic popcorn kernels . . . .

3 tablespoons honey . . . .

1 teaspoon ground or freshly grated
turmeric . . . .

Pinch of freshly cracked sea salt and
black pepper . . . .

Among the more wily cooks, turmeric is known as poor man's saffron. This neon root mimics saffron's prized ability to give everything a crazy golden glow. But unlike saffron, turmeric is cheap and can pull some serious superpower moves.

There is an impressive body of research on the health benefits of curcumin, a compound found inside turmeric. Curcumin helps to reduce inflammation in our body by interrupting the production of odious leukotrienes. That's a high-five for readers looking to relieve joint problems or chronic injuries. Turmeric is your new BAE.

To pop the kernels, heat your chosen fat in a large pan. Try not to let the oil smoke – this is crappy health-wise and taste-wise. Tip in your popcorn kernels and secure with a lid. Let the kernels pop. They are ready when the jumping slows down to one pop every 3 seconds. Remove from heat while you get going on your topping.

Gently heat your honey. After one minute, stir in the turmeric and a few twists of the salt and pepper mill. Mizzle this golden elixir over your popcorn and toss to coat. Serve straight away. Bodaciously good over vanilla ice-cream.

Wasabi Popcorn

SERVES 2–5 . . . .

3 tablespoons ghee (page 194) or
coconut oil . . . .

70g organic popcorn kernels . . . .

2 sheets of nori . . . .

2 teaspoons wasabi powder (e.g.
Clearspring) . . . .

Pinch of fine sea salt . . . .

The problem often with 'health food' is a lack of imagination. Healthy food can, and should, taste wicked. It shouldn't feel 'healthy' or sacrifice your taste buds in any way. It's not a tax! Healthy food should kick ass. Let me show you how.

Heat 2 tablespoons of your chosen fat in a deep pan on a medium-high heat. Try not to let it smoke – this is crappy health-wise and taste-wise.

Test the hot fat to see if it's ready. Drop one popcorn kernel in. The kernel must pop within 8 seconds before continuing with the remaining popcorn kernels.

Once the fat is ready for popping, tip in your kernels and secure with a lid. It should sound like fireworks. The popcorn is ready when you can hear the popping slow down significantly. Remove the pan from the heat while you get going on your topping.

Remove the lid. Using your fingers, scrunch up both sheets of nori over the popped corn. Parachute your wasabi powder over, add a few twists of the salt mill and toss before serving.

Instant Mango Ice-Cream

SERVES 2 ADULTS OR 4 KIDS . . . .

3 bananas, peeled . . . .

2 ripe Alphonso mangos, peeled . . . .

Trickle of dairy milk or plant milk . .

Sugared pecans (page 211), crushed . .

⊕ On a budget

. . . .

⏳ Much quicker than regular
ice-cream

This recipe is a luscious treat with a healthy twist. Kids love it. BBQs want it. Mothers dream about it. Instead of white sugar and dairy, we're using frozen bananas to achieve the same sweetness and creaminess. Trade secret. The pecans are optional, but their salty-sweet crunch is explosively good and will do all sorts of funny things to your toes. And while any mango will work, Alphonso mangos are bewitching. They are sweeter and jellier than any other mango I've seduced. So juicy and dribbly are these Alphonsos, you'll need to sit in a bathtub just to eat one.

The key to this ice-cream is using slightly more frozen banana than frozen mango, but 50-50 will still work beautifully. Before freezing the bananas, chop them into small discs and freeze on baking parchment, making sure each slice does not fraternise with its neighbour. When they freeze successfully, you can store them in a recycled freezer bag.

Repeat the same method for the mango flesh. Both can be stored successfully in the freezer until an ice-cream craving hollers.

At this point, you'll need to blend the frozen fruit on the highest setting you have on your blender. A Vitamix will do this in 5 seconds; a regular blender will take 15 seconds. You'll need a splash of milk to give it some momentum.

That's it! Scoop into chilled tumbler glasses, parachute some crushed sugared pecans on top and tuck straight in. Leftovers don't refreeze. I doubt you'll hate me for it.

Instant Salted Caramel

MAKES 1 MASSIVE JAR . . . .

200g regular pitted dates . . . .

140g roasted cashew nut butter . . . .

1 tablespoon unscented coconut oil
or melted cacao butter . . . .

2 teaspoons vanilla bean paste or
seeds from 1 vanilla pod . . . .

Flaky sea salt, to taste . . . .

 Feeling flush

. . . .

 Takes 20 minutes. Can be frozen
in ice cube trays.

Every woman needs a man who spoils her with abandon and makes her laugh until her lungs hurt. Every woman needs a man who can plug in the hoover without whining. Every woman needs a man who understands what ignites her temperature. And the secret to a great relationship is that, under no circumstances, should these three men ever meet.

For every other occasion, there's salted caramel. Soft, smooth, sumptuous layers of stickiness that soothes frayed nerves and chronic disappointments. Every woman needs a pot.

Cover the dates with a little water and boil for 15 minutes, until they collapse. Then belt them into a high-speed blender with the cashew nut butter, coconut oil or cacao butter, vanilla and a generous pinch of sea salt and blitz until seductively smooth. At this stage it won't taste or smell like caramel, so chill before you judge! Decant into a jar and store in the fridge before tucking in.

Miso Caramel

This caramel is the next evolutionary step towards happiness. Miso is a fermented soya bean paste. It means 'impossible to describe but hits the spot and makes my tongue jiggy' in Japanese.

To make a miso caramel, just replace the sea salt in the recipe above with 1 tablespoon of sweet white miso paste and follow the same method.

Freezer Shortbread, 3 Ways

More expensive than the commercial stuff

Hallowed be the freezer!

We like almonds for their cargo of calcium. But almonds also have a stonking amount of a powerful antioxidant called vitamin E. This vitamin can battle with filthy toxins lurking in our bloodstream, waiting to bomb our complexion.

When combined with vitamin C, vitamin E can be 'reloaded' in our system to disarm further oxidants. Score! You can almost feel the goodness moonwalking to your skin. With that in mind, I recommend adding freeze-dried strawberries to these no-bake almond shortbread recipes to get your vitamin C on. Any leftover freeze-dried strawbs can be used in the white chocolate caramels on page 250. You're so welcome!

MAKES 25

100ml extra virgin coconut oil

120ml good honey or maple syrup

250g ground almonds

1 unwaxed orange, zest only

3 tablespoons ground ginger

Good pinch of fine or flaky sea salt

40g dark chocolate, melted

Chocolate Orange Gingers

This shortbread will take a mere 3 minutes to whip up, 5 minutes to cook and 2 seconds to devour. But the benefits last all day, my beauties.

Fire up the oven to 180°C. Line a baking tray with non-stick baking paper.

Gently melt the coconut oil and your honey or maple syrup in a saucepan. Remove from the heat and fork through your ground almonds, orange zest, ginger and some sea salt. Mix well to form a squidgy dough ball. Gently place on a sheet of greaseproof paper and cover with another large sheet. Using your palm, press into an oblong shape, similar to a pizza base, about 1–2cm deep. Freeze on a breadboard or similar flat surface for 15 minutes.

Remove the dough from your freezer, cut out cookie shapes and place on your lined tray. Bake in the oven for 5 minutes and remove before they start to brown or colour. (Or store your shortbread in the freezer for another day, to bake straight from frozen.) Allow to set firmly on the tray before blessing with glorious melted chocolate.

No-Bake Probiotic Shortbread

MAKES 10–20 PORTIONS . . . .

80ml extra virgin coconut oil . . . .

7 tablespoons good runny honey . . . . .

250g ground almonds . . . .

4 tablespoons raisins, dried blueberries, goji berries, dried cherries and/or mulberries . . . .

4–6 probiotic capsules or probiotic powder . . . .

Pinch of ground turmeric (optional) . . . .

If feeding your family healthy food feels as easy as fox-trotting up a glass wall, then this shortbread recipe is for you. Kids love it. Teens dig it. And adults can't keep their mitts off it.

Try to find a local raw honey where you live – it will have impressive antimicrobial and antibacterial properties. These work like a giant Pac-Man in the bloodstream. Heat-treated mainstream honey cannot boast the same benefits and can be cleverly adulterated.

You'll find a consignment of vitamin E in almonds. This vitamin works synergistically with vitamin C to pimp up our immune system and front-line defence. How cool is that? I kept the best bit until last … a nifty cargo of live probiotics! You and I can neck probiotic capsules when our bodies feel like a Petri dish. But our little ones? They need our help.

Gently melt the coconut oil with your honey. Try not to kill the honey's health benefits with intense heat if you managed to get your mitts on some fabulous local raw honey. Tumble in the ground almonds and dried fruit. Now parachute each opened probiotic capsule or powder into the shortbread dough and the optional turmeric for extra nutrition. Mix thoroughly. Some cooks prefer to do this step in a ceramic bowl with a wooden spoon should the live bacteria revolt against the metal. I've found both ways to be equally successful.

Spoon onto a sheet of baking parchment and squash together with the palm of your hands. Using another sheet of parchment on top, exercise a rolling pin over the surface and flatten the dough to a depth of 5mm to 1cm. Freeze for 2 hours.

When the kids return from school hollering for a treat, remove the dough from your freezer and carefully cut into shards of shortbread. These are designed to be eaten straight from frozen, like ice-cream cookies. They need no baking and can be stored like this for up to three months. Thunderous hurrah!

Ninjabread Men

MAKES 4–8. . . . .

4 tablespoons extra virgin coconut oil . . . .

100g ground almonds . . . .

3 tablespoons maple syrup . . . .

1–2 teaspoons ground ginger . . . .

Pinch of unrefined salt . . . .

Toddlers just adore these gingerbread men. A note for wily mums: you can replace some of the ground almonds with milled flaxseed or hemp powder to inject some omega-3 artillery into your little ones. You can also add 1 teaspoon of barleygrass powder and use a shamrock cookie cutter for St Patrick's Day.

Gently melt your coconut oil in a small pan over a shy heat. Remove from the heat and stir through the remaining ingredients. Scrape the mixture out over a sheet of baking parchment. Press it into a rough dough ball, then place another sheet of parchment over it and flatten with a rolling pin to a depth of 5mm to 1cm.

Transfer to the freezer for 10 minutes, until barely set. Alternatively, you can freeze this for up to three months and let the dough thaw for 5 minutes before cutting into gingerbread men. Choose a cookie cutter and off you go! No need to bake. We store ready-to-eat ninjabread men in a recycled freezer bag, waiting for unexpected playdates and midnight munchies.

Vegan Cookies, 4 Ways

Feeling flush

....

The cookie dough can be frozen in batches

My inner sugar junkie is always looking for a sweet and salty hit. These cookies are bodaciously good, especially if you're trying to wean yourself off Jaffa Cakes and candy. Brown rice syrup and barley malt syrup can be purchased in health food stores and savvy delis nationwide. Maple syrup, honey and agave nectar don't work as well in this recipe. Only Harold McGee and God can tell you why.

Walnut and Rosehip Cookies

MAKES 18–24 COOKIES

130g walnuts . . . .

120g brown rice flour . . . .

80g oat flakes . . . .

1 teabag of rosehip tea, ripped open . . . .

1 teaspoon ground ginger . . . .

½ teaspoon baking powder . . . .

125ml extra virgin coconut oil, melted . . . .

135ml brown rice syrup . . . .

½ teaspoon flaky sea salt . . . .

You can store the cookie dough in the freezer, rolled up like a log. When the mood arrests you, unleash your inner Cookie Monster and high five your genius.

Preheat your oven to 180°C. Line two baking trays with non-stick baking paper.

Briefly pulse the dry ingredients in a food processor until they resemble big breadcrumbs. This includes the walnuts, flour, oats, the contents of one bag of rosehip tea, ginger and baking powder. Now add your melted coconut oil and the fabulously sticky brown rice syrup. Pulse again until a big dough ball forms in the bowl of your food processor. Parachute some flaky sea salt on top.

Freeze half the mixture for another day (cracking idea, no?). With the remaining dough, pull off an apricot-sized piece and roll it into a ball between your palms. Press down on your lined baking tray, using two or three of your fingers to make a nice cookie indent. Mine work out at about 2–3mm thick.

Bake in the oven for 10–12 minutes depending on their size (but no longer, promise me!). Don't worry if they seem soft or undercooked – the cookies harden once cooled. Flipping fabulous.

Chocolate Chip Chestnut Cookies

MAKES 18–24 COOKIES . . . .

135g unsalted cashews or walnuts . . .

130g chestnut flour . . . .

90g oat flakes . . . .

½ teaspoon baking powder . . . .

145ml rice malt syrup, brown rice
syrup or barley malt syrup . . . .

125ml extra virgin coconut oil,
melted . . . .

30g dark chocolate . . . .

½ teaspoon flaky sea salt . . . .

We know that sex without flirting is not as tasty. Right? Same with cookies. (Stay with me.) Getting all the right ingredients together in one place, letting them mingle and cavort with each other, then agonising over The Wait while something magical starts to unfold that's greater than the sum of the parts. All this heightens the enjoyment of that first bite.

So can we ditch that packet of cookies, please, and start making love to your kitchen. There's a party for one in the kitchen, and you're invited.

Preheat your oven to 180°C. Line two baking trays with non-stick baking paper.

Pulse the nuts, chestnut flour, oats and baking powder in a food processor. You want them to resemble breadcrumbs but not a fine flour.

Now add your syrup and melted coconut oil and pulse until the dough tumbles into a big playful ball. The key to these cookies is finding a malty syrup like rice malt syrup or barley malt syrup. I get mine in savvy delis or health food stores. Brown rice syrup is easier to find, and also excellent. Honey and maple syrup won't work.

Chop your chocolate into gloriously uneven chunks and parachute them into the dough ball along with a generous smattering of flaky sea salt.

Pull off a little dough and roll into a dinky ball between your palms. Lightly flatten with a spatula on your lined baking trays. You're looking for each one to be about 1cm in depth and of uniform size. Repeat until all the dough has been used up, although I usually freeze half the cookie dough for another day.

Bake in the oven for 10–12 minutes depending on their size, being mindful not to cook them any longer. Don't worry if they seem soft or undercooked – these cookies harden as they cool. Serve with a bubble bath and earplugs.

Aniseed and Sea Salt Cookies

MAKES 18–24 COOKIES

130g unsalted cashew nuts . . . .

130g brown rice flour . . . .

90g oat flakes . . . .

1 tablespoon milled flaxseed or
milled chia seed . . . .

½ teaspoon baking powder . . . .

125ml extra virgin coconut oil,
melted . . . .

145ml brown rice syrup or barley
malt syrup . . . .

½ teaspoon whole aniseed . . . .

½ teaspoon flaky sea salt . . . .

Here's one way you can start switching out processed white flour and white sugar for something more wholesome. The ingredients in these cookies are totemic of a modern wholefoods whore: oats, raw nuts, brown rice flour, flax, chia, Ayurvedic spice and barley malt. They'll have your nostrils twerking.

Preheat your oven to 180°C. Line two baking trays with non-stick baking paper.

Finely grind the cashews, flour, oats, flax or chia and baking powder in a food processor until it resembles breadcrumbs. Try not to aim for a flour, as this would be too fine a consistency.

Add your melted coconut oil, the gorgeously glossy syrup, a smattering of whole aniseed spice and the sea salt. Pulse again until a big dough ball forms in the bowl of your food processor.

Pull off an apricot-sized piece of dough and roll into a ball between your palms. Flatten with a spatula on your lined baking tray. You're looking for each one to be about 1cm in depth. Repeat until all of the dough has been used up – I usually bake the cookies in batches or freeze half the cookie dough for another day. Cook for 10–12 minutes depending on their size (but no longer, promise me!) and remove from the oven before they turn a shade darker. Don't worry if they seem soft or undercooked – they will harden as they cool down. Overcooking them will result in a crumbly cookie rather than a snappy, chewy cookie. Leave to cool completely before you bake another tray load. This way, you'll know whether you've hit the sweet spot or whether you need to keep them in the oven for 1 minute longer next time. Either way, they're bloody delicious.

Salted Caramel and Cashew Cookies

MAKES 18 BIG COOKIES . . . .

125g unsalted cashew nuts . . . .

120g brown rice flour . . . .

80g oat flakes . . . .

1 teaspoon ground ginger . . . .

½ teaspoon baking powder . . . .

135ml brown rice syrup or rice malt
syrup . . . .

125ml extra virgin coconut oil,
melted . . . .

½ teaspoon flaky sea salt . . . .

Salted caramel or miso caramel
(page 291) . . . .

These are closer to souped-up Custard Creams, but undeniably healthier. If you're trying to impress that vegan hottie in your yoga class, this is for you. No need for drastic measures like swearing off meat for eternity or subscribing to Alicia Silverstone's blog. Just knock up these cookies and let your serotonin somersault. Move over, Buddha, there's a new deity in town.

Preheat your oven to 180°C. Line two baking trays with non-stick baking paper.

Finely grind the dry ingredients in a food processor until they resemble breadcrumbs. Try not to aim for a flour, as this would be too fine a consistency. Add the fabulously sticky syrup and the melted oil (I get my rice malt syrup and brown rice syrup in savvy delicatessens or health food stores). Pulse again until a big dough ball forms in the bowl of your food processor. Parachute some sea salt flakes on top.

Freeze half the mixture for another day if you fancy. With the remaining dough, pull off an apricot-sized piece and roll into a ball between your palms. Press down on your lined baking tray, using the back of a fork to make a nice cookie indent. Repeat with the rest of the dough.

Bake in the oven for 10–12 minutes depending on their size, but not a moment longer. Don't worry if they seem soft or undercooked when the cookies come out of the oven – they will harden as they cool down.

While the cookies are baking, you can whizz up your choice of instant caramel (page 291). No thermometers or patience involved, I promise!

To assemble the cookie, sandwich some caramel between two cookies. Repeat until exhausted by desire.

Chocolate Chai Lollipops

MAKES 12 . . . .

12 Medjool dates . . . .

Generous handful of walnuts . . . .

1-2 chai teabags, torn open . . . .

4 tablespoons raw cacao or cocoa
powder . . . .

3 tablespoons extra virgin coconut
oil . . . .

Smattering of flaky sea salt . . . .

4 tablespoons sprouted buckwheat
groats or buckwheat pops (page 207),
to coat (optional) . . . .

 Reasonable
. . . .

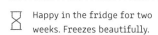 Happy in the fridge for two
weeks. Freezes beautifully.

These treats satisfy everyone from grumpy grandparents to pugnacious thugs (and other such playdates). They are The Snazzlejazzle with a smooth, rich bite and playful pops of sea salt.

The mere whiff of chocolate has the ability to vaccinate us against lousy moods. Try eating these while staying cross. It's physically implausible. That's because our serotonin thrives on the stuff. Something explosive happens in my brain. Scientists tie this experience to a neurochemical called dopamine. Once stirred, dopamine can initiate an electrical cavalry through the veins and even service our yoni. Yup. It's little wonder why chocolate sends our pheromones into orbit.

We're using teabags in this recipe to replace individual spices. Hear me out. Buying six different spices will crank up the price. A stealthier trick is to purchase uncaffeinated chai teabags (I use the ubiquitous Pukka brand available from supermarkets and health food stores). Vanilla chai, for example, has ginger, vanilla, black pepper, cardamom, cinnamon and chilli. You can tear the teabags open and tip them into any chocolate recipe. Namaste.

Destone the dates before dropping them into a food processor. Medjools are juicier and creamier than regular pitted dates and can be found in most supermarkets now.

Add the remaining ingredients except the buckwheat groats and whizz on a low speed for 1–2 minutes. If you pinch the mixture together, the crumbs should hold.

Using a generous teaspoon, mould into bonbons. Your hands will become slippery, naturally helping the process. Expect to get around 12 bonbons from the batch, depending on how many times the teaspoon fell into your mouth. Roll in sprouted buckwheat groats or your homemade buckwheat pops for optional crunch.

Chill in the fridge. Once set, insert a lolly stick into each bonbon, then return to the fridge for storage. These can also be transferred to a freezer storage box ready for those manic playdates and chronic toddler attacks.

Miso and Medjool Swiss Rolls

MAKES 1 LARGE LOG. . . . .

300g Medjool dates, stones removed

3 tablespoons sweet white miso (or a pinch of flaky sea salt) . . . .

3 tablespoons coconut flour or ground chia seeds . . . .

3 tablespoons your preferred nut butter (cashew is excellent) . . . .

Soft desiccated coconut, for the filling . . . .

 Reasonable
. . . .

Lives in the freezer, awaiting your call

I'm all about finding sweets to love that will love my body back. I enter a state of limerence milling into these pinwheels. How can something so healthy taste so unstintingly sinful? Bringing the right combination of flavours together is nothing short of bewitching. When the list of ingredients is short, like this one, and requires absolutely no cooking, a tingly infatuation takes control of my motherboard. I morph into a culinary Steve Irwin, telling everyone what's happening in my wild kitchen life.

These delectably gooey pinwheels were birthed by the One Part Plant movement. They are cleverly stored in the freezer, which is almost the same as having treats on tap. This is real fast food, brothers and sisters, with a nutritional slam dunk.

Using a food processor, blitz the Medjools, miso or salt, flour or ground chia and the nut butter until a rough dough ball forms. Splendid. Now smooth it onto a piece of parchment paper using a silicone spatula. Depending on how squishy your Medjools are, this can be straightforward or damned messy.* Be patient. You're looking for this to be about 5mm thick. I find it easier to manipulate the dough under a second piece of non-stick parchment.

Neaten the edges, ensuring a similar depth across the dough. Go for a rectangle rather than a square. Shake some desiccated coconut over. Freeze on a flat breadboard for 1 hour.

Take it out of the freezer and roll up like a Swiss roll sponge. Use the parchment paper to help you, as you would do with sushi. The first bit is the trickiest, as you tuck the 'tongue' under to facilitate rolling. I use one hand to pull the parchment away from the dough and the other hand to push and roll the dough. Work with what you have, sister. Keep rolling into a log until you've reached the end, then smooth over the seam with damp fingers. Return to the freezer wrapped in parchment, where it will live until your guests arrive (at which point, slice rounds from the log and serve straight from frozen).

*It all depends on the water content of your Medjools. If they are dry-ish, you can roll it straight away. If they are squishy and wet (yummo!), you'll need to freeze the dough for 2 hours before rolling.

Index